Career Patterns

A KALEIDOSCOPE OF POSSIBILITIES

SECOND EDITION

Liz Harris-Tuck
CAREER HORIZONS
MARICOPA COUNTY COMMUNITY COLLEGES

Annette Price
CHANDLER-GILBERT COMMUNITY COLLEGE

Marilee Robertson
INTERACTIVE TRAINING DESIGN

Upper Saddle River, New Jersey
Columbus, Ohio

Library of Congress Cataloging-in-Publication Data

Harris-Tuck, Liz.
Career patterns : a kaleidoscope of possibilities / Liz Harris-Tuck, Annette Price, Marilee Robertson.—2nd ed.
p. cm.
Includes bibliographical references and index.
ISBN 0-13-110965-0
1. Vocational guidance. I. Price, Anette. II. Robertson, Marilee. III. Title

HF5381.H17 2004
650.1—dc21

2003049821

Vice President and Executive Publisher: Jeffery W. Johnston
Senior Acquisitions Editor: Sande Johnson
Assistant Editor: Cecilia Johnson
Editorial Assistant: Erin Anderson
Production Editor: Holcomb Hathaway
Design Coordinator: Diane C. Lorenzo
Cover Designer: Thomas Borah
Cover Art: Corbis
Production Manager: Pamela D. Bennett
Director of Marketing: Ann Castel Davis
Marketing Manager: Christina Quadhamer
Compositor: Aerocraft Charter Art Service
Cover Printer: Phoenix Color Corp.
Printer/Binder: Courier Kendallville, Inc.

Photographs from Corbis Images, Digital Graphics, Digital Vision, EyeWire, and PhotoDisc royalty-free resources.

Pearson Education Ltd.
Pearson Education Australia Pty. Limited
Pearson Education Singapore Pte. Ltd.
Pearson Education North Asia Ltd.
Pearson Education Canada, Ltd.
Pearson Educación de Mexico, S.A. de C.V.
Pearson Education–Japan
Pearson Education Malaysia Pte. Ltd.

10 9 8 7 6 5 4 3 2 1
ISBN 0-13-110965-0

Brief Contents

Contents

NOTE: Every effort has been made to provide accurate and current Internet information in this book. However, the Internet and information posted on it are constantly changing, so it is inevitable that some of the Internet addresses listed in this textbook will change.

Preface

We all want to know how our personal dreams and aspirations will coincide with the current and future work world. Making career decisions and planning our work lives can help us visualize our niche in the world. Thoughtful planning can help guide and direct our actions, increase self-confidence, and add a sense of purpose to our lives.

Our intent in writing this text is to introduce students to new ways of thinking about career planning and to provide proven tools to help them turn their career dreams into reality. Throughout the text, we examine changing trends in the workplace and encourage students to anticipate and prepare for continuous change. We believe the right question for people making career choices is "What needs doing?" This is a bigger and more important question than "What do I want to be?" Seeking an answer to this question keeps your career on track with your personal development and with the evolving changes in the workplace. Discovering what needs to be done is the foundation for career resiliency and lifetime employability.

Students today want to make sense out of an uncertain world. Building on our premise that learning about the workplace is just as important as learning about oneself, this new edition emphasizes career management strategies critical for finding and keeping work today. Our marketing-based work search techniques help readers tune in to the marketplace and get results. We have added new information about trends, more Real-Life Perspectives, and tips for success once you've landed your new job.

Resources available for the instructor include an instructor's manual and a downloadable PowerPoint presentation. Resources for students include our Companion Website, which can be accessed through www.prenhall.com/harris-tuck. This site enhances the text by providing new ideas and useful links.

Acknowledgments

Many people have generously offered their special talents to help us realize our vision—bringing this book to life. This book is truly a collaborative effort, and we are indebted to those who have contributed their support. Thanks to you all.

In the early stages of planning, Tracy Tucker guided us into the world of publishing. Robin Atchison introduced us to our publisher, Prentice

Hall. Sande Johnson, our editor, has enthusiastically provided ideas and support throughout the writing process. Cecilia Johnson and Christina Quadhamer were always available with information when we needed it. Once again, Gay Pauley has enriched our writing during the publishing process. We are grateful for her editorial assistance. We have relied on the expert advice of our reviewers: Jim Caffiero, Gavilan College; Connie Egelman, Nassau Community College; Theresa Ervin, The University of Mississippi; Frederick Gallegos, California State Polytechnic University, Pomona; Jacqueline Hing, Rice University; Marilyn Joseph, Florida Metropolitan University; and Alice M. Fairhurst, California State Polytechnic University, Pomona.

We are again especially indebted to Terry Long, who tirelessly read our revisions, enlivened our writing, and offered many suggestions to add clarity. Her feedback, editing talents, and eye for detail were invaluable.

Nik Harris and Andrew Price gave us invaluable advice about the perspectives of college students and recent graduates as well as access to their network of friends. Alex Price served as a model for what a young careerist can achieve. Zobie Nieto, Alice Anderson Tomé, Rob Decker, and Chris Tomé helped us refine the scenario process by serving as willing subjects. Our clients at Rudolph Dew & Associates provided many insights into the reality of the workplace. Thanks to our students at the Maricopa Community Colleges for their input and real-world stories. You were our inspiration.

Since the publication of the first edition of *Career Patterns: A Kaleidoscope of Possibilities*, we have presented concepts from the book at the National Career Development Conference, the International Career Development Conference, the American Society for Training and Development National Conference, the Arizona Career Services Conference, and the Australian Career Counsellors Conference in Adelaide, South Australia. We are indebted to the positive response and thoughtful suggestions our colleagues have offered on these occasions. This second edition incorporates many of their ideas.

We're grateful to Chris Helms, Assistant Director of Career Services at Arizona State University, and Lynne Ross, Assistant Professor and Division Chair, Speech Communication, Theatre and Dance Department at Kansas State University, whose experiences added to our perspective. Special thanks to Rita Bresnahan, Phyllis Harper-Rispoli, and Sheryl Spohn, who read our manuscript, contributed ideas, and encouraged us throughout this project.

A special thanks to Judith Barrette for her understanding and support.

Throughout the book we have included quotations from many experts in career exploration and related fields. They are too numerous to name here, but we want to thank all of those people whose work we have read and learned from and who are represented in these pages.

And finally, our deepest gratitude goes to our families, who supported us through long hours and understood when we missed family events. Neil and Donna Tucker provided gracious hospitality when we needed a retreat. Rob Decker and Tom Tuck were always willing to shoulder our responsibilities when we couldn't be there. A special thanks to Kate and Ted Decker for providing the inspiration to wonder what the world of work will be like in the mid–21st century.

About the Authors

After 15 years as a successful entrepreneur, **Liz Harris-Tuck** changed careers. She now expresses her personal interests as a career counselor, seminar presenter, and workshop facilitator. Assisting students, young adults, and mid-careerists from all walks of life, Liz understands their concerns. Since 1986, Liz has been affiliated with the Maricopa Community College District. She directed Scottsdale Community College's Office of Career Planning and Placement and currently teaches career planning courses.

Annette Price combines organizational expertise and teaching experience to prepare people for future success. As an internal consultant for a large organization, she conducts career development workshops, presents seminars on career planning, and counsels employees regarding career decisions. She led a team that created a career website to help employees prepare for the future needs of the organization. Annette has taught career exploration courses for the Maricopa Community College District for the past 13 years. Her students include young adults, reentry students, and mid-career changers.

Marilee Robertson brings real-world experience—corporate, business, and entrepreneurial expertise—to career planning. For the last 20 years, she has assisted college students, downsized employees, women reentering the job market, corporate managers, and executives to explore career options and successfully gain new employment. Marilee has provided outplacement services to a variety of industries, from coal mining to health care. As president of Interactive Training Designs, she consults with organizations to develop training solutions and designs interactive training for employees and managers.

Introduction

Imagine creating your future—the possibilities are limitless. The second edition of *Career Patterns: A Kaleidoscope of Possibilities* provides practical, proven methods to obtain the career you've always imagined. The accelerated rate of change today is creating exciting new possibilities for work that never before existed. Adaptability is the new reality of career planning for today and the future. This book provides ways to develop a flexible plan that will adapt to career opportunities that you haven't even imagined yet. By planning for the future, you'll be ready to capitalize on whatever opportunities come your way.

A student in a course just like the one you're taking asked a question. He asked, "I keep reading about how the workplace is changing, how jobs are disappearing, and how I can expect to have seven or eight careers in my lifetime. If all that is true, how can I possibly plan my career? Why should I invest in an education for a career that may not exist when I graduate?" Students with questions like these motivated us to write this book. We developed practical ways to help students not only plan for an uncertain future but also learn skills for lifetime career planning. We have written this book to help you prepare for your future and ensure that the education you invest in today will continue to add value and increase your future work options.

Although the future looks complex, confusing, and unpredictable, we see wonderful possibilities. Today, people have more options to choose from than ever before. More people are living the lives they want and finding meaning in their work. In our work and our research, we found people who love what they do and look forward to unknown possibilities. They have reinvented their careers by taking advantage of opportunities hidden in change. Their advice and suggestions appear throughout this book.

Often, career planning focuses on personal discovery—what is it you like to do? What are your interests, skills, and values? Although these elements are still very important to consider when choosing a career, it is just as important today to research and study the outside world. You will learn ways to identify the trends that will change or impact the career choices you make so that the future doesn't bring as many unwanted surprises. By learning to think and research like futurists, you will be better prepared no matter which future comes true.

How This Book Can Help You

This book will help you create your own flexible career plan. You'll learn how to analyze your strengths, desires, skills, and interests to create work opportunities. *Career Patterns* uses the model of a kaleidoscope. Just as a kaleidoscope creates endless patterns, your skills and talents can combine to create unlimited career options. This flexible approach to career planning allows you to adapt your skills throughout your working life to create new and varied work possibilities.

You'll also learn how to plan for new opportunities that you can't anticipate now, as well as find resources and ways to discover trends. We studied how businesses prepare for uncertainty using a process called *scenario planning*. In this book, you will apply this concept to career planning so you are prepared no matter what kind of future arrives.

Our goal is to guide you in creating a flexible career plan that adapts to emerging opportunities in the world of work. We've developed the *career kaleidoscope* so you can try out several options and adapt them in the future. Inside the back cover, you'll find "My Kaleidoscope Elements," your personal career kaleidoscope. The kaleidoscope is a hands-on tool to help you integrate all the intriguing information you'll discover about yourself in Chapters 3 and 4. As you complete each self-discovery activity, you'll record the results in your career kaleidoscope. In Chapter 4, you'll learn how to arrange and rearrange your kaleidoscope elements to form various career patterns. Each pattern holds the key to several career ideas uniquely suited to your preferences.

Whether you want to be an employee, a free agent, or an entrepreneur, you will learn proven strategies on how to search for the work you want and communicate effectively with employers. If you are starting college, you'll learn how to plan your education, find out what to major in, and what to do while you're in school to prepare for the real world of work. If a degree isn't in your plans, you'll find out how to continue your learning and apply what you know to new opportunities.

The last four chapters of this book provide you with the tools to gain work. You'll learn how to stand out in an interview by communicating your value to employers, design a resume targeted to the work you want, develop and use a professional network, and manage your work search.

Features of the Book

- **Real-Life Perspectives.** These stories describe events in the lives of real clients, students, employees, and employers, offering ideas you can apply to your situation.
- **Career kaleidoscope.** The kaleidoscope activities guide you from self-discovery to employability. This hands-on tool integrates all the information you'll discover about your preferences and uncovers potential careers uniquely suited to you.
- **Advice from experts.** Don't just take our word for it! We've inserted comments and advice from business owners, recruiters, and successful

employees. Find out how others have discovered work they love to do and how they started their careers. Obtain practical ideas you can use to increase your contribution and value to any organization.

- **Activities.** All of the chapters have exercises to encourage self-discovery. Gain new insights about yourself—what you love and where your talents lie. Learn how to translate your passions and talents into a satisfying career.

- **Internet resources.** As it rushes from infancy to widespread use, the Internet explodes with information about careers and work. There is no greater storehouse of up-to-date information. We've listed useful websites where you can read articles and discuss ideas with people who are actually working in careers that may interest you.

Using This Book

One thing we know for sure—you control your future. Although this book offers an excellent structure and system to lead to career satisfaction, you are in charge and must decide how to manage your own career. Creating a career plan that results in success requires a great deal of effort. At times, you will feel anxiety, uncertainty, and frustration. Resist the temptation to look for a quick solution, and take the time to discover what is best for you. Invest in your future by completing the activities, trying out new perspectives, and researching the future. The more effort and work you invest in planning your future, the better the results. We know it is worth the effort.

We're excited about the career opportunities that the future holds. We hope this book helps you share our enthusiasm. We believe career satisfaction is in your future—just use the ideas and strategies contained in these pages.

Career Patterns

A KALEIDOSCOPE OF POSSIBILITIES

SECOND EDITION

CHAPTER ONE

1 New Perspectives

UNDERSTANDING THE WORLD OF WORK

How is the workplace changing?

What new rules do you need to know?

Are certain jobs going away?

How is technology changing the way work gets done?

What trends are driving these changes?

Entering a career exploration class, students seek direction to help them navigate their futures. They hope to find answers to questions like: "What should I major in?" "What jobs pay the most?" "What are the best fields to go into?" "How will I find a job that's right for me?"

As students begin to discuss the future workplace and the promise it holds, valid concerns often underscore their thinking. "There are so many layoffs, cut-backs, and confusing messages. One minute, companies are hiring and the next, they're downsizing and you're gone." "How can I plan when the future is so uncertain?" "I'm afraid the company I work for will go under and I'll be out of work with no back-up plan."

Every time you open a newspaper or watch the news on TV, you hear something about the way work is changing. Now, more than ever, it is important to take the time to sort through the advice you hear and the facts you read to discover how change will impact you. Although you can't predict what your work will be like in 20 years, you can be sure it will be different from what it is today. This chapter examines your beliefs and assumptions about work to find out if they still hold true. It explores how work has changed over the last century and provides clues to explain the chaotic changes happening in our world today. It introduces major trends affecting the way we work, including the varied opportunities these trends are creating for new college graduates.

Change is inevitable, except from a vending machine.

Myth or Reality?

Your beliefs and assumptions act as filters, evaluating information and creating your worldview. Those you embrace as reality connect you to your past and shape your perceptions of the present. They can continue to influence your decisions even when they are no longer true. Most schools still dismiss students for the summer in June, even though students no longer spend summers harvesting crops. The no-school-in-the-summer tradition is left over from our agrarian past—when farm kids had to leave school to help in the fields. Other outdated social traditions may continue to shape your thinking.

Outdated myths and assumptions limit possibilities and impact the way you think about your future. If you're like most people, you may have difficulty separating myth from reality. Without realizing it, you may be relying on outdated advice as you plan for the future.

Myths die out slowly. Before you start making career decisions, separate fact from opinion. Check advice you've heard against the following facts.

FIGURE 1.1 *Student views.*

"My bilingual skills will give me a niche in developing markets in Central and South America."

"I plan to make $1,000,000 before I'm 30."

"High-touch skills will be in big demand—companies will always need people who relate well with others."

"Computer science is where technology is going. In the next 5–10 years, technology will do a 500-year leap. It will be like going from the Dark Ages to the 1900s in a decade."

"You have to see a need and make a job for yourself."

"I want to major in a high-demand occupation. I see too many temps where I work now."

"If I can just discover something I love to do, I'll be successful."

Myth: Company loyalty is rewarded with job security and a secure retirement.

Reality: Job security is a thing of the past. Career-savvy employees create financial security by choosing projects and opportunities to help them stay in demand as employees. Many employees find it more lucrative to change companies. People who continually develop new skills in their professions and seek new work opportunities earn more than their counterparts who remain loyal to one company.

"The myth is loyalty. Reality is it's a deal-based world."

JAMES TAYLOR AND WATTS WACKER, *The 500 Year Delta*

Loyalty can also be a disadvantage. If you've worked for only one employer, you may be seen as inflexible and afraid to try new things. Security is now defined in new terms—the ability to continually secure work through marketable skills that are in demand.

Myth: Good-paying jobs are available without a college education.

Reality: Most good-paying jobs now require specialized education. The earnings gap between college graduates and those without specialized skills continues to widen. Family income for high school dropouts fell 10 percent. For college graduates, it has soared up to 28 percent, says Cleveland-based economist John Burke. Clearly, workers with the best earning potential have specific marketable skills—skills acquired through higher education.

"High-tech international workers will account for more than 60 percent of the income earned in the U. S. by the year 2020."

JEREMY RIFKIN, *The End of Work*

The skills required for most jobs are increasing. One out of every four new jobs is technical. Almost all work requires the use of computers or other sophisticated electronic devices. Even jobs we once thought of as nontechnical now require computer literacy. The washer repairer uses a laptop to order parts, invoice clients, and access repair information. The automobile mechanic operates sophisticated diagnostic equipment to fix your car. The receptionist now coordinates employee communication systems—from voice mail and videoconferencing to managing e-mail. Nurses, who used to follow the directions of the doctor they assisted, now consult expert software to make independent decisions as home health care providers. As work changes, the workers who don't acquire the requisite new skills may lose their jobs.

Automated technology has replaced factory and manufacturing jobs—jobs associated with high pay for brawn. The work of the future demands mental, not manual, dexterity. Manufacturing work in the future will require engineering, computer, and other technical skills.

At the same time that high-paying blue-collar jobs decline, opportunities abound in low-paying service jobs. Although people without college degrees and specific marketable skills may easily find work, most of these jobs offer little future and also fail to provide the opportunity to develop marketable skills. Advancement opportunities and earning potential are decreasing for the unskilled worker. The gap between lifetime earning potential for college graduates and non-graduates is continually widening.

Myth: A college degree guarantees a good job.

Reality: A college degree doesn't come with any guarantees. A recent MBA graduate was complaining that even though unemployment was only 2 percent, she had no luck finding a professional job. When asked about the focus of her job search, she responded, "Oh, whatever, I just want to get my foot in the door." When asked if she had developed professional relationships or contacts while in school, she replied "Not really—I was too busy studying." When asked about relevant work experience or internships, she had none.

Graduates (even those with good grades from a good school) without a focused career goal and without exposure to the workplace will have difficulty finding that first professional job. College students tend to worry most about graduating from college. That makes sense and it's important! However, the sooner you develop a career target, the more time you can devote to exploring work through internships and other activities. College is about more than going to classes—it's about finding ways to fulfill your dreams.

"Within ten years, less than 12 percent of the American workforce will be on the factory floor, and by 2020, less than 2 percent of the global workforce will still be engaged in factory work. Over the next quarter century, we will see the virtual elimination of blue collar, mass assembly-line workers from the production process."

JEREMY RIFKIN, ***The End of Work***

Myth: The best jobs are in large corporations.

Reality: Large companies used to offer more advantages, including job security and career advancement opportunities, than smaller companies. That gap is narrowing. Since 1980, the proportion of the American workforce employed by Fortune 500 companies has shrunk by 25 percent.

Some of the best opportunities are in small companies. The real growth and opportunities for rapid advancement will come from micro-businesses (those started with fewer than four employees), venture-capital-backed start-ups and entrepreneurial-venture start-ups within large companies (Boyett and Conn, 1991).

Myth: Go to work for a good company and move up the career ladder.

Of the Fortune 500 companies listed in 1980, only 50 percent were still in existence in 1990.

Reality: In the past, many Americans worked for large companies where they had opportunities to move up and build careers over 20 or 30 years. New college graduates entered management training programs and followed predictable career paths, with periodic promotions. Fast-track employees conformed to organizational expectations. If it required a stint at corporate headquarters, you packed your bags and moved. Those days are over. Today, the responsibility for career advancement and employability has shifted from the company to the employee. Although companies may offer assistance through tuition reimbursement and training programs, the clear message is that you are responsible for developing your own career path, including finding ways to identify and learn the skills you'll need for continued success.

"People who think that they can develop a passion for something by desiring money are often doomed for failure. If you have a true passion for something, the money will eventually follow if you work hard."

ANTHONY P. CONZA, president, Blimpie International

Myth: Find the hot industry and you'll always be in demand.

Reality: Jobs and industries appear and disappear faster than the click of a mouse. Today's hot industry may be tomorrow's dead end. In the heyday of the '90s, everyone thought the dot-coms would survive and sustain employment for the thousands who went to work for them. Many workers who were laid off chose their next job in a traditional company, rather than stake their future on new start-ups. Hot predictions can result in a glut on the market as many undecided students switch to that major or industry. Instead of searching for today's hot industry, base your career decisions on your interests and capabilities. Too many students follow predictions only to end up disliking what they do.

Myth: Don't try to change jobs after age 40.

Reality: This year, approximately 26 million Americans will change jobs. Some workers will carefully make this choice, but many others will be surprised to learn their jobs have been eliminated. Of the workers polled in a 1997 Labor Day survey, two-thirds say they have switched careers. Millions have started their own businesses—most in mid-career.

Record numbers of adults are returning to school to pursue new opportunities. From 1980 to 1990, the enrollment of students age 25 and older increased by about a third, while that of students younger than 25 increased by only 1 percent. The average age of students at some commu-

Truth or Fiction? *Activity 1.1*

Instructions: List advice you have heard about working. Also list the source of the advice. Place a check mark in the first column if you believe the advice is no longer valid. Below is a sample to show you how to do it.

Example:

	SOURCE	ADVICE
✓	Dad	Go to work in government or education; you'll always have job security.
✓	Mom	You're always arguing; you should go into law.
✓	Bob Jones	Go to work for a big company—you'll always have job security.
?	Sally Frost	Once you get your foot in the door, meet the right people—it's who you know, not what you know.
?	Joe	Go into business; that's where the money is.

Your Turn:

	SOURCE	ADVICE
___	________	________________________________
___	________	________________________________
___	________	________________________________
___	________	________________________________
___	________	________________________________
___	________	________________________________

nity colleges has gone from the 20s to the 40s. The average age of students in executive MBA programs is 37, with an average of 13 years of previous work experience.

Jobs—The Past

"Jobs are not part of nature. They are historical products."

WILLIAM BRIDGES, *JobShift*

Observing how the structure of work has evolved over the past 100 years can give you pointers on how work might change in this century. The predictions of leisure time replacing work didn't materialize. Work is definitely not going away. However, it certainly seems that work will be packaged in a different way. Work hasn't always been organized neatly around jobs.

Until the mid-1800s, jobs didn't exist. Three out of every four workers farmed and lived in the countryside. They worked at whatever needed doing—shoeing horses, building barns, planting crops, and chopping wood. Most also sold or traded services to make money in the winter or when crops failed. Men, women, and children all worked hard on a variety of tasks—their schedules were set by the sun, the weather, and the needs of the day. People didn't choose careers or find jobs.

By 1810, industry was growing in America, with 75,000 workers employed in manufacturing. By 1875, farmers made up less than half of the labor force. Technological changes, such as the introduction of oil as a fuel and the harnessing of electricity, forever changed our lives and packaged work in a radical new way—jobs. William Bridges, in his book *JobShift*, describes the creation of jobs. He states, "The modern job was a startling new idea—to many people, an unpleasant and even socially dangerous one. Critics claimed that it was an unnatural and even inhumane way to work. They predicted that most people wouldn't be able to live with its demands. Americans even once talked about the job as *wage slavery* and contrasted it with the farmer's and craft person's freedom and security."

How will technology impact the future?

"After I thought more and more about it, and gave myself a headache thinking about it, I decided that the best thing I could tell you was: I don't know. And you don't know."

DEAN KAMEN, inventor of the I Bot

By 1900, less than one-third of workers were still farming. As Henry Ford made the automobile affordable, workers became mobile. Americans were moving from farms to the cities and finding jobs. The assembly line created specific jobs, where workers labored hour after hour repeating the same tasks. Modern factories needed fewer workers to produce the same amount of goods. Frederick Taylor published his *Principles of Scientific Management* in 1911, and American businesses began to search for efficiencies in every task.

Jobs became classified as unions rose in power to improve working conditions. Unions negotiated tasks and defined member eligibility based upon jobs, such as machinist or garment worker. The military classified work into jobs to clarify ranks and match skills with work. The civil service system, designed to eliminate nepotism, classified civil service work into specific jobs.

Now, it seems commonplace to define and organize work through jobs. Typical workers' remarks include: "My job is to process orders." "That's not part of my job." "That's Bill's job down in purchasing." In the past, work occasionally fell through the cracks when no one thought it was part of their job. Job descriptions would then be revised to accommodate the needed changes. The concept of jobs worked very well until recently. Today, jobs must be constantly redefined in response to changes in the way we work and do business.

Eyewitness

Activity 1.2

Because approximately 40 percent of the jobs that will be available in the next 10 years haven't been created yet, you may begin to wonder about the incredible world you will soon face. What kind of work will be created, and what will happen to today's jobs? In 1900, the thought of being an airline pilot was inconceivable. Today, 232,000 pilots and mechanics work in an industry that some naysayers said would never get off the ground! Let's say riding the rails was more your style, and you were among the 2,076,000 people who occupied railroad industry positions in 1920. Today, the trains still roll and still need workers, but the work has changed and the number of employees has shrunk to 231,000. As new industries emerge and familiar industries evolve, work will continue to change in response to social, economic, technological, environmental, and political factors.

Make a list of the major technological changes that have occurred in the last five years:

- ____________________
- ____________________
- ____________________
- ____________________
- ____________________
- ____________________

Select one of the changes you listed and answer this question: "What jobs have ended and what jobs have been created as a result of this new technology?"

____

____

____

____

____

____

Today, technological change happens faster, creating obsolescence sooner. Not only are DVDs quickly replacing videotapes—the entire distribution of entertainment is being challenged through Web-sharing technologies and cable-on-demand solutions. Today, it is hard to imagine that just a few years ago, most executives didn't know how to type and relied on secretaries to answer their calls, make appointments, and type their letters. Accurate typing was a skill in high demand before computers and spell check.

The Good Old Days

In an uncertain world of rapid changes and vanishing beliefs, it's easy to long for the good old days when life was simpler, work was certain, and you could count on the past to predict the future. When you think of days long gone, however, nostalgic memories often distort the reality of how things were.

Consider being a wage earner in most nineteenth-century factories. You could expect harsh working conditions with a strict floor boss or owner whose idea of discipline was a beating with a strap or a dunk in a water barrel! Your day would begin promptly at sunrise and end at sunset. In the summer, this could mean 14-hour days, and don't forget to add commute time—which could be as long as an hour each way, on foot! Accidents were common, and running a machine was a lot like "operating at your own risk" because there were no safety standards. The factory floor could be hot and damp in summer, and cold in winter. Coffee breaks were few and far between, and if you became ill—too bad, you could get fired and replaced. Sound grim? Read on. In the early 1900s, newspapers carried headlines* like:

Girl Conductors Operating Street Cars

Steel Mills Want Women

Women Print Liberty Bond in U. S. Bureau of Engraving. All but Presswork Done by Feminine Labor

Women Make Good Shingle Packers

- In 1890, only 19 percent of all women worked outside the home, and their choices were mostly limited to schools, hospitals, libraries, and social service.
- The average annual earnings of industrial workers in 1900 were less than $490. Included in that figure were some 1.7 million children who labored for as little as 25 cents a day.
- In the first six months of 1919, there were an estimated 2,093 labor strikes and lockouts.

As the century progressed, conditions began to improve for workers. The good news was that technology was creating bigger, faster machines. The bad news was that some workers were losing their jobs. Other workers struggled to keep up with increasing work demands while still collecting meager paychecks. In the 1950s, workers began working two years later and retired five years sooner. Paid holidays doubled and vacation days increased 63 percent.

*Headlines and background information from Philip S. Foner, *Women and the American Labor Movement—From World War I to the Present,* 1980.

Jobs—The Future

Some futurists, such as William Bridges, predict the end of the job concept. Work is increasingly being parceled into specific chunks that need to be done. The work may be done by full-time employees, outsourced to subcontractors, or completed by temporary or part-time employees. Industry will continue to look for ways to chunk work into manageable pieces so it can be quickly and cost-effectively completed.

Today people are inventing their own job titles: Vice President of Cool, Creatologist, Consultant, Knowledge Engineer, Vice President of Progress, Intangible Asset Appraiser.

Most of us still define ourselves by our job: "I'm a manager" or "I'm a computer programmer." The reality is that our work seldom fits into a neat job description. In actuality, we find people with the same job title doing very different types of work. See Figure 1.2 for old and new work rules.

Certain industries, such as the film industry, evolved without full-time jobs. Movie producers contract and cast the staff they need to work each production. People are hired based on the skills needed, from animal trainers to set designers to leading actors. Construction and farming are similar, con-

The old rules vs. the new rules. FIGURE 1.2

OLD RULES	NEW RULES
Loyalty to company	Loyalty to profession
Job security	Lifetime employability
Career ladders	Successive projects based on skills
School, work, retirement	Work, play, and learn continuously
Learning happens at school	Learning happens everywhere
Work to finance fun	Work is fun
Years of experience determine pay	Actual contributions determine pay
Boss controls your career options	You control your career options
Hierarchical management structures	Self-managed teams
Internal bureaucracies	Outsourcing, profit centers
Rigid	Fluid
Beat the competition	Partner with the competition
Base work options on past experience	Base work options on emerging opportunities

tracting for services as they are needed. No one knows how work will be packaged in the future or which of these models it will follow. However, work will look different for most of us as we enter the twenty-first century.

THE CHANGING WORKPLACE

We've described historical events that radically changed the landscape of the workplace. Although no one can accurately predict what further changes will happen, we know it will continue to evolve. The current outlook differs from the past in several ways, as we discuss below.

"The new vocation is not in the field of electronics, genetic engineering, or international trade. The new vocation exists within every field, for it requires not that one produce some particular new thing, but rather that one develop a new way of being productive."

WILLIAM BRIDGES, *JobShift*

1. Organizational Structure

All organizations today—whether large or small, government or nonprofit—focus on achieving results and building shareholder or public value. Each unit within an organization is treated as a business entity, responsible for contributing to profits and/or meeting customers' expectations. Because employees have access to information and work in teams to produce results, organizations are flatter—there are fewer levels of management between front-line employees and executives.

In 2000, 21 million people worked remotely.

Employment Policy Foundation

Companies retain full-time core employees whose work directly benefits the customer. Companies hire contingent workers during peak seasons and then terminate them during slow periods. Staff positions that support the business but don't directly serve the customer, such as those in accounting, billing, human resources, and even middle management, are often outsourced to professional firms that specialize in these services.

Nonstandard Jobs—A New Look

According to the Bureau of Labor Statistics, instead of holding a full-time job, more people are working in temporary or part-time jobs. The economy now includes as many as 5.6 million contingent workers—and many millions more if part timers are added to the mix.

2. New Work Contract Between Employer and Employee

Managers in the traditional workplace did not trust employees to perform work unless they constantly monitored and directed them. A parental relationship developed. Companies took care of employees and promised lifetime employment as long as the employees performed the job and met the expectations. The contract between employer and employee is different today. Employers no longer take on the parental role. There is no promise of lifetime employment. People are expected to perform every day, learn new skills, and take on new assignments. Employees have more freedom to make decisions about their work, and more responsibility to make a contribution and add value to the organization. It's a challenging world full of new possibilities, and employees are responsible for deciding what opportunities they want to pursue. They can no longer count on the company to design a career path for them.

3. New Work Values

After all of the layoffs, mergers, and restructuring in the workplace, employees no longer rely on organizations to think and plan for them. During the 1950s and 1960s, most employees were on a treadmill, performing the same jobs for years at a time. They traded autonomy for the security of lifetime employment. Today, employees want more freedom and a say in decisions that affect their work. Workers want to contribute in a meaningful way and see results from their efforts. If workers don't believe they are making a difference, or that they are appreciated, they may quickly move to another employer.

A survey in March, 2001, found that flexible work arrangements were the number one coveted employee benefit, beating out even healthcare.

LIFECARE BENEFITS COMPANY

4. More Work Options

Not only have the sheer numbers of companies in the United States increased significantly, but the ways employees contract their services to employers have also increased. Corporate layoffs forced employees to try new employment roles. Many people have tried the new work approaches and now would not trade them for employment that is more traditional. These new ways of working provide more autonomy and opportunity for new challenges. Employees who want continuous employability put more faith in situations that provide the opportunity to develop new skills than in full-time positions without these opportunities. With so many options

Work Options at a Glance

Core employee. Permanent employees are being referred to as core employees. The number of core employees is shrinking as companies increase their reliance on other hiring options. Core employees are directly involved in the products or services provided—in a manufacturing firm, they design, test, produce, and ship product.

Contingent worker. All types of nonpermanent employment—such as contract, temporary, free agent, and part-time work—engage the services of these workers. Contingent workers may contract directly with employers or they may be paid through a temporary agency, a contractor, or a consulting firm.

Concurrent worker. Working at two or more different careers at the same time is called concurrent work. An example is the computer programmer who writes code on a flex schedule that allows him to spend evenings and weekends pursuing his career as a rock musician.

Free agent. These highly skilled contingent workers are loyal to their profession rather than to one particular employer. Free agents look for interesting and challenging work that allows them the freedom to use their knowledge and provides opportunities to improve their skills.

Job sharer. Sometimes the best person for the job is two people. The advantage to the employer—there are two minds instead of one. The advantage to the job sharers—they can decide the work schedule that suits them best.

On-call worker. On-call workers are called into work when needed and aren't guaranteed a set number of hours. For example, an occupational therapist is called by a hospital or clinic when a patient needs his or her services.

available, it's important to learn about them and evaluate which are best for you at a particular stage in your career.

Mega-Trends—Transforming the Way We Work

The massive changes impacting work seem chaotic and confusing. We've attempted to organize this chaos into manageable chunks—five mega-trends redefining the way we live and work. These trends are not conclusive. They are ever evolving. We share excerpts from experts and try to present differing viewpoints. Throughout this text, you will be referred to websites, books, and magazines for more in-depth information on future trends.

Learning about new trends and understanding how they impact work will help you prepare for the future. As you read about these five trends and consider the questions we pose, imagine the opportunities you could create for yourself.

FIVE MEGA-TRENDS

1. Global Marketplace
2. Creativity
3. Interconnectivity
4. Generosity
5. Real Time

1. ONE BIG GLOBAL MARKETPLACE

American industries are opening offices around the world, while international companies are expanding into the United States. To compete globally, they are learning new approaches to manufacturing, marketing, and customer service. Global companies recruit the best and the bright-

REAL-LIFE PERSPECTIVE

FREE AGENTS

Imagine being your own boss, in charge of your own time. You wake up in the morning and decide how to structure your day, what projects get priority, whom to contact, how many hours you spend working, and where you want to work. Your office may be in the basement of your home, an area off the bedroom, or a space designated somewhere else in your home. Going to work means getting up, putting on your slippers, pouring a cup of coffee, and walking down the hall to your office. You could be dressed in your pajamas, slippers, and robe and decide to shower at noon. You determine your own work structure.

WHAT FREE AGENTS SAY

- "Working as a consultant, you have to do your own marketing, which means that you have to allot time to that process as well as put on a different mind-set. I personally found that very hard work. I also had to deal with the natural feelings of rejection when speaking to potential clients who didn't buy my services."
- "I must say that I like it. Money and a certain amount of freedom."
- "Typically, there is more variety in assignments."
- "You can have more flexibility in your schedule."
- "Big possibility of making less money (you only get paid when you have billable hours and clients willing to hire you)."
- "There are no buddies to meet in the hallway or bounce an idea off of. I've got a network of folks to call now, but it takes a while to set that up."
- "If you have nobody to do your support work, you have to do it yourself. Making copies, keeping the books, buying office supplies, putting handouts together . . . all that takes valuable time away from revenue generation."
- "I personally have to discipline myself to get dressed before I go to my basement office, or I find myself in front of my computer at 3:00 P.M. still in my jammies!"
- "Companies expect you to be at your best at all times, no ups or downs, because they are paying you premium bucks to be the best. You need to guard your emotions and mood swings so that you are always professional and prepared."
- "Autonomous freedom is wonderful—especially if your previous experience was micro-managed. On the other hand, you may (and probably will) find yourself working much harder and for longer hours than you ever did for someone else."

INDEPENDENT CONSULTING ARRANGEMENT RIGHT OUT OF SCHOOL?

- "It's important to build your experience with the real world some place, and doing it as an independent is not the best way. If you link up with a consulting company that places you on assignments, that's different. But, there is certainly a need to work with other experts while you learn the ropes and build skills up front."
- "The rule of thumb is three to five years to get established, make a name for yourself, set up networks, and start earning enough money so you won't break into a cold sweat when the monthly bills are due. A college student with few contacts and little experience will probably find it extremely difficult to get established."

Source: Thanks to Nigel Higgs, Communication Skills & Change Skills Consulting; Paul Buerk, APLAN Information Services Inc.; and Molly Samuels, The Molidori Group, Inc. for their insights.

10 Advantages of Working in the Twenty-First Century

- More career opportunities—new fields are emerging every day
- More flexibility in how and where work is performed
- Greater opportunity to contribute your ideas and express yourself through work
- The chance to work on innovative projects, products, and services
- Greater diversity in the workplace
- The ability to go in your own direction, rather than a course set by your employer
- Greater opportunity to work on teams that break barriers to innovation
- Freedom to create situations or positions where you can fill a need in the marketplace
- More opportunities for entrepreneurs, free agents, and independent contractors
- The flexibility to reshape your career as your values and interests change

est—individuals who can handle responsibility, are sensitive to cultural differences, and are eager to bring new ideas to the marketplace.

As global offices continue to expand with workers from all parts of the world, employees face new challenges. People must connect across organizational boundaries as well as national boundaries. National borders lose their importance as commerce thrives over the Internet. Information work can be produced from anywhere. Time zones, rather than geographic locations, determine work teams. Software developers in the Far East may pass on their work to team members in Europe, who then pass the project on to their colleagues in North America, resulting in a 24-hour production day. Competition for commodities has been global for some time. The rise and fall of foreign stock markets affects the cost of materials used around the world. The price of soy beans depends on worldwide weather and economic conditions.

As borders shrink, global opportunities expand. You can tap into the global marketplace by learning which companies have foreign subsidiaries or interests.

How is the global marketplace changing the way you work now?

How will globalization impact you in the future?

2. CREATIVITY IS ESSENTIAL

The United States was founded on American ingenuity—finding new and better ways to do things. Today, it's not enough to bring one great innovative solution to market. Organizations (and workers) must constantly look for new and better ways to solve customers' needs. When change was incremental instead of monumental, slight adaptations worked. Today, you must learn how to create what has never been created before, not just improve on what already exists. Creativity is no longer a nice-to-have characteristic, but a crucial asset for survival.

"The world will not evolve past its current state of crisis by using the same thinking that created the situation."

ALBERT EINSTEIN

In the past, American business generally discouraged creativity. Workers completed their jobs as well as possible and left the creative thinking to the top executives, the design engineers, and the advertising department. Worker involvement changed with the total quality movement (TQM). No longer were workers expected to check their independent ideas at the factory door. Today, workers are asked to look for innovative solutions to improve quality, and creative thinking techniques are taught in corporate training rooms. Creative thinking is an essential skill we all have and can strengthen. Each time you have a novel idea, solve a problem, or put old ideas together into new combinations, you are creative. Creative people believe that failure is not a waste of time. They strive to see what works and what doesn't work, using their failures to trigger new ideas.

"Imagination is more important than knowing."

ALBERT EINSTEIN

Many of us think only artists are creative. In reality, everyone has the potential to be creative. Land and Jarman (1992) said:

> Even though some have long maintained that a few chosen humans are special because they're creative, the undeniable fact is that even atoms behave in ways that could be defined as *creative.* So do molecules, cells, plants, and animals. They invent novel forms, shift to new behaviors, combine in unpredictable—and unprecedented—ways. Far out in the nether reaches of the universe, stars form and galaxies coalesce in a creative process. The noted scientist and philosopher Karl Popper concluded, "The universe, is in a sense, creative." Unleashing the creative spirit within each of us will happen only when we recognize the natural creativity that lies within everything and everybody—and willingly remove the tight barriers that have us convinced that only a few special people are creative.

When was the last time you felt creative?

What were you doing?

What creative ideas have enhanced your work?

3. INTERCONNECTIVITY CREATES VALUE

"This century is going to turn our world upside down. The Internet combines people and ideas faster than they have ever been combined before."

TIM BERNERS-LEE, director, WWW Consortium, M.I.T.

The haves and have-nots of tomorrow will be defined by interconnectivity. Whom can you connect with and how quickly? Interconnectivity is not just about networking between computers and accessing information. Interconnecting with people and developing relationships are more important than ever—both online and in person.

Even though telecommuting and home offices allow you to work alone, connecting with others is still crucial. Whether chatting with other home office workers at Kinko's or sending instant messages, staying connected to other humans is a priority.

"The new vocation is not in the field of electronics, genetic engineering, or international trade. The new vocation exists within every field for it requires not that one produce some particular new thing, but rather that one develop a new way of being productive."

WILLIAM BRIDGES, *JobShift*

Organizations now expect workers and suppliers to collaborate to solve problems. Today, most employees in companies with more than 50 employees work in self-managed or problem-solving teams. Workers are expected to be team players from the start. Team members change as work and problems change. Employees must demonstrate the interpersonal skills to connect and get along with everyone.

As networks expand, their value increases. The value of the Internet increases with each person who logs on. Sharing resources increases their value. LISTSERVs® have become increasingly popular as people share information with colleagues and use word of mouth to increase the value of the network. It is estimated that LISTSERVs® on the Internet are growing at 5 to 10 percent per month. The more people connected to the list, the more valuable the information. It's possible to pose specific professional questions to 3,000 knowledgeable people and in a matter of minutes, receive replies from colleagues around the world.

The rules of the game have changed. It's no longer about who wins and who loses. The new rules involve finding ways to network together to increase the value for everyone involved.

How can you develop professional relationships?

In what ways could interconnectivity change your work?

4. GENEROSITY CREATES WEALTH

In the past, natural resources defined wealth. The law of supply and demand drove up prices as a commodity became less available. Scarcity created value. In the Information Economy, the rules have changed. Power now comes from abundance rather than scarcity. The more common something becomes, the more it pays to stick to that standard. For example, as Windows NT proliferates, more companies buy Windows NT and soon it becomes the standard. As AA batteries become the norm, the demand for AA batteries increases. As more people use Yahoo! as a search engine, the more Yahoo! becomes the standard. This dramatic shift in the way wealth grows has changed businesses and work. In the 1980s, no one would have guessed that:

- VCRs and DVDs would make movies more popular and increase attendance at movie theaters.
- Giving away software would build market share.
- Fast-food restaurants would sell more burgers when they're across the street from each other.
- Microsoft would invest in its competitor, Apple.
- Competing chip manufacturers would partner together to share training resources and recruit employees.

What new partnerships are influencing business today?

Who could you partner with to build career opportunities?

5. WORKING IN REAL TIME

Time seems compressed. Everything seems to be moving faster and faster. Consumers demand faster and better service in everything from express hotel check-out to instant loan approval.

Idea-to-market time has decreased dramatically in most industries as companies utilize new technology to anticipate and meet customer needs.

"Change gives us psychic whiplash."

JAMES TAYLOR AND WATTS WACKER, *The 500 Year Delta*

"The future is out, now is in."

REGIS MCKENNA, *Real Time*

Sony has produced a new version of the Sony Walkman every three weeks since it was introduced. Tylenol markets more than 41 varieties of its pain suppressant.

Fashion designers used to take a year to develop the fall or spring line. Computerized sewing combined with ink-jet fabric printing now allows clothing designers to reduce the design-to-runway time to mere days. Obviously, the next step is consumers designing their own clothes and having the fit customized and the clothes delivered immediately. Already, you can order a custom pair of jeans, designed to fit your body perfectly.

Increasingly, customers' expectations define the product. Middlemen are eliminated as production-to-customer links grow and expand. Regis McKenna (1997), a pioneer in modern marketing, calls this *real time*. "Real time occurs when time and distance vanish, when action and response are simultaneous." Work is redefined in terms of what the customer wants today. Although many real-time experiences are obvious, most are not. You operate in real time when you:

- Obtain instant credit approval
- Withdraw cash from your ATM 24 hours a day
- Watch live events from around the world on TV
- Participate in a teleconferencing call with people from around the world

"We will increasingly find that the technologies of speed will not give us the time to see or plan beyond the horizon. We will have to think and act in real time," says McKenna.

Long-term plans don't work like they did in the past—no one knows what work will look like in 10 years, let alone 40 years. Practice and sharpen your short-term thinking to make real-time decisions to carry you through the long run. Marathon runners don't train by running marathons daily. They train for the long race by running sprints and short distances. By continually adapting their pace and form, they build up stamina and prepare for competition. Like marathon runners, if you continually practice and adapt your skills, you can prepare for a successful future. Career planning is no longer a one-time event. Planning in real time means creating a series of short-term plans that you can adapt to meet changing needs. Although you can't prevent the surprises lurking around the corner, you can develop the skills to effectively maneuver through them.

How is your world moving faster than before?

How have your expectations as a consumer changed?

Summary Points

- Myths shape your perceptions and expectations about work. By recognizing which myths are outdated and which new ones are emerging, you can evaluate the new realities. These realities impact your career choices and the way you will work.
- High-velocity changes in technology have eliminated the need for many jobs. Jobs disappear, but the need for work never does. New work is created based on social, economic, technological, environmental, and political change.
- Work will look different in the future. Five new mega-trends can help you redefine the way you live and work and plan for the future.

CHAPTER TWO

2 Careers

THINKING IN NEW WAYS

How has career planning changed?

How do you plan in uncertain times?

What is the connection between your career goals and your beliefs?

How do self-confidence and adaptability build career resiliency?

Planning a career is like driving a car at night. When you're driving, you can't see any farther ahead than the area illuminated by your headlights. It does help to have a destination and purpose for your trip. But no matter how well you've planned your trip, a lot can happen along the way. Sometimes, even a quick trip to the supermarket involves unforeseen events—an unexpected detour suddenly appears, you stop to buy gas, you remember to buy a birthday card for Uncle Albert, another driver needs assistance, or you have to return home because you forgot your wallet. In spite of all of these factors, if your headlights are on, you can make the whole trip.

We live in a turbulent, constantly changing environment where old assumptions and beliefs no longer help us navigate. When planning your career, you can't always see as far ahead as you might like. But that shouldn't discourage you from starting the trip. It helps to have a purpose, but in the new work world, you can expect your destination to change along the way.

"Writing a novel is like driving a car at night. You can only see as far as your headlights, but you can make the whole trip that way."

E. L. DOCTOROW

A sudden detour on a trip is frustrating, especially when you are pressed for time and have a definite destination in mind. However, detours can lead to interesting sights and encounters—it just depends on your attitude. If you plan too precisely, you'll miss opportunities for new experiences. The adventurous see unplanned events as the chance to develop, grow, and do surprising things. They set a direction and let the adventure unfold.

That's what we're asking you to do as you read this book. You'll be setting a direction, and then letting your career evolve as new opportunities arise. We're asking you to embrace different expectations about work and your career. Instead of setting your sights on job security, replace it with a more realistic objective—lifetime employability. Your employability depends on your ability to adapt to change. Will you bounce back from the uncertainties, innovations, and business changes you'll face during your worklife? What's fundamentally different now is that you are in charge of your career, as though you're in business for yourself. You'll be responsible for keeping your eye on the horizon to sense new trends and the opportunities that come with them.

"Today the materials and skills from which a life is composed are no longer clear. It is no longer possible to follow the paths of previous generations."

MARY CATHERINE BATESON, *Composing a Life*

Maneuvering successfully through the maze of changes in the workplace is like driving at night. We've interviewed many people with their headlights focused on the near future. We've identified the strategies they use to keep moving in the sometimes-treacherous landscape of work and organizations. We're asking you to use these same strategies as you plan your adventure through the world of work. We've discarded the traditional career-planning question, "What do I want to be when I grow up?" A better question to ask is, "What kind of life do I want to create?" Asking the right questions today—"What work has to be done now?" and "How do I want to contribute to the work?"—will help you set a course toward personal satisfaction and meaningful work.

"Alice asked, 'Would you tell me, please, which way I ought to go from here?' 'That depends a good deal on where you want to get to,' said the cat. 'I don't much care where,' said Alice. 'Then it doesn't much matter which way you go,' said the cat."

LEWIS CARROLL, *Alice in Wonderland*

How People Make Career Choices

Some people define a career as work that one enjoys. Actually, your career is the sum total of all of the work you do in your lifetime—regardless of how much you enjoy it.

If you're like most people, your career choices up to now have been hit or miss. You began formulating your ideas about work as a small child when you pretended to put out fires like a firefighter or twirl like a ballerina. Ordinary events and everyday experiences shaped your perceptions of who you are and how you might fit into the work world. Often, without asking, you received feedback from teachers, family, and friends about what you do well: "You're really good at arguing; you should become a lawyer" or "You're a whiz at math; go into engineering." In addition, you hear various and often conflicting messages about work. All of these messages influence your decisions. For example, you might hear: "Medicine doesn't pay what it used to, find something else." "You need to learn computers to get a good job." "Women are breaking through the glass ceiling." "Women can't do that."

You develop beliefs about various kinds of work and whether you think the work will provide you with the things you want: "Go into programming like Jane—she's a programmer, and she has a beautiful new house." "I want to become a teacher so I can make a difference in children's lives." "I want to make the environment safe for future generations."

"Focus on computers, continuous education, networking, and career planning that emphasize mobility across different industries that are increasingly interrelated (such as communications and entertainment) and whose boundaries are increasingly porous."

ROBERT REICH, former Secretary of Labor

As a final step, you look at the jobs that appeal to you and determine which ones you think you could do. For example, you may think that lawyers have just the lifestyle you're looking for, but if you don't think you're smart enough to go to law school, you discard that choice and look at occupations where you think you can be successful. Or, perhaps you gave up on deciding for yourself and took a job recommended by a friend or relative.

This hit or miss approach has many problems. Often the advice you get from family and friends is the advice they wish they had taken. Such advice says more about them than it does about you. Most of the information you hear is incomplete, leaving you with a slanted, and sometimes false, view of work. Second, the jobs you hear about are only a small fraction of the work that is actually available. Everyone in your family may be in education or law, so that's the work you hear about. If you live in a small town with one major employer (everyone you know works at the automobile factory) that may be the total universe of jobs to you. Third, your belief in your abilities is a big contributor to the decisions you make. If your experience is limited or your self-esteem is low, you may be talking yourself out of work you can do. Deciding your future in this way, while common, often yields poor results.

The History of Career Planning

The profession of career development arose to help people take a more organized approach to selecting a career. At the time, jobs were stable and relatively unchanging. Career planning helped answer the question, "What do I want to be when I grow up?" Career counselors usually emphasized an assessment of your interests and preferences. Once you identified your traits or strengths, you could identify the job that matched those traits. This approach fit the linear thinking of the times: First, you get an education, then you get a job using that education, then you work at that job for a number of years, and then you retire. Using the traditional planning model, career options were evaluated by looking at average salaries, occupational demand, working conditions, and the required skills and education necessary to perform the work.

"Because the future is not linear, you cannot prepare for it with one single plan."

MICHAEL MICHALKO, *Thinkertoys*

Planning was based on the underlying assumption that everything would go according to the *plan*. This thinking worked well when work stayed the same and you could count on the job being there until retirement. Today's chaotic work world, however, demands more flexibility when planning your career.

"The critical issue today is not how to get there. It is where do you want to be?"

JAMES TAYLOR AND WATTS WACKER, *The 500 Year Delta*

In today's reality, job descriptions and job titles are disappearing and work is increasingly defined by projects that change with the introduction of new technology and different needs in the marketplace. Using a decision-making process that reaches a permanent conclusion (one perfect job for life) sets people up for unemployment. The rules *have* changed, so the way you plan your career should change too—it must be flexible and constantly evolving. Your career search should answer the question that fits today's reality: "How do I maintain employability throughout my work life?

Planning for Uncertainty

You may be wondering if there is so much change occurring, what good does it do to plan a career? It isn't that planning won't work, but this new work world requires a new planning perspective. How do you plan for today's reality?

Although we can't know exactly what the future holds, we can create flexible plans that allow for uncertainty. We can reframe our idea of planning into a flexible, evolving process. *Reframing* is the ability to see problems, situations, things, or people from a new angle with a different perspective (see Figure 2.1). To think of your life without a box labeled retirement is to reframe it. To conceive of learning as a continuous process that you manage, rather than as a classroom you attend, is to reframe it. To imagine work as 2,000 hours a year, instead of five days a week, is to reframe it. The way to reframe career planning is to change it from a long-term, do-it-once-and-it's-done process to a continuous, constantly changing strategy.

An excellent resource for how to get out of linear thinking about careers is Richard Bolles's first classic book, *The Three Boxes of Life.*

Plan your career to keep up with continuous changes in the world of work. When some jobs are disappearing and work is constantly changing, your career planning must evolve. The purpose of this text is not to help you choose one job or career but to give you methods to maintain employability throughout your lifetime. Asking good questions leads to finding out what's really happening so you can take advantage of new opportunities. This book is based on the premise that an awareness of technological

FIGURE 2.1 *Reframing helps you stay flexible.*

REFRAME FROM	TO
• Things will go according to my plan.	• Some parts of my plan won't work, and I can't know which ones until I get there.
• I can control the events in my life.	• Unexpected events are bound to occur.
• Unexpected events are problems to solve.	• Unexpected events are new opportunities to explore.
• The status quo is comfortable.	• The status quo is obsolete.
• I plan what I want to be.	• I plan what I want to be doing in the future.
• This plan worked last year.	• Following any plan for too long, no matter how successful in the past, leads to obsolescence.
• I choose a career.	• I grow and learn to maintain employability.

and marketplace developments is just as important as knowing your personal strengths. Career planning is a creative, flexible process involving a dynamic interchange between identifying your assets and discovering the needs of those organizations that will contract for your skills for a finite period of time. You cannot assume that any set of circumstances will stay the same, or you will be left behind. As William Bridges (1994) says:

> We are moving beyond jobs today as surely as we moved into them almost 200 years ago. At that time there was a very popular story about a man who went to sleep and awoke to find that enormous changes had taken place and that life had passed him by. Washington Irving's character, Rip Van Winkle, didn't fit into the job world that was just then emerging, for he had what his creator called "an insuperable aversion to all kinds of profitable labor, although he was always ready to lend a hand at the old communal tasks of barn raising." The modern Rip Van Winkles are in danger of repeating his mistake and waking to find themselves old people in a world that they cannot any longer understand.

FLEXIBLE CAREER PLANNING

A flexible career plan is not a linear step-by-step process or a cookbook recipe for success. It prioritizes your values and distinguishes unrealistic wishes from achievable goals. It helps you set targets for achievements and encourages you to take advantage of emerging opportunities. A flexible career plan is:

- **Time limited—**Instead of a search for one perfect job that will last a lifetime, ask, "What do I want to do for the next one to six years?" Remember that you are driving in the dark on a rapidly changing road full of unknown detours! By following the strategies outlined in this book, you will be able to anticipate changes that affect you and your future work.
- **Framed by your core focus—**Discover work that is meaningful to you. Finding work that connects your talents to real needs is the secret to satisfaction. Your core focus can serve as a guide to finding worthwhile opportunities.
- **Continually shifting—**You will change your work frequently throughout your lifetime as technology and global competition impact the world of work. The new requirement of success for workers today and tomorrow is the ability to adapt and stay employed.
- **Ever-evolving—**You'll design your career plan to take advantage of new opportunities created by technology and evolving job markets. Your ability to anticipate and adapt to change is the litmus test for your success. You must continually assess your profession and the marketplace, searching for answers to questions like these: "What problems can I solve with my skills?" "What new technology is impacting my work?" "What do I have to learn to remain employed?"
- **Thinking of yourself as your business—**Manage your work life like a business plan for the future. Whether you work for an employer or you're self-employed, base your decisions on market needs, not just your expertise. Reframe your thinking from "I'm a journalist," to "What problems can

For anyone interested in career-related news and websites: www.careerpronew.com

be solved with my journalism skills?" In this age of information overload, we don't need more information as much as we need journalists to help us find relevant information, sort truth from fiction, and apply knowledge from one field to another. Continually look at the marketplace and, like the journalist, ask, "What are people's needs, and how can I use my skills to fulfill these needs?"

- **Considering alternative work options**—This is good news for those who enjoy variety. As businesses outsource more services (hire the work from outside providers rather than do the work themselves), your work structure may change frequently. Even high-level executives are finding the world of contract employment to be a lucrative, satisfying alternative to a permanent job. In your lifetime, you may work as a core employee, contract employee, and entrepreneur. Sometimes, you may work for one employer at a time; other times, you may have two or more concurrent sources of employment.

CAREER KALEIDOSCOPE—A TOOL FOR FLEXIBLE PLANNING

Up to this point, we've emphasized the changes that will occur in the workplace. However, what about you? You're just as likely to change as the workplace. You'll have new experiences, learn new skills, and develop new interests. You'll want different things from your career at different stages in your life.

We've met and talked to many students at different points in their lives. For a variety of reasons, they wanted to take a new look at themselves and redirect their careers. Some students were promoted to management positions, and then learned they didn't want to be responsible for the work of others. Students on the fast track at work wanted enough time to raise their families. Some took early retirement and then discovered they weren't quite ready for the golf course full-time! Like you, these students wanted a new way to discover their work preferences and motivations. They wanted a method that recognized they would change throughout their lifetime. A new tool that accommodates flexible career planning and your personal development is the career kaleidoscope.

Think about your career as though you were looking through a kaleidoscope. When you hold a kaleidoscope toward light, pieces of colored glass are reflected on mirrors, creating a collage of color. Each time you turn the kaleidoscope, you rearrange the glass pieces to form new patterns. Although only a few pieces of glass are contained in the kaleidoscope, endless patterns can be created from them.

Instead of glass, a career kaleidoscope contains your skills, interests, preferences, education, abilities, and knowledge. These elements can combine in various ways to form many patterns or work choices. Like the students we interviewed, you'll want to add new elements to your kaleidoscope as you gain different experiences, acquire new skills, and learn new knowledge. You may also decide to remove some elements as your interests and values change. By turning your kaleidoscope this way, you bring new career options into focus. Even a slight shift in your kaleidoscope creates a new view—a pattern of surprising career opportunities you may never have considered. Just as a kaleidoscope is constantly changing and evolving, so will you and your career.

In Chapters 3 and 4, you will complete self-assessment activities and create your own career kaleidoscope. Your kaleidoscope will be filled with career elements—your values, preferences, interests, and skills. You'll shift your kaleidoscope so you can see a wide variety of career options. Your career kaleidoscope is a tool that makes flexible planning and lifelong personal development possible.

Career Management Strategies

1. **Self-Management.** Choose an empowered mindset by developing self-confidence and adaptability.
2. **Self-Awareness.** Discover what interests, skills, values, and preferences build your career satisfaction and success.
3. **Futurist Thinking.** Continually scan the work environment to discover emerging trends and needs.
4. **Flexible Planning.** Use career information to develop and implement career decisions. Adapt your plan to meet evolving needs created by changes in the workplace.
5. **Continuous Learning.** Commit to lifelong learning that includes developing new skills to meet changing business needs.
6. **Communicate Value.** Align with new work opportunities by developing skills to market you.
7. **Obtaining Work.** Sharpen your skills to obtain or change your career or position.

HOW TO MANAGE YOUR CAREER

What's the difference between launching a career and managing it? Your career launch begins when you choose a career direction and follow it. Career management, on the other hand, is the ongoing planning and development of your career.

Managing your career is making choices along the way—deciding whether it's better to move from one industry to another doing the same work, or deciding to move up and learning how to accomplish it. Managing your career may involve new career choices, or it may involve developing new skills for the same employer. Either way, it is continuing to choose the path you want to follow as you evolve, grow, and discover new opportunities.

Your career path is your choice—a unique journey based on your values, strengths, and interests. You won't find your path spelled out for you in a book, website, or personnel handbook. Your path is your own creation. We have developed seven Career Management Strategies to guide you on your path. Each one is designed to keep your headlights on—focused on the landscape ahead. In this book, you'll work with each strategy so you can launch your career successfully.

One of the greatest challenges you're likely to face throughout your life is learning to live with change and uncertainty. Some changes are inevitable; others are necessary. When you learn to anticipate change and deal with uncertainty, change can be advantageous. The Career Management Strategies will help you anticipate change and prepare as transformations in the workplace impact your previous decisions. Used continuously throughout your working life, these strategies allow you to take charge of your career, whatever circumstances you face. Using them will maintain your employability and bring continuous career satisfaction.

Self-Management

Managing your career is a paradox: On the one hand, remaining employable requires you to be more responsible than previous generations for managing your career; on the other hand, work is changing so rapidly it's harder than ever to know how to manage your career successfully.

You are the person in charge of your career. That's good news for people who know what they want and have the self-confidence to obtain it. But for those who are less sure of themselves, this might sound imposing. Each of us creates a mental framework that holds our beliefs about our capabilities. We make daily judgments about what we can or cannot do. Based on our beliefs, we talk ourselves into or out of our choices. Deciding on the work that is most meaningful to you begins with an open mind, free from self-imposed restrictions and constraints.

The first step toward successful career management is choosing an empowered mindset. Empowerment is a way of thinking about yourself and your goals. It's an approach to life giving you permission to strive for your aspirations. Without this mental outlook, the career choices you make will remain dreams. It takes empowerment to turn dreams into reality.

"Creative people shape their lives with a profound sense of personal meaning. They are not manipulated by circumstances. They are responsible, free, and fulfilled. They love and enjoy their lives, their work, and the people around them. They are energized by purpose. They continually discover new resources and possibilities. They feel great satisfaction and peace of mind flowing from the contributions they make in shaping a better life and world."

GEORGE LAND AND BETH JARMAN, *Breakpoint and Beyond*

To feel empowered, you'll need two competencies: self-confidence and adaptability. Self-confidence is believing in yourself and your ability to achieve your goals. Adaptability allows you to cope with unexpected events and bounce back. Both adaptability and self-confidence are learned behaviors—which means it's not to late to acquire them!

Self-Confidence

Why are some people able to set goals and attain them while others drift through life, trapped in dead-end jobs? Self-confidence, rather than talent or training, usually makes the difference.

Self-confidence is your belief in your own competency. Your confidence is a perception—and it isn't necessarily based on reality. What do

REAL-LIFE PERSPECTIVE

LAUREN

Although Lauren knew that she wanted to go to college, she was still trying to decide on a major. Lauren had always loved animals, particularly horses. She had spent every spare moment riding and caring for her horses for as long as she could remember. Based on her interest in animals, becoming a veterinarian seemed a natural choice for her.

However, Lauren immediately rejected the idea. She believed that she wasn't good at math. Though she had excelled in science classes in high school, she deliberately chose not to enroll in any higher math courses. Now she feels it's too late to start learning algebra. She believes her career dream is out of reach.

you believe about your abilities? Is your appraisal realistic, or do you tend to underrate yourself? Psychologists are studying the connection between thoughts, beliefs, and behavior. They have discovered that people choose to do what they think they can attain. Rarely do they choose to do what they think is impossible. As Henry Ford once said, "If you think you can't or you think you can, you're right."

"If it is to be, it is up to me."

In Figure 2.2, Bill is not a very happy person. He believes things are not really within his control. The arrows represent his perception—events are always happening *to* him, controlled entirely by the outside world. This perception leads him to avoid making decisions or taking action to achieve his goals. He often sees himself as a victim of the system or other people. He doesn't know what he can do about that. Bill has quit trying to succeed. He often feels helpless and hopeless. Examples of how he interprets events: "If only . . . ; there's nothing I can do; that's just the way I am." If someone suggests a solution to a problem, his response is always, "Yes, but . . ." He has reasons readily available to show why any new idea wouldn't work.

Sam, on the right, is a happy, confident person. He takes action to make things happen to his benefit. By setting goals and planning, Sam systematically works to achieve his goals. He knows that not everything is within his control—unforeseen things do happen. However, he believes he can overcome obstacles. Sam feels that some of the best things in his life have happened as a result of an obstacle or change he didn't predict. His interpretations of events: "I can choose a different approach; I will . . . ; I control my own feelings." When he has a problem, he welcomes suggestions from others about how to solve it. He refuses to believe he is helpless and is optimistic that things will work out for the best.

"What lies behind us and what lies before us are tiny matters compared to what lies within us."

RALPH WALDO EMERSON

How do you perceive the world? FIGURE 2.2

Are you more like Bill or Sam?

Bill and Sam both have a frame of reference, or belief system, that influences how they perceive reality. Their beliefs color their interpretations of events and act as filters for new information. Both of them, like all of us, tend to notice information that coincides with their viewpoints and tend to ignore information that contradicts what they already believe. These filters are partially conscious and partially unconscious. If you identify your hidden filters and consciously question your assumptions, you will be more able to accept new information. As you learned in Chapter 1, holding on to old assumptions hinders your ability to prepare for the future. Accurate information about yourself and what is happening in the world of work will help you make intelligent choices.

CONNECTIONS BETWEEN BELIEFS AND SUCCESS

Martin Seligman, a psychologist, studied the difference between optimists and pessimists. Through his extensive research, Seligman has shown that the way a person explains events is a strong predictor of success. Pessimists explain life's events as permanent ("These things always happen to me"), pervasive ("Everything is ruined"), and personal ("It's all my fault"). Optimists respond to adverse events by explaining them as temporary setbacks, limited to those events, and external (not their fault). Seligman has conducted many studies to demonstrate that optimists are more successful than pessimists. In one study, people who didn't meet the usual hiring criteria but scored high on Seligman's optimism scale were hired to sell insurance. They outsold—by 88 percent—experienced salespeople who were pessimistic.

"Everyone has inside him a piece of good news. The good news is that you don't know how great you can be! What you can accomplish! And what your potential is!"

ANNE FRANK

If you would like to acquire greater self-confidence, the first step is to identify your assumptions about yourself. Once you understand that your interpretations of reality affect your thoughts and behaviors, it's possible to change them. You can choose to see reality from a different perspective. You can discard outdated beliefs and form new ones. How do you interpret events in your life? Are you generally optimistic or pessimistic? One way to identify your attitude is to think about borrowing money. Do you usually believe that you shouldn't borrow money because you won't be able to pay it back in the future? Or, do you feel confident that things will work out better in the future, so the loan will be easy to pay back? If you tend to see the world as a pessimist, worrying about money in the future, you can consciously change that belief.

Earlier in this chapter, you looked at ways to reframe your perceptions about work and careers. Reframing is a process of seeing a problem from a different viewpoint. It involves countering assumptions that limit your thinking. You can use the same technique to reframe your beliefs about yourself and your capabilities. Read the example below of how Annie reframed her beliefs to gain self-confidence and increase her career options.

Your self-confidence is not constant. Everyone has days when they make a mistake, or they fail to achieve a goal—those days when they think they can't do anything right. On those occasions, you might find you are blaming yourself for what happened. Without knowing it, you may judge

REAL-LIFE PERSPECTIVE

ANNIE

"I barely graduated from high school. I feel I was lucky to get my diploma—most of my grades were C's and D's. Occasionally, I would get lucky and receive a B! At the time, I valued socializing, not learning. Consequently, I grew up believing I was intellectually inferior—I wasn't smart enough to do well in school. After all, my grades reinforced my beliefs. After high school, I wondered what to do with myself; college was certainly out of the question. My parents believed I could do well as a hairdresser because in high school I enjoyed creating new hair designs for my friends. So, off to cosmetology school I went. I completed the year-long training program and actually graduated in the top of my class. I obtained work as a hairdresser but knew this wasn't what I wanted to do forever. I decided to confront my old belief system about not being smart enough to do well in school and enrolled in a psychology course at a local community college. I enjoyed learning about human behavior and received an A for my hard work and effort. The experience changed my life. By disputing old realities and beliefs about my abilities, I was able to pursue a college education and change my career path. I now have a master's degree in educational psychology and work as a counselor in the field of human services."

Annie reframed her beliefs about school, which expanded her career choices.

Old Beliefs

I can't do well in school.

I'm not smart enough to go to college.

College is too hard for me.

New Beliefs

I can achieve good grades.

I can pass the course.

By applying myself and working hard,
I can succeed in college.

your feelings, thoughts, and actions in a critical way. *Stop the negative thought immediately* and reframe it into a positive one. Jake found himself thinking, "I'll never be able to get this job. They won't hire someone like me—straight out of college with no real experience." He caught himself and decided to turn that thought into a positive one. Jake told his roommate, "If I identify the skills I can use for this position, the employer may hire me." By reframing his thought, Jake increased his options. If you aren't achieving your goals, examine your beliefs underlying your self-talk. Your thoughts may be contributing to self-defeating behaviors.

The body makes millions of changes each day to adapt to the environment. In fact, if your cells aren't changing, you're not alive.

Everyone has some areas where they don't feel competent. These are opportunities to improve your skills and reframe your beliefs. Build on your strengths in small ways to increase your self-confidence. *Building self-confidence comes from repeating successful behaviors.*

Your self-confidence determines the choices you make and the actions you take. Self-confidence motivates you to move forward to achieve your dreams. You decide which dreams you want to turn into reality. It's important to set realistic career goals, but be careful you aren't lowering your expectations because you lack the self-confidence to attain them.

REAL-LIFE PERSPECTIVE

JANE

"Your 20s are supposed to be an exciting time—full of new experiences, exploring the world, and finding your own identity. I had my moments: I graduated from college and had a couple of successful jobs. But, by the end of the decade, I went through a divorce and lost my job as my husband's business partner. At 29, I had less identity and self-esteem than I had when I was 20. The only bright spot in my life was my 3-year-old daughter. I started reading every self-help book I could lay my hands on, but nothing seemed to get me back on track and into the swing of things. I guess I hoped one of those books would personally tell me I was OK, but the only person who could do that was me. One day, I realized I just had to get out and start living my life. I couldn't sit home and wait for my self-esteem to improve. I had it backward. I had to get a job and get on with my life; then, my self-esteem would return.

I went to a career counselor who gave me permission to dream. She encouraged me to discover my interests and admit I had skills. I set a direction and found a job that would get me started—although I still had doubts that I'd really end up where I wanted. It's now about 13 years later, and I've done all the things I dreamed of and then some! I used to think problems were proof that I didn't deserve something I wanted. I've learned not to take them personally. I see problems as challenges I have to overcome somehow. My self-esteem is a lot better. I focus on what I've done well, and I've stopped dwelling on what I could or should have done better."

Activity 2.1 Reframing

Instructions: Read Jane's story. In the chart provided, write down Jane's old beliefs in the left column. In the right column, reframe Jane's beliefs into positive statements.

OLD BELIEFS	NEW BELIEFS

REAL-LIFE PERSPECTIVE

ELISA

Elisa believed that she wrote poorly. Her grades in English had always been the lowest in her elementary class. She struggled through high school, dreading each research paper. Her belief that she was unable to write caused her to avoid writing whenever possible. Even though the rest of her family communicated online, Elisa even avoided e-mail, joking that she always preferred to talk in person or at least on the phone. Elisa didn't want to become a professional writer, but she did want to feel comfortable enough with writing to be successful in college.

For Elisa to increase her self-confidence in writing, she first had to develop her skills. She knew that she needed a new approach to overcome her fear about writing. She decided to begin with her strengths. One of Elisa's biggest strengths is her ability to get along well with children. She excelled at understanding their viewpoints. Currently, she is volunteering part-time at a shelter for abused children. Elisa felt very self-confident about bringing happiness into children's lives. Elisa decided to start keeping a journal about her experiences at the shelter. She began to document each child's progress. She started writing concise notes and practiced capturing her thoughts in writing. Elisa is on her way to reframing her belief about her writing skills.

Reframing My Career Beliefs — Activity 2.2

Instructions: Identify your own beliefs about your career. Then, reframe them in the chart below.

CURRENT BELIEFS	NEW BELIEFS

REAL-LIFE PERSPECTIVE

MAX

Max was a successful food photographer who owned his own studio. He photographed food items weekly for grocery store insert ads in newspapers. Max knew that photography was changing dramatically with digital imaging; however, he refused to believe that it would impact his business. Even though the photos he provided were digitally scanned by his clients, he cited many good reasons not to go digital and why it wouldn't work for him. Max knew a couple of colleagues who had switched completely to digital equipment to stay in business, but he was sure any equipment changes wouldn't impact food photography. Eventually, Max lost his main account when they discovered they could easily download stock images of food over the Internet and save the cost of weekly photo sessions. Max's business came to a screeching halt because he refused to adapt. If Max had assessed the advantages and disadvantages of adapting, he would have realized the changes he had to make to keep his business viable.

Adaptability

If you drop a frog in a pot of boiling water, it jumps out quickly and hops away. However, if you put the frog in a pan of water and slowly increase the temperature, the frog will relax in the warm water with no sense of the danger, content until it's too late.

Like all living creatures, we naturally adapt to changes in our environment. If the changes are monumental, we react immediately, like the frog dropped in boiling water. However, when the changes are incremental and happen a little every day, we often overlook them until it's too late. Generally, most of us prefer to stay in our comfort zone. When you're in a familiar environment, it's easy to ignore the facts and believe that things will always be the same. Trying new things can expand your thinking and open your eyes to new possibilities.

"Change demands continuous adaptation."

PETER SENGE, ***The Fifth Discipline***

As the rate of change accelerates, it's more important than ever to be able to adapt. There is no indication that the speed of change will slow down anytime soon. You can learn adaptability by recognizing old habits and replacing them with new behaviors. We're caught up in the process of change either as a catalyst causing change to happen or as a victim of change triggered by external forces. It's better to be a player in the game rather than an observer on the sidelines, wondering what kind of world you live in and lamenting how you were passed by. The successful person is a change agent. Knowing what changes will be happening in your profession, learning new skills, and applying them in new ways are all part of being successful.

REACTING TO CHANGE

People react to change in different ways. Some changes are easy to take in stride; other changes are more difficult to accept. *Sometimes, people don't admit change is occurring or they don't believe that it will affect them.*

Dukes of Habit

Activity 2.3

Dukes of Habit always do things the same way, must have everything scheduled, and are at a loss if something violates their plan. Because everything in their lives is precisely labeled, predicted, and planned, Dukes of Habit are limited problem solvers. They lack resiliency. You can learn flexibility by deliberately programming changes into your daily life. Make a list of things you do by habit. Most of the items will probably be those little things that make life comfortable but also make it unnecessary for you to think creatively. Next, take the listed habits one by one and consciously try to change them for a day, a week, a month. For example:

- Take a different route to work.
- Change your sleeping hours.
- Change your working hours.
- Listen to a different radio station.
- Read a different newspaper.
- Make a new friend.
- Try different recipes.
- Change the type of restaurants you visit.
- Change your recreation: Try tennis instead of golf.
- Watch a different TV news anchor.

HABITS	CHANGE I INTEND TO TRY

REAL-LIFE PERSPECTIVE

MOLLY

Molly's supervisor asked her to learn a new software program that the department had just acquired. At first, Molly was angry that one more task had been added to her heavy workload. Then, Molly talked to a coworker who suggested she should learn the software. Molly realized she didn't have a good attitude about this change and decided to analyze what it would mean to her job. Molly compared the advantages and disadvantages to help her decide whether to learn the new software program.

Molly's example

Advantages	Disadvantages
My skills will be up-to-date.	Learning requires effort and practice.
I will be regarded as an expert in my field.	Some tasks will take longer while I'm learning.
People will ask for my advice.	I will feel like a novice.
I will enjoy my work more.	I won't be an expert for a while.
I will feel competent at my work.	My work will feel chaotic.
My work will be less boring.	
I will be more marketable.	

Molly looked at the advantages of adapting and realized they outweighed the disadvantages. To help herself adapt, she addressed the issues that she described in the right-hand column, the disadvantages of adapting.

Here's how she did it. She realized that she would feel like a novice but reminded herself that everyone does when they learn something new. She remembered that she had successfully learned other new programs and that feeling like a novice wouldn't last long if she spent time practicing the program. She listed resources she could use while she was learning the new program: the trainer, the manual that came with the software, and the technical support provided by the publisher.

Although it's true that she wouldn't be an expert right away, she was signing up for the training before other people in her department so she would be the first to master it. Certain aspects of her job would seem more chaotic as she spent time away from her usual duties. However, the time she would save once she mastered the program would be worth it.

Writing out the advantages and disadvantages helped Molly see that the change was important to her career. Once she identified ways she could get help while learning the new program, she was able to adapt. As you can imagine, people in her department seek her out when they have problems with the program!

When Dramex announced a merger, Misha and Mark were both stunned. They knew it meant jobs would overlap and that some jobs would be eliminated. Misha thought about the changes and determined that she would use this change as an opportunity. She immediately began talking to the managers in operations about other opportunities in the company. She also contacted colleagues outside the company to let people know she was looking for another job. Within a month, Misha had three positions to choose from, all with an increase in pay.

Mark, on the other hand, wasn't worried. As payroll administrator, Mark knew his job was secure—no one else knew the payroll software. Mark was devastated when he was let go six weeks later. He couldn't believe the company had decided to outsource the payroll function.

Misha and Mark both had the same information, yet they chose to react to it in different ways. Misha became a change agent, while Mark chose to deny change. By embracing the inevitable and exploring ways to use change to her advantage, Misha was able to enhance her career.

One way to become a change agent is to evaluate the pros and cons of adapting to a change (see Activity 2.4). When you see your list of advantages, it may convince you to take action—even if it's difficult, uncomfortable, or scary. You may decide that it's in your best interest to adapt, even though you'll have to step out of your comfort zone.

What to Expect— Putting the Pieces Together

In this textbook, you'll learn strategies to help you decide your career and find work that is meaningful for you. As you learned in this chapter, your career will change and flexible planning is essential.

The strategies you'll learn in Chapters 3, 4, 5, and 6 will help you plan your career in a constantly changing work world. Through the activities, you'll discover elements of your career kaleidoscope that will help form work patterns for your future. As with any book with exercises, just reading about the exercises won't add much value. Completing the activities will help you understand your unique kaleidoscope and discover ways you can refocus it to continually find new work options.

In Chapters 7, 8, 9, and 10, you'll learn strategies to market yourself and obtain employment opportunities. You'll learn interviewing skills and develop a resume that gets noticed by employers. You'll learn strategies based on marketing principles, rather than traditional job-hunting techniques. Whether you are a first-semester freshman, a student about to graduate, or between jobs, these strategies will help you integrate new concepts of career planning with workplace realities. Our goal is to provide you with information and practical strategies for creating your future.

Activity 2.4 Evaluating a Change

Instructions: Think about a change in your life that is going to impact you in some way. Examples might be getting a new job, taking new courses, moving out on your own, or learning a new skill. Fill in the two columns with the answers that occur to you when you consider the change. Do the advantages outweigh the disadvantages?

MY CHANGE:

ADVANTAGES OF ADAPTING	**DISADVANTAGES OF ADAPTING**

If you strive for career resiliency and continuous employability, you'll have to become a change agent. Anticipate the future and prepare for it. Rather than waiting for change to affect you, you can learn to create change and embrace it as an opportunity.

Summary Points

- Traditional career plans were based on the assumption that jobs, professions, and organizations were stable and relatively unchanging.
- Career planning requires constant scanning of the work horizon to see advancing changes in technology, organizational structure, and ways to align with organizational and customer needs.
- The beliefs you form about your capabilities and skills influence your behavior.
- The way you interpret and explain the events in your life is a strong predictor of your success.
- You can reframe or change your beliefs and assumptions about yourself that limit your thinking and success.
- You can increase your self-confidence by building on your strengths.
- To adapt to change, first recognize and accept its existence. Evaluate the advantages and disadvantages of change and consider its impact on your life.

CHAPTER THREE

3 Discovering Your Values

FINDING CAREER MEANING

What creates meaningful work for you?

What are your work values?

What are your preferences about work?

How can you balance your work and your life?

Has this been happening to you? Faced with making a career choice, you try out various ideas in your head. You read about a hot career, a friend tells you about a great job opening, someone else advises you to go into computers. On Tuesday, that hot career seems perfect, but by Friday, you wonder how you ever considered it. It seems like a poor idea. So it goes—ideas spinning in your head with no idea how to choose. Eventually, nothing sounds attractive, and you are tempted to give up. You may wonder if a college education is really worth pursuing after all. On the other hand, you may consider majoring in something—anything—and decide you'll worry later about work options. Or, you may decide just to wait and see what happens—take the first job that comes along after college, and let that define your career.

In the next two chapters, you'll discover how to resolve this dilemma. The first step out of this confusion is learning more about yourself—what is important to you, how you define satisfaction, and what you enjoy doing. If you base your career decisions on these factors, you'll achieve self-direction and resilience in a world of constant change.

Many students approach career planning by asking the question, "What do I want to be when I grow up?" This asks the wrong question. It reflects the obsession in our society with equating work and identity. You are, after all, much more than what you do for a living. These chapters guide you to answer two different questions: "What do I want?" and "What do I want to do?" The first question allows you to consider your career as one aspect of your life—not the sum total of who you are. The second question will help you focus on action instead of a job title. Both of these questions recognize work as a means to get what you want from life, rather than something separate from your goals and ideals.

Success is not just doing your job—it's caring about it, the people you work with, and the results you achieve. Success requires a large dose of self-discovery to find what you care enough about to pursue.

During your exploration of this chapter, you may occasionally react by thinking, "I already know this about myself." That's as it should be—after all, you've been living with your preferences for quite a while! At other times, you will be surprised by your revelations. Answering a third question, "Who am I?" helps you organize what you already know, strengthens your self-awareness, and helps you discover new insights about yourself.

As you define who you are, you will gain a sense of direction in a world of continuous change. Self-awareness is the foundation for finding and pursuing meaningful, satisfying work. If you know who you are, what you want, and where and how you do your best work, it is surprisingly easy to decide what career to choose. Self-knowledge helps you understand the value you can add to an organization.

Finding career satisfaction is an individual process. It includes discovering your values (what gives you direction and meaning), your talents and skills (what you do well), your interests (what you care enough about to dedicate your talents and time to), and your preferences (what kind of environment matches your needs). You will also identify your core focus (what makes work meaningful for you). You will clarify who you are so that when you look at career possibilities, you can decide which ones would fit you best.

Once you have completed your self-assessment, the next step is to research professions, industries, and companies to find exactly where you can find work that matches your values, talents, and interests. For example, a person who likes meeting people, discussing ideas, and working with others to solve problems would be frustrated sitting behind a computer all day with no one to talk to. This person might enjoy marketing, training people to use software, or consulting with businesses about technology. You'll learn exciting, innovative ways to research work opportunities in Chapter 5. Research enables you to develop a career plan that is future-focused, flexible, and connected to new opportunities.

Career Kaleidoscope Elements

- *Core focus*—A frame of reference that points to meaningful work
- *Values*—Give direction and personal meaning to your work
- *Preferences*—Where and how you do your best work
- *Interests*—Activities or knowledge areas you care enough about to dedicate your time and talents to them
- *Skills and talents*—What you're good at and like to do

The more time and effort you spend discovering who you are and researching possible career choices, the more likely you will be to set yourself on a path toward satisfaction and continuous employability. Don't expect to find the one perfect career. If you approach choosing a career as an indelible decision, you will be saddling yourself with a heavy responsibility. Worrying that the wrong decision will ruin your life is an irrational belief. Instead, look for a career that interests you enough to explore it further. Remember that one career isn't likely to last your entire lifetime. More likely, you will spend no more than five or six years working before the field you choose evolves and changes. You may enjoy the transition. If not, additional research will help you make incremental changes to find a new niche in the workplace.

It's impossible to know precisely what you and the workplace will be like in 20 years. The self-assessment techniques in these chapters can be used repeatedly to continually reassess what you want to do. Use them throughout your life to stay employable and satisfied with your career.

This chapter and Chapter 4 are full of activities to help you discover what brings you satisfaction. Although you may not choose to complete each exercise, take the time to thoughtfully complete some activities in each section. Using several methods for self-evaluation helps you see what is most important—what leaps out as information that you cannot ignore. Second, write in this book! Writing down your thoughts, feelings, and experiences as you explore the activities is a highly effective tool for self-examination. You will discover new insights when you see your experiences and desires in writing. So use this book—write in it; doodle; and look for connections, patterns, secret desires, and hidden talents. Have fun exploring a unique world—you!

Building a Career Kaleidoscope

A new way to think about your career is to see it as though you were looking through a kaleidoscope. The elements in your career kaleidoscope (your values, interests, skills, and preferences) combine to form many patterns or work choices. These elements are a reflection of you and your potential contribution to the world of work.

Your career kaleidoscope is a visual model to display your unique attributes—what is important to you—as you search for ways to express yourself through work. Turning your kaleidoscope slightly brings into focus new career possibilities. The more elements in your kaleidoscope, the more potential you have for various career patterns. At the end of each self-discovery section, you will determine what's most important to you. These insights become the elements of your personal career kaleidoscope and will be entered into the shapes of *My Kaleidoscope Elements* (see the cards placed inside the back cover of your book). When you have identified all of your kaleidoscope elements, you will try out various ways the elements can be arranged. Just as a real kaleidoscope creates unlimited patterns with colored glass, your career kaleidoscope elements can be rearranged into many career options. As you enter, arrange, and rearrange your kaleidoscope elements, ask yourself:

What stands out?
What connections do I see?
What possibilities do I see?

You may see themes repeated throughout, or perhaps one element jumps out from all of the others. Seeing the connectivity between your values, interests, and skills gives you ideas for the types of work that will bring you satisfaction.

The career kaleidoscope you create now captures you at this moment. Over time, you will evolve, and so will the patterns you create within your

BUILD YOUR KALEIDOSCOPE

1. Discover your career elements
2. Arrange your elements
3. Look for compelling elements and connections
4. Identify potential careers
5. Rearrange your elements and look for additional possibilities

kaleidoscope. You can add elements to your kaleidoscope as you develop new skills through work experience. As you do this, your kaleidoscope shifts to create new patterns—new ways to work. You can emphasize different elements within your kaleidoscope, shifting your kaleidoscope again to create still more work possibilities. In a few years, you may choose to delete elements from your kaleidoscope as your interests and values change. Each time you add or remove elements, you adjust the pattern in your kaleidoscope—and create new career possibilities.

To see how a kaleidoscope can shift to create new work patterns, read Rob Decker's Real-Life Perspective. Figures 3.1–3.4 show the elements in Rob's kaleidoscope. See if you can match the elements with each of his career choices. Some elements stayed in every pattern he created. Some elements dropped out, while others were added as a result of his experience and education. Analyzing his kaleidoscope helped him broaden his perspective from photography to imaging. He also researched new technology and then decided to add new elements to his kaleidoscope to create new patterns and work opportunities. Changes in technology and business needs diverted his original plans, but they didn't keep him from finding satisfying work.

"It's hard for me to guess what I'll be doing at the end of my career—I don't know what I'll be doing in five years. Technology is changing the way we do everything. However, I'll still probably be involved in the imaging business in some way."

ROB DECKER

REAL-LIFE PERSPECTIVE

ROB DECKER

Rob Decker's interest in photography began when he was in high school and continues to be a prominent element in his kaleidoscope. Figure 3.1 shows the elements for Rob's career kaleidoscope. He has already shifted the pattern several times. After graduate school, with an MFA in photography, he wanted to teach photography on the college level (see Figure 3.2). Soon, he realized that the only opportunities for teaching were one-year contracts, which required moving yearly. After much research, he chose the city he wanted to live in and created an opportunity to open a chain of one-hour photo labs (see Figure 3.3). After a few years, Rob noticed that photography was changing. Some of his customers were going next door to use color copiers rather than paying for photo reprints. Rob began learning about digital imaging and became an expert in this growing area. He saw opportunity in helping companies digitize their photographic operations, so he sold his interest in a declining photographic market to sell digital imaging systems (see Figure 3.4). This opportunity gave Rob the chance to once again use his teaching skills. Rob anticipated the next shift in his kaleidoscope, consulting for graphic arts departments to resolve imaging problems and adjust color corrections. Photo processing has been hard hit by both Japanese competition and new technology, but Rob saw these changes as opportunities. The key to his success is his ability to reframe his work options by rearranging his kaleidoscope elements (skills, interests, and abilities) into new options. Notice that all elements aren't used in every pattern; Rob picks and chooses the elements he wants, focusing on market needs.

Elements in Rob Decker's career kaleidoscope. FIGURE 3.1

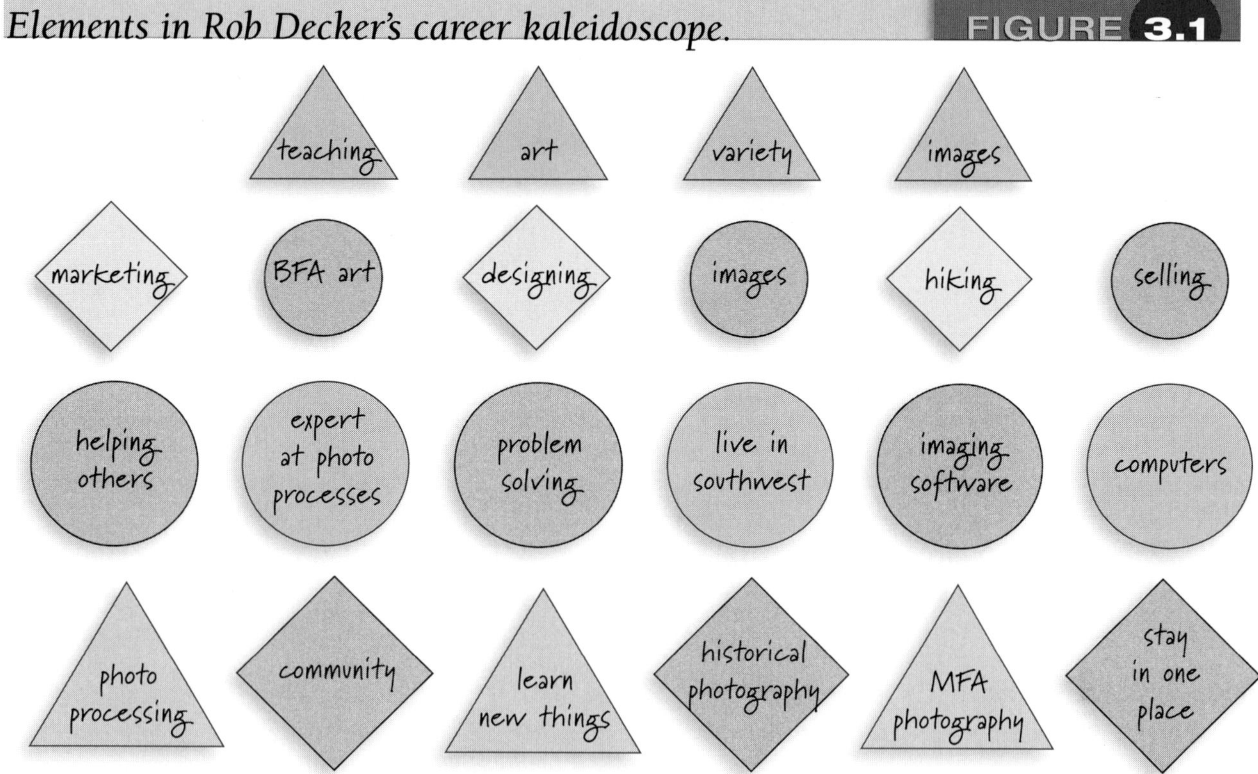

Rob Decker's career kaleidoscope—College professor. FIGURE 3.2

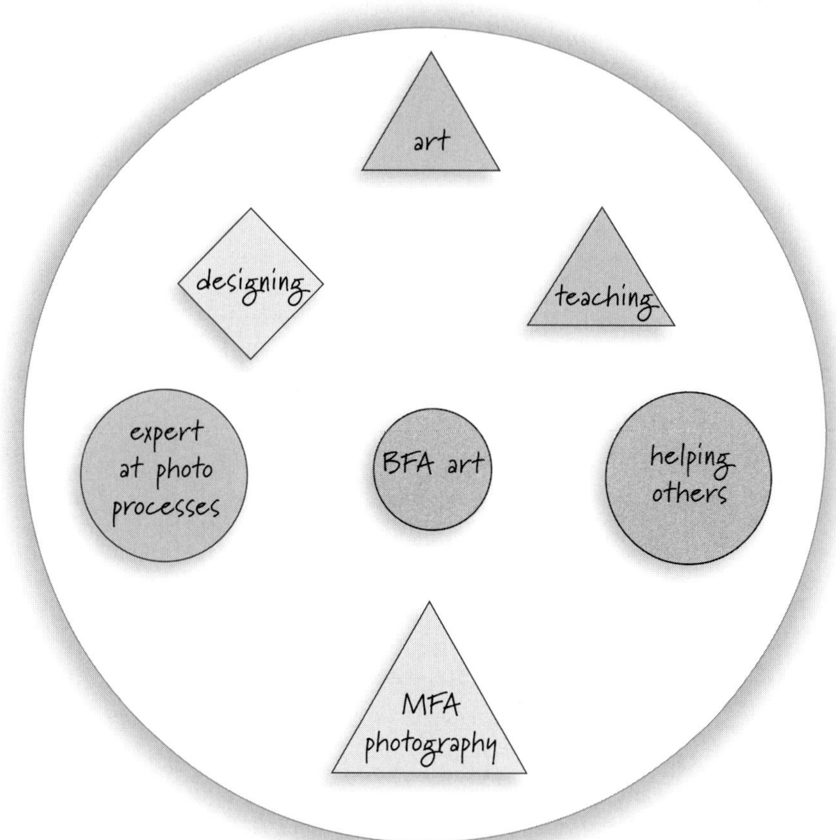

FIGURE 3.3 *Rob Decker's career kaleidoscope—Photo processing store owner.*

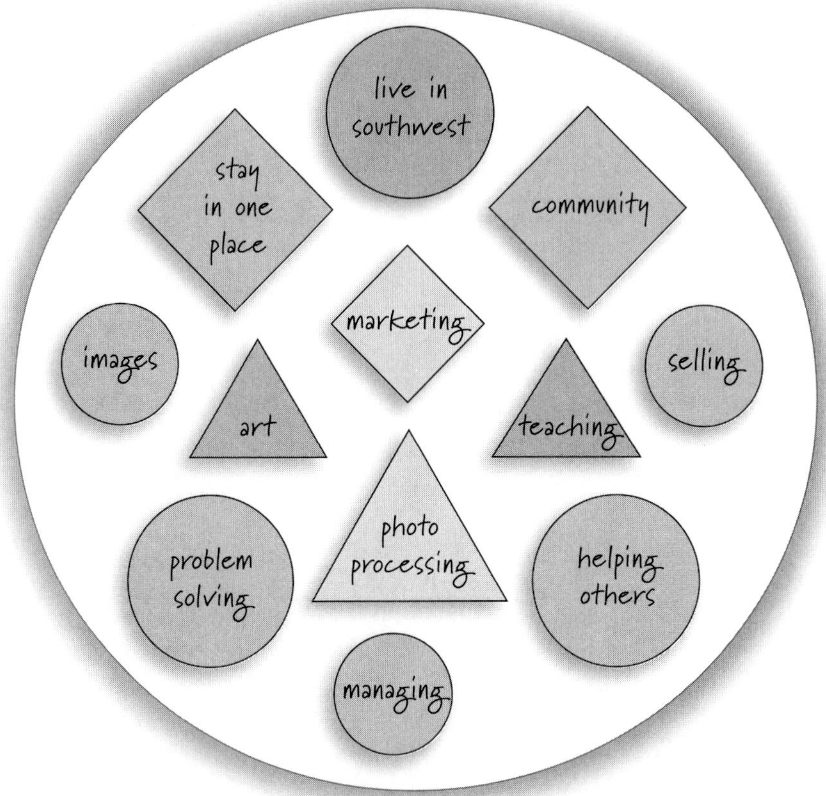

FIGURE 3.4 *Rob Decker's career kaleidoscope—Digital imaging equipment sales.*

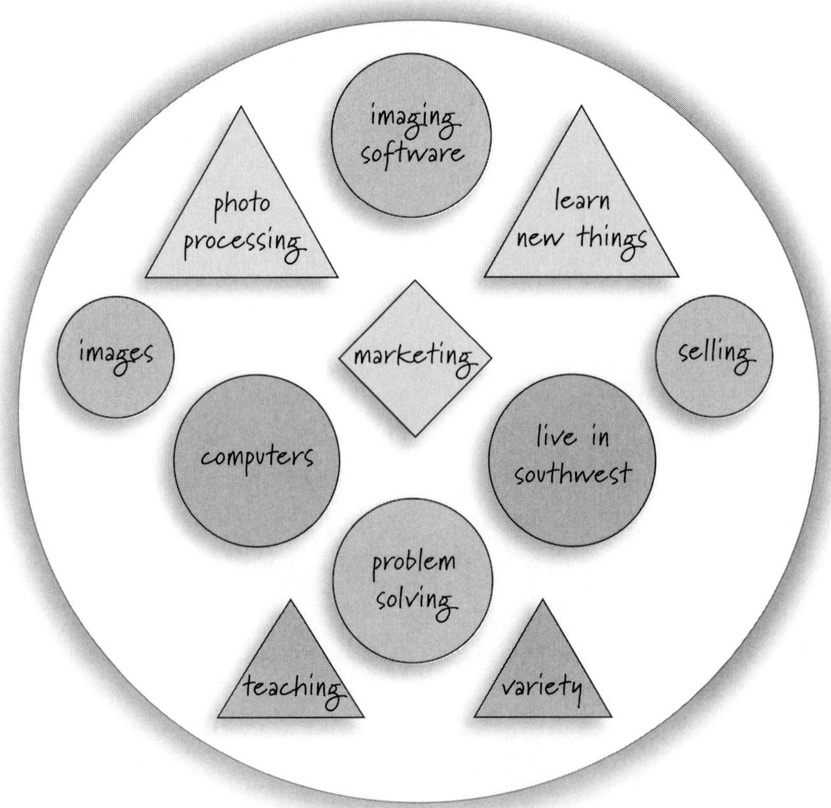

Discover Your Career Elements

Now, it's your turn to identify what's important to you in making a career choice. The first elements to place in your kaleidoscope are your values. Your values are what you want to get from work. When your work is aligned with your values, you'll feel a sense of satisfaction. We begin by examining your core focus.

CORE FOCUS

What's important to you? In past generations, people looked for secure work that provided for their families. Most people focused on finding out what jobs were available, rather than striving for work that would create personal satisfaction. However, when the baby boomers experienced downsizing, layoffs, and restructuring, they realized that following the company career path doesn't always pay off. Generation Xers, who are the baby boomers' children, learned the same lesson by watching the pain of their parents. They, too, want work to be something more than a paycheck. Most of us want to perform useful work and contribute to society as well as provide for our families. Often, people say, "If I have to spend more than half my life at work, I want it to be meaningful."

"What makes work meaningful?" is a question that produces different answers. Everyone is unique and motivated by different kinds of accomplishments. What is it that drives you to want to be productive, to work hard to overcome obstacles? What motivates you to move toward your goals, creating energy to achieve what you set out to do?

Today, there are many paths to meaningful work. No one has to settle for a life of unsatisfying work. Work can be drudgery, or it can be exciting, fulfilling, and productive. The difference is whether you make the effort to discover your talents, use your imagination to create dreams, and develop plans to make your dreams reality. The choice is yours. Will you settle for what's available, or will you follow your dreams?

There are five different ways people achieve a sense of meaning from their work. Some people may prefer a combination of these core values; others may achieve a sense of purpose and satisfaction by focusing on one of the following:

Passion

Competence

Dedication to a cause

Self-expression

Entrepreneurship

Discovering your core focus helps you determine a frame of reference and a sense of identity around the content of your work. This reference point will ground you in turbulent times and help you search for ways to be productive and useful. Though your work may change frequently during your lifetime, your core focus is likely to remain steadfast.

Which of the following best describes your core focus? Once you have decided which focus is most meaningful for you, answering the key question for that focus will help you discover a sense of direction.

CORE FOCUS

Passion: to be absorbed by work

Competence: to produce tangible results

Dedication: to make a difference

Self-Expression: to express ideals, values, and self

Entrepreneurship: to start something new

Passion

You want work that you love to do. Work, for you, is a way to merge your talents with how you spend your time. Work becomes meaningful and satisfying when you discover a talent for something and find work that lets you use that talent. People who focus on passion want to be absorbed in their work, meet new challenges, and continuously develop their talents.

Key Question: What do I love to do?

A focus on passion: "My father was a welder, and what I learned from him is that, whatever I do, I have to love it and be the best at it that I possibly can. Growing up, I loved making cookies. It was my hobby. I was always the kid with the cookies. I went through two years of college trying to decide what I wanted to do and, during that time, I decided that I wanted to do what I really loved—and that was making cookies and sharing them."

DEBBI FIELDS, president, Mrs. Fields Cookies, in *First Job, Great Job*

Competence

You want work to have tangible results. Your reward is seeing the results of your efforts. Your primary concern is developing and using a set of skills to produce a product, a service, or a system. Ultimately, you would like to be recognized as an expert in your field. People who focus on competence are persistent, determined, and quality-oriented.

Key question: To what do I want to devote myself?

A focus on competence: "Early in my career, I noticed that I felt a lot of satisfaction when customers said they liked my work. Of course, my goal has always been to make a living, but the biggest reward for me is when people compliment what I've done. I like knowing I did a good job—it's the difference between quality work and shoddy work. I like to know I've done a job well enough to put my name on it."

TOM HOWARD

Dedication to a Cause

You want to make a difference. You see work as an opportunity to make a contribution that benefits others. There is a cause—whether it's the environment, children, literacy, health, emotional well-being, or family well-being—that matters to you and that you would do anything to help.

Key question: How can I make this world a better place?

A focus on dedication to a cause: "At first my cause was personal—I just wanted to learn how to share parenting with my ex-husband after our divorce. I didn't realize I had done anything unusual until our son returned home during a break from college. Drake told me none of his friends had an experience similar to his. They had been forced to choose between parents after a divorce. He said, 'Mom, you have to write a book about this!' I went to graduate school to get a degree in counseling. I was discussing my parenting ideas with an instructor, who said, 'I see you have a cause you're very dedicated to.' I found this very empowering. Since then, I have specialized in co-parenting and have written two books about it. This work is very hard. Sometimes I ask myself, 'Why am I doing this?' But having a cause keeps me going and gives me direction in my career."

KAREN TODD

Self-Expression

You want to express yourself, your values, and your ideals through work. You enjoy work that is creative and full of variety. People who focus on self-expression want to be in touch with their inner selves and their view of the world. They enjoy influencing others through their creative expression.

Key question: How do I want to express my ideas?

A focus on self-expression: "I was taught as a child that it isn't good to fantasize or daydream. As I got older, I discovered that daydreaming about success is good. If you constantly continue to work, even at a turtle-like pace, to achieve your dreams, then what you dream about can eventually come true. It's amazing what fantasizing and imaging can do in terms of conditioning your mind as to what your lot in life is to be, assuming you're willing to work for what you want. Once you create goals, think hard about what it will take to achieve those goals, and then work toward achieving them."

JIM MCCANN, CEO, 1-800-Flowers, in *First Job, Great Job*

Entrepreneurship

You want to build a company, create something new, or leave a legacy. Founding a company and building it to achieve goals is exciting to you. You want to know that your creation was the result of your efforts. You are willing to take risks and overcome obstacles to reach your goals. People who focus on entrepreneurship desire autonomy and control over their life. They want to work and live in their own style.

Key question: What kind of problem do I want to solve?

A focus on entrepreneurship: "Entrepreneurs, by definition, are people who start something new and fresh. The novelty and excitement of a new enterprise is appealing. Control is a big issue for people who start their own businesses. Entrepreneurs and executives are equally interested in liking their work, feeling challenged and stimulated, and building wealth. But, entrepreneurs are much more likely than executives to be satisfied with how they're doing in these areas. They're also more likely to say that having control over their lives, as well as the ability to influence important decisions and shape corporate culture, is very important in the career choices they've made."

DIANE CRISPELL, *The Lure of the Entrepreneur*

Activity 3.1 Finding Your Core Focus

Instructions: What makes work meaningful to you? Some college students gave these responses. Can you determine the core focus for each student?

- Work should be a place where I feel comfortable and happy. I want to be appreciated for who I am and what I do.

  Core focus: ______________________________

- When a job is self-fulfilling, it becomes meaningful to me. To know that I am recognized and respected for my accomplishments and to work with people I truly enjoy.

  Core focus: ______________________________

- I want to find work that is fun, that keeps me interested in learning new things. I would hate a boring job that is always the same.

  Core focus: ______________________________

- Being able to help someone or make a difference makes work meaningful to me. I want to know that I've impacted someone's life in some way.

  Core focus: ______________________________

- When I go home at night, knowing that I accomplished something productive.

  Core focus: ______________________________

- When I can see the results of my efforts and I am valued by management.

  Core focus: ______________________________

- My work has to influence other people and make a difference in someone's life, as well as be fun.

  Core focus: ______________________________

- Making a contribution to the planet.

  Core focus: ______________________________

- I want to start my own company where employees are glad to come to work every day.

  Core focus: ______________________________

Core Focus Assessment

Activity 3.2

Instructions: What is most important to you in your career? Read each item and the choices that follow it. Place a checkmark (✓) by the phrase that is most true for you.

WHEN SOLVING A PROBLEM:

- ◯ I want the solution to make a difference to people
- ◯ I like to be absorbed in finding the solution
- ◯ I want the solution to express my point of view
- ◯ I like to see practical results
- ◯ I take full responsibility for the solution

I WANT MY WORK TO:

- ◯ have an impact on the lives of others
- ◯ incorporate my vision and goals
- ◯ produce tangible results or have a practical application
- ◯ provide the chance to do my own thing
- ◯ use my talents and interests

I WANT TO USE MY WORK SKILLS:

- ◯ to build a new enterprise
- ◯ to create a lasting impression
- ◯ to enjoy what I do
- ◯ to make the world a better place
- ◯ so others will recognize my expertise

PEOPLE WOULD DESCRIBE ME AS:

- ◯ caring
- ◯ expressive
- ◯ focused on results
- ◯ passionate
- ◯ resourceful

DURING MY CAREER, I WANT TO ACHIEVE:

- ◯ a legacy
- ◯ innovative ideas
- ◯ making the world a better place
- ◯ recognition as an expert in my field
- ◯ work I enjoy

I PREFER TO WORK:

- ◯ as the leader of a team
- ◯ as a knowledgeable contributor to a team
- ◯ as the creative contributor to the team
- ◯ for team harmony
- ◯ on teams that have fun while they work

I LIKE ACTIVITIES THAT:

- ◯ are unstructured
- ◯ are goal-oriented
- ◯ are enjoyable to do
- ◯ challenge me to perfect my skills
- ◯ contribute to others' well-being

I WOULD DESCRIBE MYSELF AS:

- ◯ aggressive
- ◯ conscientious
- ◯ creative
- ◯ enthusiastic
- ◯ giving

LIFE IS A SEARCH FOR:

- ◯ achievement
- ◯ joy
- ◯ dedication (excellence)
- ◯ ways to express myself
- ◯ ways to make the world a better place

I AM:

- ◯ imaginative
- ◯ optimistic
- ◯ passionate
- ◯ persistent
- ◯ strong-willed

I WANT A CAREER THAT:

- benefits others
- develops my competency
- influences others
- is competitive and challenging
- uses my talents

I LIKE WORK THAT:

- achieves goals
- helps others
- influences others to accept my ideas
- is aligned with my interests
- uses my expertise

I WOULD FIND WORK MEANINGFUL IF I:

- achieved recognition for a job well done
- did what I love
- found a new way to do something
- made a difference
- put my name on something

Look back at the phrases you marked with a check. Which core focus seems most like what you want from work?

____

____

What is the key question related to the core focus you've chosen?

____

____

____

When you have completed this activity, go to the cards inside the back cover of your book, entitled My Kaleidoscope Elements. *Enter your core focus in the diamond shape.*

VALUES

Your values determine what you want from work. Values define the outcomes that bring you satisfaction. When your work aligns with your values, work isn't just a way to pay the bills; it's fulfilling and exciting. Your values help determine the kind of company, work environment, and industry where you will feel satisfied. Your values are also elements of your career kaleidoscope and help define the pattern of your work.

Exploring Values—Childhood Dreams *Activity 3.3*

Every child dreams about what he or she wants to be as an adult. Although it may not be practical to follow these childhood dreams, they often reveal basic values that are still important to you. When Leslie was asked, at the age of 50, what she had wanted to be as a child, she replied, "a ballerina." Because she was now out of shape and hadn't had a dance lesson since the age of 8, obviously this was no longer a practical choice. When asked why she had wanted to be a ballerina, she replied, "It wasn't that I wanted to be a star or even a dancer—it was to be part of a ballet troupe, to be part of a team that put on a production." Leslie realized that these values were still important to her, and she used them to reassess her current job. As a supervisor, she recognized she could view her department as a troupe. She dedicated herself to coaching her entry-level employees to learn good work habits and new skills. She taught them how to communicate better and to function as an integrated team to accomplish their work. Leslie uses skills that align with her values, and she feels useful in her job.

1. What did you want to be when you were a child?

____

____

2. Why was this important to you?

____

____

____

____

3. What values are still important to you?

____

____

____

____

Activity 3.4 Exploring Values—Work Scenarios

Instructions: Read the following work scenarios and decide the values represented by each one. Create a list that includes 8 to 10 values from each scenario. Your complete list will reflect 40 to 50 different values. When your list is complete, individually rank your top 10 values 1 through 10, with 1 being most important.

Meiko is part of an organization without the typical organizational chart. The defining system of operation in her company is the team. Work is distributed to more than 100 self-managed teams. People come together to work creatively and solve problems. Employees know their strengths, and roles are defined based on what skills and knowledge they contribute to the project. Leadership changes depending on the expertise needed at various stages in the work process. Meiko's team operates with very few rules. Without a typical organizational chain of command, the ability to get resources and results depends on her ability to persuade others to support her. The variety of projects helps develop flexibility and broad expertise. She knows her success depends on the success and respect of others and their motivation to succeed.

Jim enjoys projects for which he is personally responsible for the outcomes, and he is recognized for results. He seeks out challenging work and determines project goals and deadlines. He uses his intellect to solve complex problems. He enjoys breaking down a problem into its elements and reaching a solution. The work requires research and data analysis. The value he contributes to the organization is a result of his own initiative and specialized expertise.

Jennifer's work centers on the belief that the world and its inhabitants deserve respect and care. She is constantly on the move, working in different places around the globe. Her knowledge and education assist people with improving their environments and communities. Her organization promotes international goodwill. Her work is filled with unexpected events requiring mental flexibility. She is free from routine activities and predictable work schedules. To Jennifer, success means following the direction of your heart.

Richard's experience as an entrepreneur started when he was in his late 20s. With four years' experience in business, he started his own company. He enjoys creating his own working conditions, having flexibility and freedom, and being able to choose the projects he finds most interesting. He continually develops his skills and abilities by pursuing a variety of activities. Richard constantly finds ways to do new things, to keep learning, and to have fun.

(continued)

Sergio works with a small group of people designing computer games. The office space where he works was specially designed to resemble a game lab. He has access to a wide-screen TV and DVD, arcade machines, game tables, and a variety of other play activities. The company is on the leading edge of creativity and innovation in game design technology. "Leading Change" is the company's motto. The employees believe anything can be done and that possibilities are unlimited. The company is expected to triple its employee base in the next year. Employee salaries and opportunities are considered to be some of the best in the industry.

My top 10 values, ranked from most important to least important:

1.
2.
3.
4.
5.
6.
7.
8.
9.
10.

Examine Activities 3.3 and 3.4 to determine your values. Choose those that are most important to you to add as elements of your career kaleidoscope. Turn to My Kaleidoscope Elements *inside the back cover of your book, and record them inside the circular shapes.*

BALANCING WORK AND LIFE

An important aspect of career planning is deciding how work fits into your total life. Imagine that your work is meaningful to you and fits your talents and education well. How much time would you want to invest in your career? How much time would you want to spend pursuing other interests, such as family, friends, personal development, or learning activities?

Just as identifying your work-related values can guide you toward satisfying work, examining your life values and goals will lead to an overall sense of satisfaction. Allowing time for both work and a rewarding personal life will bring a feeling of enthusiasm for life. It isn't easy to find balance in today's complex world. Many people want to achieve recognition and status from their careers, excel with their children, pursue an interesting hobby, and care for aging parents. Being realistic about how much you can accomplish will help reduce the amount of stress in your life. If family, learning, or other interests are important to you, revising your career goals may be necessary to achieve balance.

The amount of time you choose to invest in your career may relate to your life stage. Many young adults are choosing to pursue education and the development of career experiences before starting a family. While their families are young, some parents either leave the workforce or scale back the amount of time they invest in their careers. They renew their dedication to their careers when their children are older. Consider your life stage as you balance your career and life goals in Activity 3.5.

PREFERENCES

Your preferences are also important elements of your kaleidoscope. Your choices about where and how you prefer to work are important aspects of work satisfaction. Some people want work that allows them to be physically active, while others are happy spending the day in an office as long as the work is creative. Some people get their best ideas during lively discussions, while others need solitude to think. Some people need structure to feel effective, while others believe structure stifles their autonomy. Matching your preferences regarding work environment and personal style with opportunities in the work world will create a satisfying work life.

Activity 3.5 Balancing Work and Life

How do you structure your day from the time you wake up in the morning until the time you go to bed at night? How do you spend your time? Think of the 16 hours or so you are awake during an average day and complete the activity below. In the blank circle, draw slices of the pie to represent how much time you spend each day on various activities. Use the categories in the list below or create your own.

HOW I SPEND MY TIME

- Work activities, including commuting
- Learning, including training, classes, and study time
- Maintenance activities, such as housekeeping, car maintenance, and shopping
- Leisure activities, such as eating out, visiting friends, watching TV, and surfing the Internet
- Parenting activities, such as interacting, helping with homework, and watching sports events
- Spiritual or personal growth activities, including worshiping, reading, and communing with nature

Now, think about how you would ideally like to spend your time. How would you like to divide your time among various activities? Use the circle below to show how you would apportion your time.

HOW I WOULD LIKE TO SPEND MY TIME

How is this circle different from your first one? What insights have you discovered about what is important to you? What can you do now to achieve more balance in your life?

Activity 3.6 Preferences—Work Environment

Instructions: Read each pair of words, and place a check mark in front of the statement that best expresses your preferences regarding work environment.

○ I prefer to work indoors	○ I prefer to work outdoors
○ I prefer to work alone	○ I prefer to work as part of a team
○ I like being a leader	○ I prefer following someone else
○ I enjoy traveling most of the time	○ I prefer not to travel
○ I like ever-changing activities	○ I like predictability and routine work
○ I prefer an unstructured workplace	○ I prefer a structured workplace with clear rules and procedures
○ I prefer a private work space	○ I prefer a shared work space
○ I like managing others	○ I prefer to manage myself
○ I prefer working with specific deadlines	○ I prefer working with broad goals
○ I'm precise and methodical	○ I'm creative and enterprising
○ I take initiative and am visionary	○ I'm responsive and practical
○ I prefer using my social skills	○ I prefer using my technical skills
○ I prefer a large company	○ I prefer a small company
○ I prefer a well-established company	○ I prefer a new and growing company
○ I thrive on pressure	○ I prefer a relaxed environment
○ I like influencing others	○ I prefer supporting others
○ I prefer to specialize in one area	○ I enjoy using multiple talents and expertise
○ I prefer compensation based on performance	○ I prefer a set salary
○ I prefer learning new skills	○ I prefer using existing skills
○ I prefer working for myself	○ I prefer working for someone else

Decide your top work environment preferences. Record them in the triangle shapes in My Kaleidoscope Elements, *inside the back cover.*

Summary Points

- The first step in making a career decision is self-discovery. Knowing who you are, what you want, and what you want to do are the keys to career satisfaction.
- A career kaleidoscope is a visual model that integrates the information you gather during your self-discovery. It is a flexible model that allows you to see all of the elements that build career satisfaction for you.
- The elements in your career kaleidoscope can be added, deleted, and rearranged to create many career patterns or options that reflect areas of interest to you.
- A career kaleidoscope is a method to evaluate career options based upon your core focus, values, interests, skills and abilities, and preferences.
- People find work meaningful when it matches their core focus—passion, competence, dedication to a cause, self-expression, or entrepreneurship.
- Your values give direction and personal meaning to your work.
- Your preferences help determine the type of company, work environment, and industry in which you will be satisfied working.
- Work should balance with the other activities in your life. Decide what is important to you and how you want to use your time.

CHAPTER FOUR

Discovering Your Interests

4

CREATING CAREER POSSIBILITIES

What can you do to discover your interests?

What skills do you want to use in your work?

What career possibilities does your kaleidoscope suggest?

What careers are you most interested in exploring?

What are your deep interests? This is the real question to ask according to human resources executive James Waldroop. "Good career decisions have to be based not just on your aptitudes but also on your deep interests. The most common mistake that people make in their career decisions is to do something because they're good at it."

This chapter continues your self-discovery. You'll be identifying your interests and skills. While your values determine what you want to receive from your work, your interests and skills determine what you want to do. As you work through this chapter, you'll put all of the elements of your kaleidoscope together and uncover potential career ideas. You'll be surprised at how many possibilities there are!

REAL-LIFE PERSPECTIVE

GLENDA

Glenda is a bright successful engineer with seven years of experience in a fast-paced computer manufacturing environment. In spite of her career success, she's frustrated because she thinks her management position is full of senseless activities that bring her very little satisfaction. When Glenda looked closely at her preferences, she discovered that she has strong vision and leadership skills but does not have the patience to coordinate or implement the vision, as a manager or supervisor would. She also enjoys working on her own individual projects. With this information, she redirected her career from management to a consulting track, which is a much better fit with how she prefers to approach work.

Interests

For many people, the secret to career satisfaction is discovering what they love to do and then finding a way to be paid to do it. Your interests influence the patterns in your career kaleidoscope.

Not everyone knows what they love to do. Sometimes, our interests have been stifled by others. Someone may have said to you, "Don't waste your time playing at that—get serious." "Don't daydream; pay attention to what I'm saying." However, our daydreams and our play reflect our interests. Have you ever really observed a toddler at play? She is totally absorbed in her world, manipulating objects, and trying to figure out how things work. She is concentrating intently—hard at work—yet in the next moment, she happily bounces on to the next thing that catches her interest. By defining your interests, you can find play at work, too.

Do you have difficulty identifying your interests? Do you like to do so many different things that it's difficult to decide which you prefer? Several activities follow to help you identify and prioritize your interests.

How People Talk Themselves Out of Doing What They Love

- **Believing they have to choose between what they love and what's practical—** "I love horses, but I need to develop practical skills, like working with computers."
- **Believing what they love will lead to poverty—**"I'd love to write screenplays, but I couldn't make any money doing that."
- **Believing they don't have the talent or initiative to achieve what they want—**"I'd love to be a motivational speaker, but you have to have charisma to do that."
- **Believing that only the lucky end up doing what they love—**"If I won the lottery, I could afford to do what I want; otherwise, I have to get a job."
- **Believing their career choice is a way to win approval from others—**"My parents want me to become an engineer. I guess that's what I'll do instead of interior design."

Exploring Interests—Reverse Thinking

Activity 4.1

Instructions: If your interests were stifled in the past and you can't think of a thing you like to do except play Nintendo, reverse your thinking: List all of the things you know you wouldn't like in your work, and then list the reverse. Note the ideas this process triggers about your interests.

Example:

THINGS I DON'T LIKE	REVERSE THINKING	WHAT IDEA DOES THAT TRIGGER?
Detail	The "big picture," creating new ideas	Developing ideas into something practical
Routine	Variety, challenge, making a difference	I like to help people solve problems
Working alone	Helping people solve problems	A career in human resources or counseling?
A boss standing over my shoulder	Work I can do independently	I want a profession where people earn respect

Your Turn:

THINGS I DON'T LIKE	REVERSE THINKING	WHAT IDEA DOES THAT TRIGGER?

REAL-LIFE PERSPECTIVE

BEN

Ben nearly talked himself out of what he loves to do. He believed he should increase his computer skills and planned to get advanced training as a network technician. Ben works in a large organization in the information technology department. He works behind a computer all day in a room by himself. He isn't happy, but everyone keeps saying, "Stay in computers."

When he assessed his interests, he realized he wants to interact with people and likes to train them and help them solve problems. Now, he is looking for ways to combine his computer experience with his interest in working with others. Ben says, "I can see that I'll be much happier when my work is more aligned with my interests. I'm glad I had this opportunity to gain more self-knowledge and learn how to adapt my work to the things I like to do. I'm excited about exploring new ways to work with computers."

Activity 4.2 Exploring Interests—Activities I Like to Do

List 25 activities that you enjoy doing. Don't worry about whether they're career oriented.

1. ______
2. ______
3. ______
4. ______
5. ______
6. ______
7. ______
8. ______
9. ______
10. ______
11. ______
12. ______
13. ______
14. ______
15. ______
16. ______
17. ______
18. ______
19. ______
20. ______
21. ______
22. ______
23. ______
24. ______
25. ______

Someone makes money through work related to every one of the interests you've identified through these activities—no matter what's on your list. For example, if you enjoy reading, a related career might be copy editor. If you spend hours upon hours playing computer games, maybe a career in programming or designing electronic games would be a good fit. If you'd rather spend your time in the woods backpacking, perhaps you might opt to be a nature guide, work for the U. S. Forest Service, or sell equipment for hikers.

To learn ways to translate interests into careers, find the companies or agencies that produce the products and services related to the interests you've identified. Go to their home pages on the Internet. See if you can find the names of some people who do that work, and send them an e-mail—you'll be surprised how often someone will respond!

Like working outdoors? Check out www.coolworks.com

Exploring Interests—Time Flies Test

Activity 4.3

Take the time flies test. Sometimes, you may be so engrossed in what you're doing that you lose track of time. Suddenly, hours have passed, and you're amazed when you finally look at the clock. Where did the time go? You might have forgotten to eat or even missed a class or some other appointment! The activity is so absorbing that you're suspended in time.

Time flies when . . .

Brainstorm careers that involve the activities you've identified in the time flies test. Write your career ideas below.

Activity 4.4 Exploring Interests—News I Can Use

In addition to enjoying certain types of activities, you may have interests in certain subjects. What do you consistently like to learn about? What subjects do you read in magazines or surf the Internet to explore? Pick up an issue of *Time, Newsweek, Psychology Today, U.S. News & World Report, Business Week,* or some other general-interest magazine. Select six articles you find most interesting, and read them from beginning to end. If you can't find six articles you really enjoy, select another magazine until you come up with a full half-dozen. As an alternative discovery method, review your favorite bookmarks, or spend an evening surfing the Internet.

What subjects did you enjoy most?

What magazine(s) or websites did you select?

Identify each article and list what interests or intrigues you.

What careers are related to these interests?

INTEREST INVENTORIES

Another way to discover your interests is to take an interest inventory. Commonly used interest assessment tools include Self-Directed Search, Strong Interest Inventory, Campbell Interest and Skill Survey, and World of Work. These inventories were developed from the work of Dr. John Holland, a psychologist who has devoted his career to studying how people make career choices. He found that people develop preferences for certain types of activities. By the time a person reaches adulthood, usually he or she has developed clusters of similar interests that can be categorized into six areas. The preferences that most people develop are related to each other so, from this observation, he categorized people into six personality types. He termed these preferences *vocational interests* and found that the work world consists of environments that recognize and reward each of these interest areas. For example, a realistic person likes hands-on, practical work that produces concrete results. Suitable environments for this personality type include manufacturing, construction, transportation, and military service. Dr. Holland believes choosing a career is a process of identifying your interests and then matching them to a corresponding work environment.

Typically, a person's interests cannot be narrowed to just one of the personality types. In fact, if you had developed interests in only one of these areas, making a career choice would be relatively simple. Most people, however, have developed more interests than can fit into one category. Usually, people use their top three interest areas to investigate careers. For example, if your top scores are Social, Enterprising, and Artistic, your personality type would be SEA. A person with this personality profile prefers working in a social setting, helping people solve problems. The enterprising interest might lead you to seek a leadership position or start your own firm. You would enjoy expressing your creativity by developing new methods to help people. Possible career choices for you include counselor, human resources representative, community organizer, or special education teacher. The career center at your college may have a copy of the *Dictionary of Holland Occupational Codes.* This resource lists many (but not all) career choices for each three-letter Holland code.

Additional career assessment tools may be available at your school's career center, and many assessment tools are now available on the Internet. Not all inventories are created equal, so examine the results carefully. If they are contrary to your own knowledge of yourself, only use whatever information is helpful. Your own real-life experiences offer strong evidence of what you like to do.

Personality Tests

If you enjoy tests and assessments, you might enjoy these websites:

- www.queendom.com
- www.keirsey.com
- www.sdstest2.com
- www.assessments.ncs.com

Use caution when taking tests. There is no magic in them—if the results don't match what your experience tells you is true, stay with what you know.

Activity 4.5 Exploring Interests—Holland's Vocational Choices

Instructions: The six general areas of vocational interest are described below. Think about your past experiences and current activities. Include work, school, and leisure activities. Then rank these areas from 1 to 6, giving a score of 1 to the area that describes you best.

___ **Realistic**

Prefers practical activities, working outdoors or with tools and machines using physical skills. Likes to achieve concrete results. Avoids social situations. Compatible environments include outdoors, manufacturing, military service, or construction.

___ **Investigative**

Prefers observing and investigating scientific or technical problems. Avoids leadership roles. Compatible environments include scientific endeavors, information technology, or education.

___ **Artistic**

Prefers creative or innovative activities in an unstructured environment. Enjoys opportunities to express self or ideas. Avoids structure and procedures. Compatible environments include the arts, publishing, or advertising.

___ **Social**

Prefers interacting with people to inform, teach, develop, cure, or enlighten them. Uses social competencies to solve problems. Avoids realistic roles. Compatible environments include medicine, social work, education, or human resources.

___ **Enterprising**

Prefers working with others to achieve organizational or monetary goals. Enjoys influencing and persuading others. Avoids investigative activities. Compatible environments include sales, leadership, or entrepreneurial pursuits.

___ **Conventional**

Prefers working with numbers or information. Enjoys detail work, following procedures and systems. Avoids artistic or unstructured activities. Compatible environments include data processing, accounting, or administration.

Look back at the interest activities and assessments you've completed. Select your top interests and write them in the squares in My *Kaleidoscope Elements,* inside the back cover.

Skills and Talents

Skills and talents are another element to include in your kaleidoscope. The skills you develop are apt to be strongly related to your interests: Research indicates that 80 percent of your skills probably overlap with your interests. If you think about it, this makes perfect sense. Anytime you became interested in something, you probably developed skills while pursuing it.

As a child, Bernadette liked to investigate things; she spent a lot of time tinkering with machines around the house, taking them apart and putting them back together. She was always asking questions and following her father around as he fixed things. Bernadette's interest in investigating how things work gave her certain skills when she grew up. As an adult, Bernadette is adept at fixing things and finding mechanical solutions. She knows how to troubleshoot problems and how to use tools as a result of her childhood interests. She's the family member everyone relies on when the faucet drips or an appliance quits working.

Brandon, on the other hand, is socially driven. As a child, he was the one the teachers always said "talks too much." From childhood on, Brandon spent his time communicating with others and developing interpersonal skills. He's the kind of person who always knows the right thing to say. Friends seek him out for assistance when they have a problem to solve. Over the years, Brandon has developed skills to inform, teach, and develop others. He knows how to get everyone together to agree on a solution.

Everyone has inherent skills like these. You may want to develop other skills—that's why you're attending school. Discovering the skills you like best is important. You'll feel passion and enthusiasm when you use these skills in your work. Don't worry that your skills aren't good enough. All skills are learned—developing skills is a gift you give yourself to create the life you want. Because your preferred skills are important to you, you'll be willing to spend time developing and improving them.

Like others, you may be asking, "What talents do I have?" Your talents may be latent, just waiting to be discovered and developed. You may have grown up in a family that didn't support and reward your particular skills, or you may not have had the opportunity to try out or discover your talents. Often, people take their skills and talents for granted. The skills you most prefer are so much a part of you that it is sometimes difficult to see them.

TYPES OF SKILLS

Did you know that ordinary people who have been taught by career counselors to recognize their skills commonly create lists with 500 to 700 entries? You probably have that many skills, too! By examining your skills, you'll discover many more career choices than you ever imagined!

Job content skills refer to abilities or specialized knowledge used in a particular kind of work. Examples of job content skills include bookkeeping, programming a computer, repairing an appliance, acting in a play, diagnosing an illness, or constructing houses. Job content skills are what most people think of first when asked to list skills.

Activity 4.6 Exploring Skills—Job Content Skills

Kate's Example:

When Kate was asked to describe her job content skills, she thought about her work and volunteer experience, listing the skills she used. Then, she looked at each item and checked off the skills she might want to continue to use in her career.

POSITION (volunteer or work experience)	SKILLS	
Administrative assistant	Use MS Word, Excel, and PageMaker	
	Lay out newsletter	✓
	Write and edit memos	✓
	Operate and repair copier	
Hospice volunteer	Act as liaison to medical personnel	
	Explain medical procedures	
	Assist with medical paperwork	
	Counsel grieving families	
	Advocate for patient rights	
	Listen to people in pain and give comfort	
Recreation aide in after-school program	Supervise school-age children	
	Teach arts and crafts	
	Plan special events for children	✓
	Entertain children with stories	✓
	Persuade children to participate	✓
	Help children feel better about themselves	✓
Jewelry salesperson	Persuade people to buy jewelry	
	Arrange displays of jewelry	
	Compute profit and loss	
	Recommend settings and jewelry designs	

Your Turn:

Instructions: Consider your volunteer and work experience. List all of the job content skills you used in each position.

POSITION (volunteer or work experience)	SKILLS	

Now, go back and place a check mark next to each skill you might like to continue to use in your work.

IDENTIFYING TRANSFERABLE SKILLS

Transferable skills are general abilities used in many different situations. For example, if you've always done well organizing things—you plan great parties—you could also organize tours, projects, or anything else that interests you. The secret to expanding your options is to first list your transferable skills, which are verbs, and then add different objects to the verbs. For example: As a jewelry salesperson, Kate persuaded customers to buy—she could also persuade juries to convict, persuade employees to perform, or persuade readers to believe her. In each case, the root verb, *persuade*, remains the same, but many options are created by changing the object that follows.

Refer to Chapter 6 to find out the skills employers want.

Activity 4.7 Exploring Skills—Transferable Skills

Accomplishments are part of your professional, educational, and personal life. You may take for granted landing the job you have, receiving a promotion, completing college, learning a skill, solving a problem, or completing a project. Sometimes, you receive recognition for your accomplishments, but other times, few people know about your achievement. It's not important whether or not you receive recognition; what's important is how meaningful the result of your efforts is to you. When you initiate, follow through, and end up with a meaningful result, you produce an accomplishment. As you look back over your life, you have achieved many results. By examining your accomplishments, you can identify the skills you used to achieve a result that was significant to you.

Your accomplishment—write a detailed paragraph about the situation. Describe who, what, where, when, and why.

List the skills you used in your accomplishment. To help you identify the skills, refer to the skills list on the next page. Circle the skills you most enjoy using.

Results—what happened through your efforts (e.g., an outcome, a product, a behavior change)?

On separate sheets of paper, write four other accomplishments. Using the format above, describe the results you achieved and the skills you used. When you look at the skills used in your accomplishments, do you see any similarities? If you do, this is evidence that using these skills gives you a sense of satisfaction.

Transferable Skills

Skills can be categorized as follows:

COMMUNICATION
Advise
Arbitrate
Articulate
Collaborate
Counsel
Define
Demonstrate
Develop rapport
Edit
Entertain
Explain
Instruct
Interpret
Interview
Listen
Liaison
Mediate
Negotiate
Persuade
Present
Propose
Report
Sell
Teach
Train
Write

CONTROLLING
Appraise
Assess
Audit
Budget
Compute
Estimate
Evaluate
Inventory
Monitor
Maintain records

CREATIVE
Apply theory
Design
Develop
Direct
Generate ideas
Imagine
Innovate
Market
Perceive intuitively
Portray images
Visualize

INFORMATION
Analyze
Arrange
Classify
Collate
Develop databases
Diagnose
Evaluate
Index
Integrate
Investigate
Observe
Organize
Problem solve
Program computers
Purchase
Record
Research
Retrieve
Sort
Synthesize
Test
Transcribe
Word process

MANAGING
Administer
Approve
Assign
Coach
Control
Direct
Govern
Improve
Influence
Initiate change
Lead
Mentor
Motivate
Schedule
Supervise
Vision

MANUAL
Assemble
Construct
Cultivate
Cut
Dexterity
Draft
Draw
Maintain
Operate
Plant
Prepare food
Produce crafts
Repair
Tend animals
Transport
Treat, nurse
Use mechanical abilities

ORGANIZATIONAL
Conceptualize
Catalog
Collect
Coordinate
Expedite
Implement
List
Make arrangements
Make decisions
Organize
Plan
Recruit
Set priorities
Summarize
Systems thinking
Team building
Troubleshooting

PLANNING
Conceive
Develop strategy
Estimate schedules
Design programs
Review
Survey

Identify the skills you want to include as elements in your kaleidoscope. Insert them in the rectangles in My *Kaleidoscope Elements,* inside the back cover.

Arrange Your Elements

BUILD YOUR KALEIDOSCOPE

1. Discover your career elements
2. Arrange your elements
3. Look for compelling elements and connections
4. Identify potential careers
5. Rearrange your elements and look for additional possibilities

Now that you've completed the self-discovery activities in these two chapters, you're ready to arrange the elements to create your career kaleidoscope. If you haven't already done so, write your choices from each activity in the blank kaleidoscope shapes in My *Kaleidoscope Elements.* Don't feel constrained by the number of elements on the chart. You do not need to write in something for every shape, and you may add others as needed. Any other elements that you have identified in class or that you feel are important may be added in the oval shapes.

The elements of your kaleidoscope hold the key to potential careers. Your elements define what you want from work, what interests you, and what you want to do. By rearranging and combining elements into three different kaleidoscope patterns, you will discover careers that match what is important to you. As you analyze your kaleidoscope, keep an open mind. Be creative as you look at your elements.

Take a pair of scissors and actually cut out all of the elements for your kaleidoscope. Place them in the circle shown in Activity 4.9. This will allow you to arrange and rearrange the elements as you work through the next steps.

REAL-LIFE PERSPECTIVE

KATE

Kate is a college student trying to decide on a college major. She had been considering a degree in sociology or education. She realized that before she could decide on a major, she had to decide what she wanted to do when she graduated. Her mother encouraged her to go into education, but Kate wasn't sure. Let's examine her kaleidoscope elements and see how she used her elements to create new career options (see Figure 4.1).

Kate compiled the elements for her kaleidoscope by prioritizing the information she developed from several activities. She has included her core focus, values, preferences, interests, and skills. Kate also wrote five other considerations in the square boxes that she wants to consider when making her career choice. Figure 4.1 shows Kate's kaleidoscope elements. When Kate looked at all of her elements, she saw several connections and realized that some elements were compelling

Kate's career kaleidoscope elements. FIGURE 4.1

Look for Compelling Elements and Connections

ELEMENTS IN YOUR KALEIDOSCOPE

Core focus

Values

Preferences

Interests

Skills and talents

As you look at all of your kaleidoscope elements, analyze what you see. Move your elements around so you can group similar elements together. This will help you see relationships and connections between them. For example, you may see several skills and interests that seem connected and you may want to place them together within the circle. You may see elements that you want to discard or think of things you'd like to add. Be creative as you look at your elements and keep an open mind.

Examine your kaleidoscope for:

- **Connections.** What similarities do you see when you examine your elements? What do your values, skills, and interests have in common? How could you combine elements to form interesting work? For example, can you see ways to use your skills with one of your interests?
- **Compelling elements.** What stands out—what can't you live without?

Activity 4.8 What Stands Out?

Kate's Example:

CONNECTIONS	COMPELLING ELEMENTS
Spanish language, culture, diversity Several interests and skills related to children Maybe I could combine my interest in Spanish and working with children	Working with children Helping others Definitely want work that lets me interact with people

Your Turn:

Examine your kaleidoscope and write down the connections you see and the elements that are most important.

CONNECTIONS	COMPELLING ELEMENTS

Identify Potential Careers

If you're like most people, you have many more elements in your kaleidoscope than you could possibly use in any one profession or career field. (That's why you have many possibilities—it would take your entire lifetime to use them all!) The next three activities give you an opportunity to look at different combinations of career elements so that you can discover a variety of career options. Figure 4.2 shows Kate's first kaleidoscope pattern and the career ideas she discovered.

Here's how to select your career elements for Activity 4.9. Start by placing all of the elements you listed in Activity 4.8 in the circle. Add other elements important to you so that your kaleidoscope contains 20 to 25 elements. As you examine this kaleidoscope pattern, ask yourself the following questions:

- How could you use your skills?
- What kind of work is related to your interests?
- What needs could you fulfill in the workplace?
- What professions or career fields are related to the pattern you've created?

Write your ideas under the heading *Career Ideas* in the lower left-hand corner of Activity 4.9. See if you can come up with at least five ideas.

Show your kaleidoscope pattern to a partner. Explain why you chose these particular elements. Ask your partner to help you think of additional ideas for this pattern and add them to the Career Ideas box. You and your partner are just brainstorming, so remember not to evaluate suggestions right now or you'll stop the flow of ideas.

FIGURE 4.2 *Kate's career kaleidoscope—Pattern 1.*

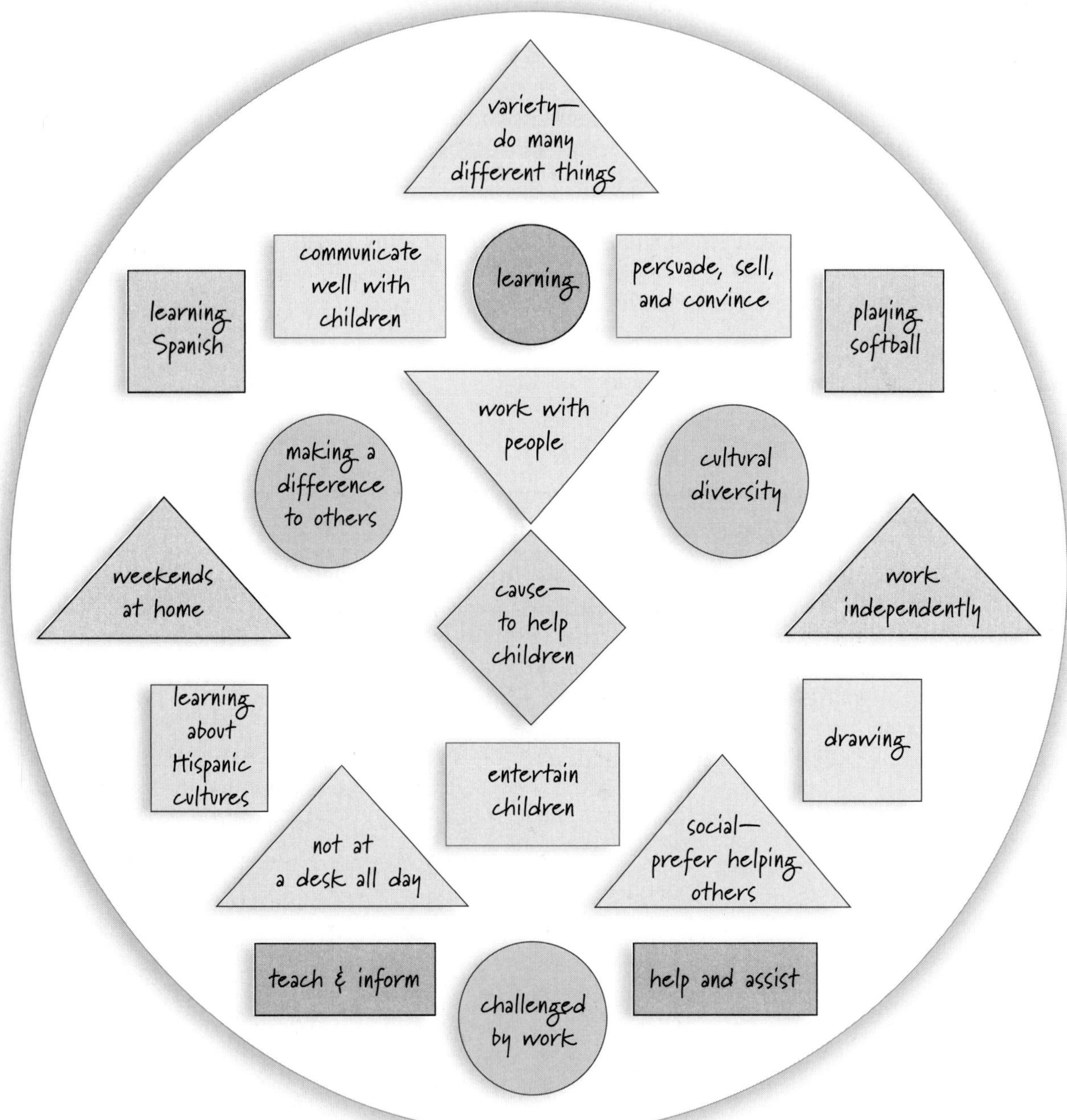

CAREER IDEAS

Bilingual teacher
Daycare administrator
Head Start teacher
Parenting skills instructor
Cultural diversity trainer
Children's entertainer

Kate developed a kaleidoscope pattern and came up with six career ideas. Everything in Kate's pattern revolves around a cause that's dear to her—helping children. Her skills seem to fit being a teacher. Her interest in Hispanic cultures and her desire to learn Spanish make being a bilingual teacher one option to consider.

Career Kaleidoscope—Pattern 1

Activity 4.9

Instructions: Place 25 elements in the circle. Then, brainstorm Career Ideas and write them below the circle.

CAREER IDEAS

Rearrange Your Elements and Look for Additional Possibilities

Now, it's time to experiment with your elements. You can add, remove, and rearrange the elements in your career kaleidoscope to create many career patterns and work options. Rearranging your elements will help you see yourself in new ways. Figure 4.3 shows Kate's new pattern.

In Activity 4.10, you will create a new kaleidoscope pattern. To do it, place your Core Focus and a few compelling elements in the blank circle. Then, add elements that are different from your first pattern. With this kaleidoscope pattern, experiment, look for new connections, and think of additional career ideas. Once you have listed some career options, brainstorm with a partner to add more to your list.

Discuss this pattern with others to come up with career ideas. List your Career Ideas for this pattern.

Activity 4.10 Career Kaleidoscope—Pattern 2

CAREER IDEAS

Kate's career kaleidoscope—Pattern 2. FIGURE 4.3

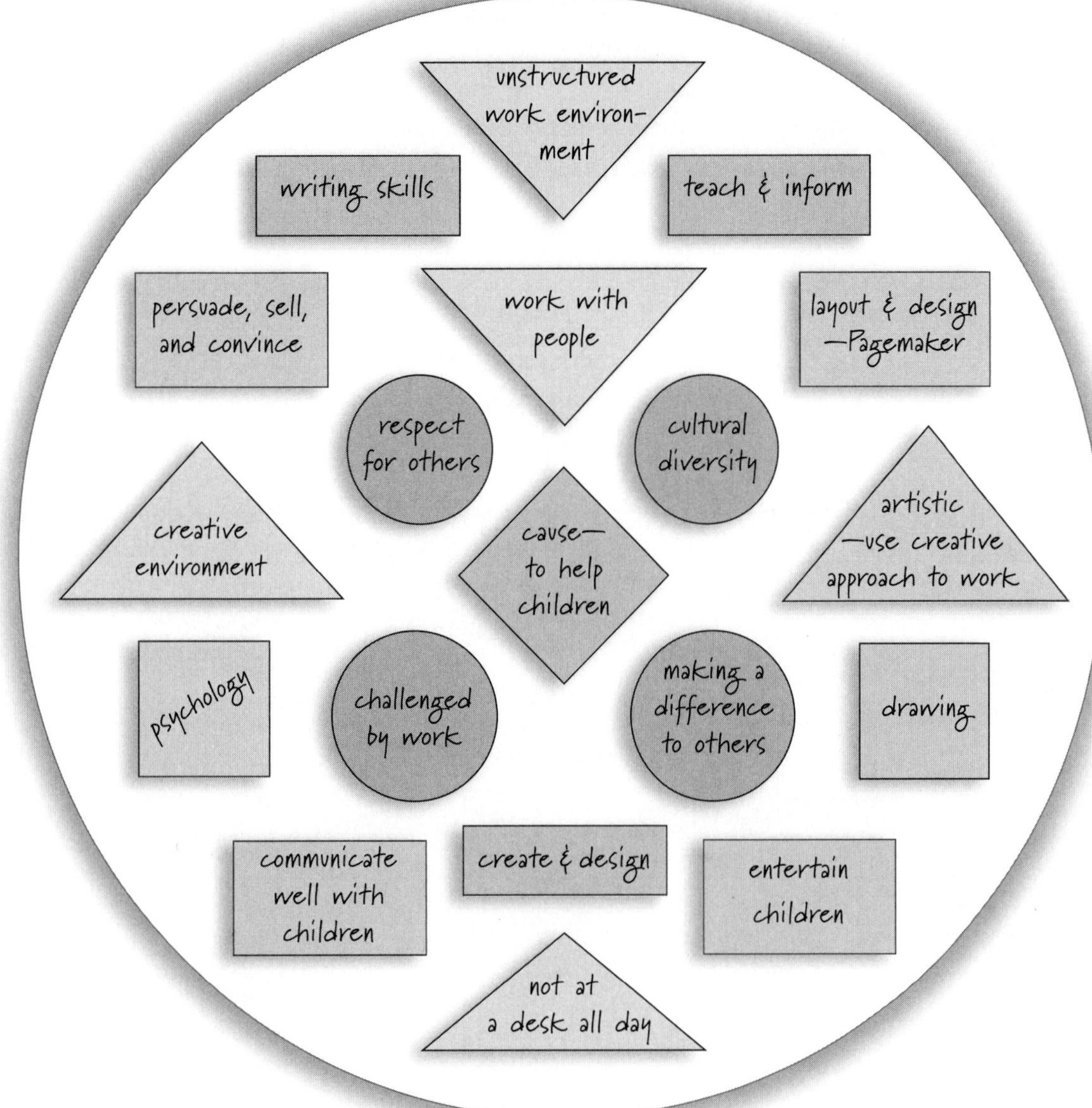

CAREER IDEAS

Design educational multimedia
Art teacher
Writer
Educational sales
Art therapist

Kate discovered new career options with her second kaleidoscope pattern. By combining her creative design skills, teaching abilities, and computer knowledge, Kate came up with the idea of multimedia designer for children's educational materials. Other career options that seem to fit include art teacher and writer. After evaluating all of her options up to this point, Kate decided to research education, looking at both multimedia design and teaching.

Your third kaleidoscope pattern (Activity 4.11) is entirely random. To create it, remove all of your elements from the circle. Without looking at the names of the elements, place 25 random selections in the circle. Again, brainstorm career ideas and ask a partner to add to your list. You may find some surprising ideas this time! Figure 4.4 shows Kate's third pattern.

FIGURE 4.4 *Kate's career kaleidoscope—Pattern 3.*

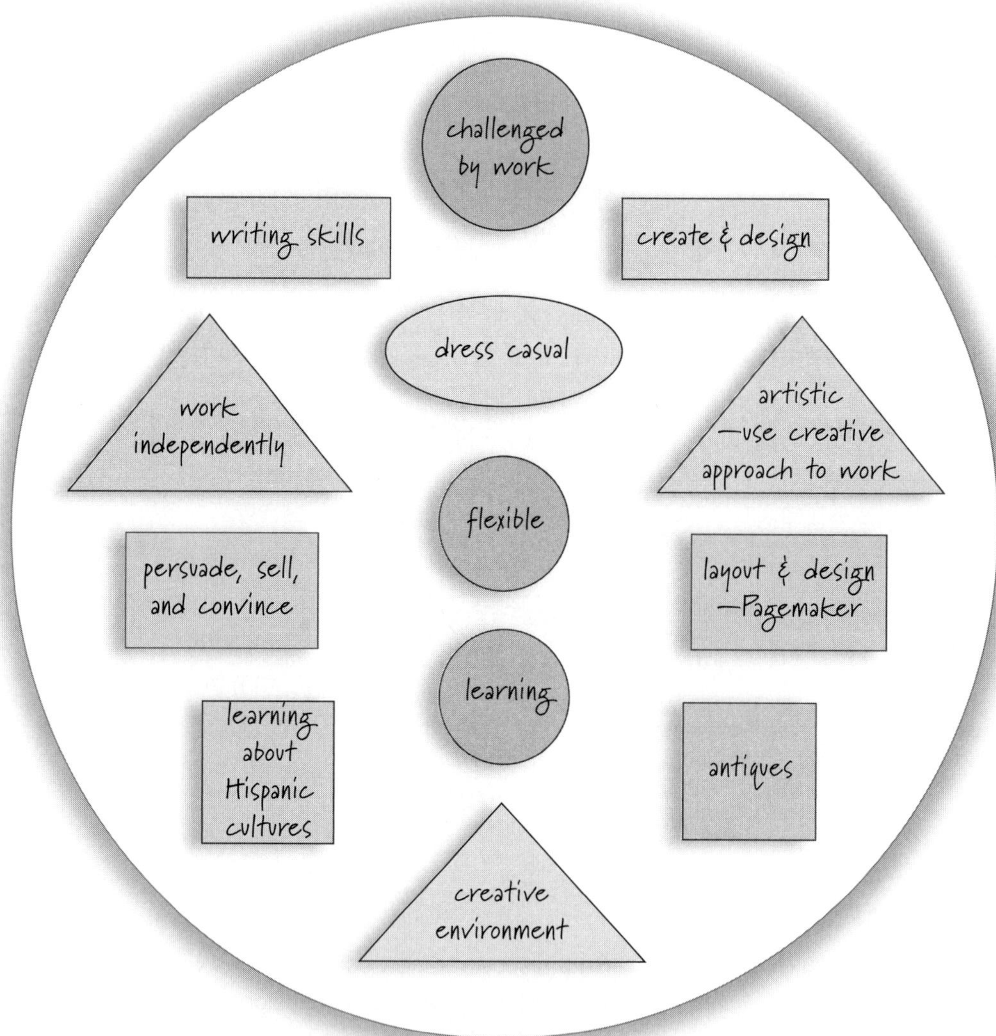

CAREER IDEAS

Antique dealer
Art importer
International liaison
Cultural exchange programs

By combining her skills to persuade, sell, and convince with her interest in antiques, Kate considered the career option of antique dealer. When she connected these elements with her interest in learning about Hispanic culture, she thought of the career option of importing art or antiques from Mexico. Both of these career options seem to fit with all of the elements in her kaleidoscope, except for core focus. Kate remembered to ask her key question: How can I make this world a better place? Kate decided to consider whether she could meet this need by volunteering.

Career Kaleidoscope—Pattern 3

Activity 4.11

CAREER IDEAS

As a final step, examine the three kaleidoscope patterns you've created and list below the career ideas you feel hold the most promise. In the next chapter, you will learn how to research these ideas to help you decide the best career fit.

CAREER OPTIONS I COULD CONSIDER:

A CAREER FIELD OR PROFESSION I WANT TO LEARN MORE ABOUT:

Summary Points

- Your personal interests can be turned into career opportunities.
- Everyone has two types of skills—job content skills that define specific abilities and knowledge and transferable skills, general abilities that can be used in many different situations.
- A career kaleidoscope is a creative way to develop options based upon your core focus, values, interests, skills, abilities, and preferences.
- You can add, delete, and rearrange the elements in your career kaleidoscope to create many career patterns and work options.

CHAPTER FIVE

5 Creating Future Possibilities

RESEARCHING CAREERS

How do you research a career?

What trends will impact your career?

Where do you get accurate information?

What resources are available?

How can you plan for uncertainties?

You have looked inward and are forming an idea of what is meaningful to you. You have carefully examined your interests, values, and skills; you shifted your kaleidoscope to view several career patterns. In this chapter, you'll turn your focus outward and explore one career pattern in depth. You'll use several innovative strategies to gather and evaluate information about what it's really like to work in the field that you've chosen to explore.

In reading this chapter, you'll discover just how dramatically the world of work is changing. You may feel somewhat overwhelmed by the rate of change and its impact on careers. The future is here—compelling, exciting, and full of new possibilities. Hang on!

Until recently, there was little need to scan the future to decide on a career. When change happened slowly over a lifetime, evaluating the way things were done in the past was enough. Researching a career was a simple process. You could talk to a reporter and obtain a reliable idea of what your life as a reporter would be like. You could read a book describing the skills and abilities needed by an anthropologist to conduct field research. From your own experiences, you could accurately describe the work of a dentist, teacher, and many other occupations. Although these are good methods to begin researching a career field, today you must know not just about the past and present, but also about the future. With various changes affecting the world of work, the past no longer reliably predicts the future. One prediction is that most of the jobs available 10 years from now don't even exist today!

Although nearly everyone agrees that it's important to check out the job market and research current opportunities before deciding on a career, how can you make sure the information you learn today will be valid in the future? How will the career fields you're exploring change by the time you graduate, or within the next four to five years? Unfortunately, information about future work is not neatly packaged and easy to find. To ensure you're choosing a field with a future, you'll search out information, speculate, and evaluate opinions. You may find more questions than answers as you begin your research.

"By studying the future, people can better anticipate what lies ahead. More importantly, they can actively decide how they will live in the future, by making choices today and realizing the consequences of their decisions. The future doesn't just happen: People create it through their action—or inaction—today."

World Future Society, *Why Study the Future?*

As you discovered in Chapter 2, your personal experiences color your view of the world and can limit what you see. When researching a career, it's very easy to seek and find information to support your choices and dismiss the opinions of those with whom you disagree. This chapter will give you ideas and strategies to think outside the box. Our goal is to help you think and see in new ways. Find the possibilities, opportunities, and challenges created by the changes impacting the career field you're exploring. Then, you can evaluate how these changes might affect you—or whether you want to twist your kaleidoscope to view new options.

Your research won't be completed at the end of this chapter or at the end of this semester. Our goal is to help you begin to think like a futurist—a skill you will need to continue refocusing your kaleidoscope throughout your career.

Studying the Future

What does it mean to *think like a futurist?* What does a futurist have to do with evaluating career options? Futurists aren't fortune tellers. Futurists know better than anyone that the future is unpredictable. Futurists seek to know what can or could be (the possible), what is likely to be (the probable), and what ought to be (the preferable). They strive to uncover possible and preferable scenarios to help people and organizations decide what actions to take to create a preferable future. They do this by analyzing world trends and forecasts.

"The Gretsky Principle: Don't skate to where the puck is; skate to where the puck will be."

JAMES BELASCO,
Flight of the Buffalo

The World Future Society is a nonprofit association interested in how social and technological developments are shaping the future. It serves as a neutral clearinghouse for ideas about the future, including forecasts, recommendations, and alternative scenarios. These ideas help people to anticipate what may happen in the next 5, 10, or more years.

Future Views—Changes for Counselors

Personal counseling is one career field that is changing dramatically. The relationship between therapist and client is not immune to the rapid change of technology. Some predict that, within five years, most counseling will be done electronically. Electronic counseling increases accessibility—the counselor is available anywhere at anytime, rather than just by appointment. Counseling on the Web tends to be more solution-focused than traditional therapy. Much of the push to electronic counseling comes from HMOs. Health care reform has already forced enormous changes in private practices over the last few years. Because of insurance reform, 50 percent of the psychologists in private practice 10 years ago are not in practice today.

When people can visualize a better future, they can begin to create it. The following is a brief introduction to thinking about the future from the World Future Society:

> Quite simply, [futurists] try to suggest things that might happen in the future, so that people can decide what they want to make happen. By looking at current trends, for example, it is possible to make a projection of what might be the case in the future.
>
> If the population of a city is growing at 2 percent a year, we can suggest that the city will have more people in the future than it has now and even calculate how many additional people it will have. But, that does not mean the city will definitely have those additional people, because a lot of things could happen to stop or even reverse the city's population growth.
>
> Knowing the possibilities of the future—that is, what might happen—enables people to choose. Unless they know the alternatives, people can't choose what they want to have happen, let alone make it happen. The first step in creating a better future is identifying the things that might happen in the future. Once these possibilities are known, we can try to make the desired possibilities become realities and prevent the undesired possibility from ever being realized.

MYTHS ABOUT FUTURISTS

Myth Futurists try to predict the future and fail miserably.

Reality Futurists try to identify events that might occur in the future. Occasionally, they make forecasts—that is, statements indicating what they think is likely to happen if people allow current trends to continue. Futurists believe, however, that predictions—statements indicating that something definitely will happen in the future—are generally impossible because of human decisions that alter the future and the many uncertainties inherent in human life.

Myth Forecasts and long-range planning are fine for governments or businesses, but they're not really useful for individuals.

Reality Forecasts can help you plan your career, make investment decisions, or even help determine where you should live. Forecasts tell people

FUTURISTS

To learn more about futurists, contact the World Future Society, 7910 Woodmont Avenue, Suite 450, Bethesda, Maryland 20814, (tel.) 301-656-8274, or visit its website at www.wfs.org

what fields will provide good employment opportunities, what sort of businesses or stocks to invest in, and how many people will be living in a metropolitan area and what transportation problems they could create—perhaps convincing you to move nearer to a subway stop. Individuals can profit by forecasts every day—from helping with major decisions to deciding whether to take an umbrella to work.

Myth It is useless to think about the future because we can't do anything to stop it.

Reality The past is finished; it's too late to change the present. The decisions that we make now can have an effect only on the future. Furthermore, we can do more about the more distant future than about the immediate future because we have more time to do the things we need to do.

Source: "The Art of Forecasting—A Brief Introduction to Thinking About the Future" (1996) from the World Future Society. Used with permission.

How Futurist Research Can Help

"The best way to predict the future is to create it."

PETER DRUCKER, *The Effective Executive*

Effective career research involves exploring and uncovering future possibilities, not just examining the way work has existed in the past. Research is one part of career planning where many people fail to devote enough time and energy. Many people only research long enough to find information to support their viewpoints. However, in our changing world, research is essential to ensure that many of the changes in the future won't catch you by surprise. Although you can't precisely predict what changes the future holds, you can be sure that no matter what career you're researching, it will change and evolve. Follow Wayne Gretsky's advice and look ahead to the future so you're ready when it arrives. Futurist research can help you in several ways:

- **Improved decision making.** When you're aware of potential opportunities or challenges that the future may bring, you can make an informed decision about whether a career field is a good fit for you. For instance, when Reuben discovered that computer-controlled surgery will be commonplace in the future, he began rethinking whether he wanted to be a surgeon.
- **Creating career resilience.** Examining how your career will change is not just a nice-to-do activity. It ensures that the career you are choosing and the education that you are pursuing will continue to provide you with a viable living.
- **Uncovering different ideas.** Your research will uncover various viewpoints to help you identify trends and opportunities. Futurist thinking involves stretching your thinking with an eye on the future. Remember, your goal is not to predict the future, but to forecast what might lie ahead.
- **Suspending your opinions.** You will be asked to suspend your opinions and view other perspectives. It isn't easy to perceive the world from someone else's point of view; however, that's the only way you can objectively evaluate the facts and prepare for the potential futures you will face. By suspending your disbelief, you will uncover new ideas that may affect your future work.

Test Your Beliefs About the Future

Activity 5.1

Your beliefs and assumptions affect the way you think. Before you actively start your research, answer the following questions to find out your views about the future. This quiz was designed with no clear right answers, so you can't fail. Peter Bishop, Associate Professor in the Studies of the Future program at the University of Houston, Clear Lake, designed these questions to stretch your mind and examine your assumptions about the future. For more information about the M.S. program in Studies of the Future, check out www.cl.uh.edu/futureweb/.

1. Can we know the future?

   ◯ Yes ◯ No

Answer: Yes. About 50 percent of people usually answer "yes"; about 50 percent say "no." Your answer, of course, depends on how you define *know.* If by *know* you mean that you can predict what will happen, then the answer is obviously "no." Efforts to predict the exact future of human systems are so prone to error that they are futile. However, if by *know* you mean what might or could happen, then the answer is a qualified "yes." Futurists hold that we can know the majority of plausible futures if we relax our assumptions and preconceptions of what is possible.

2. Are there one or many futures?

   ◯ One ◯ Many

Answer: Many. Most people say there are many futures. The idea of many possible futures gives us the freedom to influence the future. If there were only one future, we wouldn't have any opportunity to influence change.

3. Which is better for understanding the long-term future?
   a. Single clear predictions
   b. Multiple possible futures
   c. Neither
   d. Both

Answer: b. If only we could have a crystal ball to give us one clear prediction of the future! The problem is that predictions give us a false sense of certainty and precision. Multiple possible futures are the best we can do and are, therefore, better for understanding the future. Futurists believe that basing a decision on a single prediction is like putting all your eggs in one basket. The purpose of forecasting is not to be right but to avoid being surprised.

4. Which influences the long-term future the most?
   a. Trends
   b. Events
   c. Choices
   d. All influence the future equally

(continued)

Answer: d. Each of the three specific factors—trends, events, and choices—represents a theory of how the future develops. People who emphasize trends look for ways to measure and quantify change. Those who focus on events believe the future is full of unpredictability and uncertainty. Futurists who emphasize choices believe they and others control the future. In fact, each influences the future and should be considered when making decisions.

5. What is the most important characteristic for a good forecast?
   a. Accuracy
   b. Precision
   c. Usefulness
   d. Clarity

Answer: c. Accuracy and precision are supposed to make the best forecasts. People often ask futurists how often they are correct (i.e., what their batting average is). The best long-term forecasts are not necessarily accurate or precise but **useful** to decision-makers. They point out the most likely future as one possibility in a range of alternative plausible futures. Useful forecasts can even be inaccurate (i.e., when a forecast of impending doom promotes action to avert the problem).

6. Which is the most serious cause of forecasting errors?
   a. Lack of information
   b. The forecaster's assumptions
   c. External events

Answer: b. It's easy for us to blame a lack of information or external events because we are not responsible for them. Our assumptions, on the other hand, are of our own making. A reading of history shows that the most serious errors are the result of mistaken assumptions: A patent official forecasts a decline in invention around the turn of the century; a physicist said heavier-than-air flight was impossible; an office equipment executive saw no need for more than six computers worldwide. Forecasters had all the information in front of them. Their interpretation of what the information meant caused the error.

7. Telling stories about possible but unlikely futures is useful.
   ○ True ○ False

Answer: True. Science fiction stories have told highly improbable but highly engaging visions of the future. Stories capture the essence of the future without claiming to know the details. Futurists borrow the techniques of storytellers to develop scenarios to describe plausible futures. The best response to a scenario is "Yes, you're right; that could happen."

Although futurist research requires more effort than spending a few hours in the library, it is also fun and exciting to find out what other people think. It involves talking to people and listening for new ideas.

During your research, find answers to these questions:

- How will trends or technology advances impact the demand for workers in this field?
- How do you feel about the changes likely to occur in your career field?
- If these possible futures come true, will the career field still fit your skills, abilities, and interests?
- How might your future earning potential change?
- Are you willing to adapt?
- Would you prefer to shift your kaleidoscope to new options?

A Guide to Futurist Career Research

The first step in researching careers is to uncover trends that may impact your future career. This chapter presents trends that will affect the way people live and work. Your research will uncover additional trends. As futurist Peter Bishop says, you'll know you've succeeded in finding new possibilities when you say, "Aha—yes, that could happen." The next step is to evaluate the effect of these trends. Then, you can make educated choices about your future, no matter what surprises lie ahead. As you are conducting your research, three strategies will help you gather and evaluate information:

- Discover possibilities—research trends to find new opportunities
- Evaluate your assumptions—be open to new information
- Focus on the big picture—you'll have more choices to consider

FUTURIST RESEARCH

Discover possibilities

Evaluate your assumptions

Focus on the big picture

After conducting your research, you'll create scenarios to describe the futures you can envision in your career field. These stories will help you see what could happen and help you decide if this field is right for you—no matter what the future holds.

DISCOVER POSSIBILITIES

Sometimes, large trends are easy to spot; however, it's not so easy to figure out how they might change a particular career field. Consider some of the major trends that are impacting our lives that were hard for most of us to predict just a few years ago. Each trend has produced new career fields or new ways of working.

- The start of the Web began back in 1950 as a government solution to national security. At that time, no one considered the commercial feasibility of the Internet.
- Colleges predicted that the number of students would decline along with the birthrate. They didn't consider the demand for adults to reskill. Today, more people are attending college than ever before, with many universities scrambling to replace outdated facilities or investing in technology to offer distance learning via the Internet.

- When the first computer was developed, IBM announced that world-wide demand would never exceed five or six computers. Today, few industries can flourish without the aid of computer technology.

In retrospect, it's easy to fault the limited thinking that dismissed the impact of computers and the commercial use of the Internet. Will we be any better at predicting the trends that will impact our future?

Top Technologies for the Next 10 Years

- Genetic mapping
- Super materials
- High-definition energy sources
- Miniaturization
- Smart manufacturing
- Anti-aging products
- Medical treatments
- Hybrid fuel vehicles
- "Edutainment"

Source: Douglas E. Olesen "The Top Technologies for the Next Ten Years," *Exploring Your Future.*

Some Trends and Predictions

Some futurists say these possibilities are already on the way. Realistically, some of these predictions will come true and others won't. Again, don't worry about the accuracy of the predictions, rather ask, "If this were to happen, how would it impact my career choice?"

- The population of the United States is aging. People are living longer: Some predict that living past the age of 100 will soon be a reality for many. The large population of baby boomers is also aging, and 76 million people will retire in the next half-century. By the year 2010, nearly 6 million Americans will be at least 85 years old.
- The current population of the United States will nearly double in size to a whopping 394 million by 2050.
- A new industry called life sciences brings together agriculture, biotechnology, and pharmaceuticals to create new products such as organically grown plastics and cancer-preventing proteins. "Monsanto, for example, is working on a cottonseed that can produce its own colors. DuPont is working on grains that can look and taste like meat," says Greg May, a researcher at Boyce Thompson Institute for Plant Research at Cornell University.

To learn more about the technology revolution, check out this virtual think tank: www.gwforecast.gwu.edu

- By 2010, fish farming will surpass beef production. Aquaculture is growing faster than any other sector of the world food economy. Will the trend toward healthy eating continue so that sushi bars will replace steak houses?
- Textbooks will disappear as networked learning takes hold. Students will access information, read lectures, participate in discussions, and take tests online. Professors and learners will customize learning materials to meet their needs.
- Language translators will be perfected to allow seamless conversations between cultures speaking differing languages.
- Nanomedicine is expected to emerge by 2025 when nanotechnology-based therapies will reach clinical use, including machines to monitor internal processes, remove cholesterol or blood clots from arteries, and destroy cancer cells before they become tumors. Nanodevices may be able to stimulate and guide the body's own construction and repair mechanisms to restore healthy tissue.
- By the year 2020, automated highways will allow people to use their own cars without driving them.

- The human genome project and others for animals and plants will neatly catalog genetics into databases by the year 2020. Eric Lander at the Whitehead Institute for Bio-medical Research in Cambridge, Massachusetts, likens these complete genomes to the periodic table of elements, the basis for twentieth-century research in chemistry. Monica Riley, senior scientist at the marine biological laboratory in Woods Hole, Massachusetts, says, "In the near future, we will know everything that goes into making up a living cell. It's an exhilarating time to be doing science" (Carey, Freundich, and Gross, 1997).

SCIENCE & ENGINEERING

For more information on science and engineering careers, check out the website at www.nas.edu, home page of the National Academy of Sciences. Look for the publication *Science and Engineering Research in a Changing World,* from the National Academy of Sciences, the National Academy of Engineering, and the Institute of Medicine.

Some of these trends may impact the career field you are considering. You'll find some more applicable than others. For instance, Rosa is researching a career as a computer engineer. The human genome project interests her. She wonders: How might this technology impact my work in computers? With a little research, she discovers that Motorola is currently exploring the use of gene splicing and genome engineering for computing. They are using the DNA molecule as the basis to create computers that are more powerful. Her research triggered these questions:

- If we grew computers biologically, what would be the role for computer engineers?
- How would that impact computer engineering as a profession?
- How would biological computers use software?
- How soon would this happen?
- If this happens, would I still want to be a computer engineer?
- Would this career field still match the elements I want in my kaleidoscope pattern?

Rosa can't answer these questions without further research. The answers to some of these questions haven't been developed yet. However, Rosa is beginning to think like a futurist and will begin to focus her research with these questions.

Activity 5.2 helps you evaluate future trends and develop questions so you can research their impact on your field.

To Discover Possibilities, Ask These Questions:

Social Dynamics—How will people communicate and relate with each other?

Demographics—How will statistical data (age, ethnicity, population size, and location) affect the future?

Economics—How will the economic climate impact our future?

Political—How will government policies and international relations change our world?

Technology—What impact will scientific and technological advances have?

EVALUATE YOUR ASSUMPTIONS

As you learned in Chapter 2, your experiences and values filter how you see the world. Your tentative career choice is based on your exposure to work, viewpoints you've heard, and things you've read or seen on TV. You may think you know a great deal about the field already (and perhaps you do), but you have probably filled in information gaps with assumptions. One goal of your research is to determine whether the facts support the opinions you've heard and the assumptions you've made.

"It's what we know already that often prevents us from learning."

BERNARD HALDANE

Your assumptions can also influence your research. Wouldn't it be easier if your research validates what you already believe? That's why some students only look for information that confirms their tentative choice. They ignore information that suggests this field might not be

Activity 5.2 Evaluating Future Trends

Instructions: Choose three trends; then, with a group, brainstorm the potential ways they could impact the career field you are researching. Write down any questions you want to research further.

Let's revisit Kate, the college student who created a kaleidoscope pattern for a bilingual elementary teacher in Chapter 4. For each trend, Kate asked, "How might this factor impact the field of education? What kind of opportunities might it create?" She was careful not to evaluate or criticize the ideas. An open mind is necessary to generate as many ideas as possible.

Kate's Example:

TREND	IMPACT	QUESTIONS
The U. S. population, including the minority population, is increasing.	More students will create a demand for teachers. Many of the students will be minorities, which will increase the opportunities for bilingual teachers.	What's the demand for bilingual teachers? What advantage would I have if I learned Spanish? Will this demand be in my community?
Groupware systems will allow students to learn together at multiple sites.	Schools could be hooked together to allow students to work together from all over the globe. Students might stay home and attend school via computer, creating virtual schools.	Would I still want to teach if it was over computer lines rather than in a classroom? What do teachers need to know about technology?
A variety of movies, TV shows, sports, and other forms of entertainment can be selected electronically at home on demand.	Students will have more access to learning media at home than at school. Students will expect school to entertain them.	What are the opportunities to develop entertaining education for children? Will entertainment and education blur more?

Your Turn:

TREND	IMPACT	QUESTIONS

The questions you develop through this activity will guide you to gather information about how your potential career field might change in the future.

suited to them. This approach makes your research much easier, but can lead to dissatisfaction later. It's much better to choose a different path now than to make that decision after several years of disappointing work experience.

As you conduct your research, find out what it's really like to do this work—day in and day out. To gain accurate information, it's important to recognize and put aside your assumptions. The following questions will help you:

What assumptions am I making about working in this field?

Are my assumptions based on fact?

What questions can I ask to test my assumptions?

For example, Kate was researching the field of teaching and leaning toward becoming an elementary teacher. As she began to look at her assumptions, she realized she had many preconceived ideas about teaching. Activity 5.3 shows Kate's assumptions and the research questions she developed to test them.

FOCUS ON THE BIG PICTURE

"Only a panoramic view of the present can encompass all the factors we need to anticipate change and plan effectively for the future."

BEVERLY KAYE AND CAELA FARREN

Begin your research by focusing on the big picture. Examine professions and industries, rather than specific jobs. Professions are stable—many have survived for centuries. Professions meet basic needs that are easy to identify. Accountants ensure that a business is profitable. Attorneys advise clients on legal issues. Counselors help people develop psychological well-being. Scientists conduct experiments to test theories.

Individual jobs within professions change and sometimes disappear. For instance, computerized accounting systems have dramatically changed the jobs in an accounting firm or department. Accountants used to examine handwritten balance sheets to reconcile accounts; now, they use software systems. As technology changes, so do the roles of people working in the profession. Today, accountants say they spend most of their time advising managers and analyzing financial data to make business decisions. How will accounting opportunities change as expert systems and smart computers enter the everyday business world?

Find the Basic Need

What is the basic need of the profession you are considering?

As you begin researching your industry or profession, find out the basic need it meets. Photography is a relatively new profession, invented at the end of the nineteenth century. What need does it fill? As Kodak reminds us, photography meets our need to remember the past through pictures. This basic human need has been met in different ways throughout history as the media and technology have changed—from cave painting to oil portraits to photographs. Though the technology and related jobs have changed, the basic need endures.

In the nineteenth century, journalists scoured city hall, neighborhoods, and anywhere else they could to find the news. Today, many journalists don't hunt for news; they decide what is significant and relevant. Their role is changing from a provider of information to an

My Assumptions

Activity 5.3

Kate was investigating and researching the field of teaching—leaning toward becoming an elementary teacher. Let's find out what she discovered when she evaluated her assumptions. First, Kate identified her assumptions and then she developed questions to test them.

Kate's Example:

CAREER FIELD:

Teaching elementary school

ASSUMPTIONS

Elementary teachers' schedules allow them to spend a lot of time with their own children.

With summers off, teachers have time to travel.

My mom always thought I would be a good teacher because I liked school and made good grades.

Teachers work in a classroom teaching subjects they like.

Teaching is a way to help children feel good about themselves and develop a love of learning.

QUESTIONS TO ASK TO TEST MY ASSUMPTIONS:

What hours do teachers work?

Do elementary teachers have summers off?

Is being a good student a good predictor of success as a teacher?

Would I earn enough money to be able to travel?

As technology develops, will teachers have the same role in the classroom?

(continued)

Your Turn:

CAREER FIELD:

____

ASSUMPTIONS

____

____

____

____

____

____

____

____

____

____

____

____

QUESTIONS TO ASK TO TEST MY ASSUMPTIONS:

____

____

____

____

____

____

____

____

____

____

____

____

interpreter of information, saving time for people in a world saturated with information.

As you consider future trends affecting work roles and job responsibilities, you may discover that some day soon, the work won't match your interests, skills, and preferences as much as you thought it would. If your image of reporting is dashing from one scene to the next, and you learn that now most newspapers rely on syndicated news services to gather the news, you may decide being a reporter isn't for you. Does this mean you should abandon journalism altogether? Not necessarily.

Kate discovered that, during her lifetime, teaching could look very different from today. As technology redefines the way education is delivered, there may be few opportunities for the person who likes personal interaction in the classroom. Gathering this information, although initially disappointing, saves Kate the disillusionment of entering a career that won't satisfy her.

Kate has another alternative, however. Instead of looking for another career choice, she can focus on the big picture and expand her options by looking at the whole profession of education. She uses a process called *mind mapping*. Generally, when we think of education, we see a school and identify a handful of jobs: teachers, counselors, advisors, and administrators. The education mind map illustrates many other careers involved in the delivery of education.

When she looked at education this way, Kate realized that although she didn't think she'd want to be teaching in the classroom of the future, she could still follow her passion in other ways. After doing further research, Kate decided the field of educational media was just right for her. She could develop streaming videos and animation for television and online learning. She'd still be helping children learn, and her new choice would be a good match for her other interests. As a media developer, she would have the opportunity to use her artistic abilities and computer knowledge.

Activity 5.4 will help you expand your career idea and consider options within a career environment or profession that you might not have considered. After your research, you may find that one of these ideas is a better fit for you than the one you originally identified.

Conducting Research

Good research requires planning and organization. As you plan your research, look for resources that tell you things you don't already know. The resources listed in this section are a good starting point. A good research strategy will help you discover what a particular career field is like. You'll also learn what people are saying about its future. If you spend a day observing someone in a profession, you'll learn a lot more than just reading about job requirements.

"Change is the law of life. And those who look only to the past or present are certain to miss the future."

JOHN F. KENNEDY

Activity 5.4 Expanding Career Ideas—Mind Mapping

Instructions: Choose one career environment that interests you:

- Health
- Manufacturing
- Social services
- Business (including services to consumers or businesses)
- Education
- Government
- Communication/entertainment

"What we play is life."

LOUIS ARMSTRONG

"Whatever you can do or dream you can, begin it. Boldness has genius, power, and magic in it. Begin it now!"

GOETHE

Expand your thinking about this career field. Create a mind map (see Figure 5.1 for an example), capturing as many related work opportunities as possible. A mind map is a creative method to help you record creative ideas. Begin your mind map with one central career environment. Create branches off this environment, listing related occupations. The further you can branch out on your mind map, the more likely you will be to arrive at creative possibilities.

Your Turn:

Create your own mind map in the space below.

An example of mind mapping. FIGURE 5.1

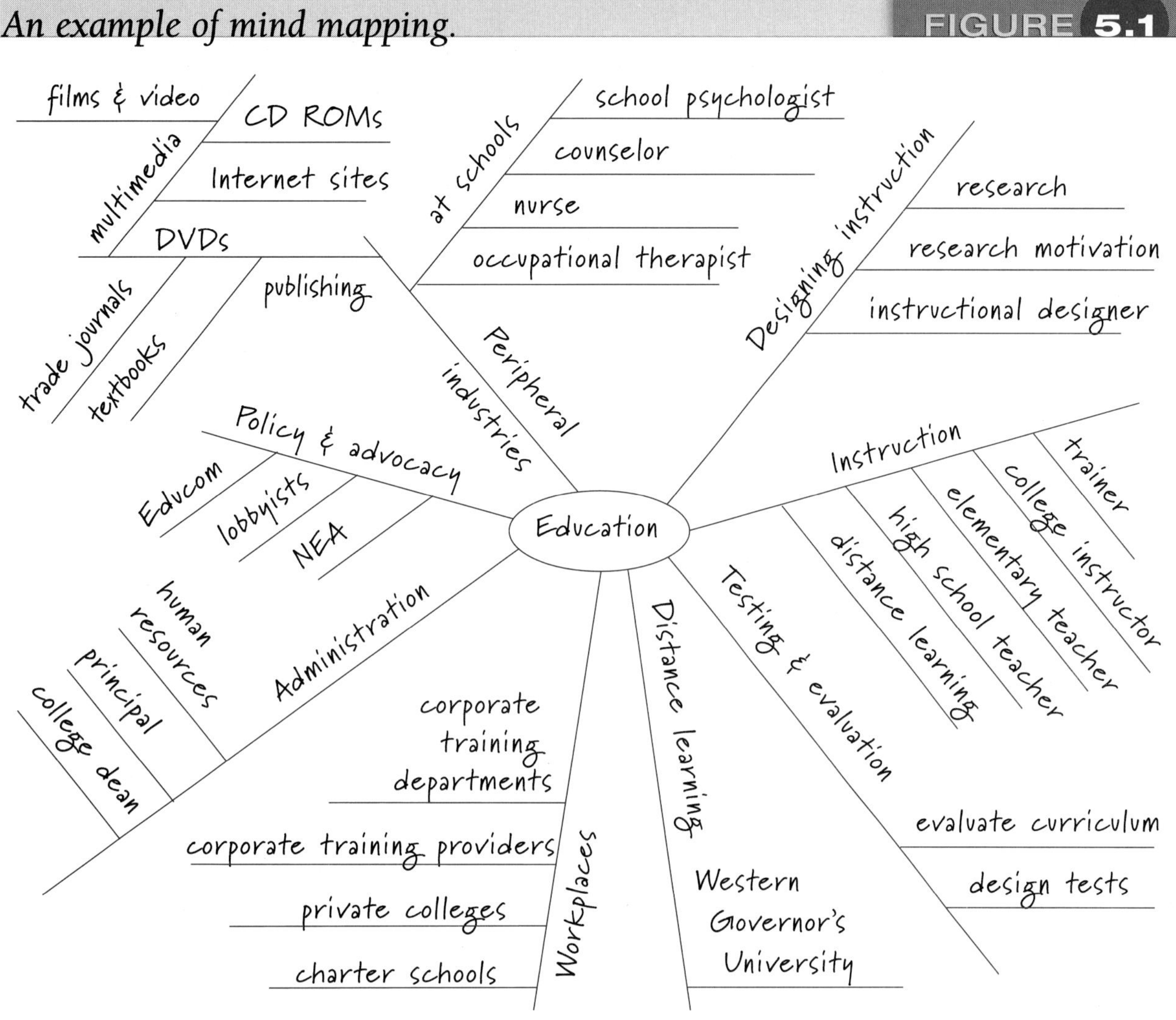

RESEARCH RESOURCES

Career centers. Colleges and universities currently offer a variety of career counseling services, which can include career counseling, internships, interviews, field trips, career fairs, employer listings, student employment, and alumni services. Don't wait until you're about to graduate to visit your career center. Career counseling staff offer consultation and information regarding specific career opportunities, effective job-seeking techniques, and career planning for undecided students as well as for students with declared majors.

The resource library in the career center contains information regarding majors, careers, graduate/professional schools, employers, employment trends, videos, and other resources. Computers are usually available to students for creating resumes, researching information, and reviewing Internet information.

Many career centers also offer an alumni program that enables you to contact alumni for assistance with career information questions. You can contact alumni by mail, by telephone, or in person regarding your career interests. Alumni can be a valuable source of real-world information.

Activity 5.5 Research Plan

Instructions: Use the worksheet below to plan your research. Write down the questions you developed in the previous activities in this chapter. The next section helps you identify resources you can use to find answers to your questions. Then, fill in the last column and you're ready to start searching for information. Check off each question as you answer it.

✓	MY QUESTIONS	RESOURCES I'LL USE

Many career centers are online and can be accessed through the Internet, even if you're not a student at the institution. Online career centers provide links to other Internet resources where you can research professions, industries, and companies.

Visit the Internet Public Library to find associations: www.ipl.org/ref/aon.

Trade magazines. Nearly every profession has at least one trade magazine. Most are also online. Go to the library, and read trade magazines relevant to the field you are considering, keeping an eye out for indications of how the field is changing. Reading the advertisements can give you good clues. Studying the topics at annual seminars and conferences is another good way to spot trends.

For example, Darrin is considering majoring in communications. One of the patterns in his kaleidoscope is focused on corporate training. He is investigating becoming a trainer and has discovered the professional association of trainers, the American Society for Training and Development (ASTD). For more information on corporate training, check out ASTD on the Internet at www.astd.org.

Using Computer Discussion Groups

Discussion groups on the Internet cover every imaginable topic. E-mail messages are sent to all members on the list. Most students prefer to *lurk*

Favorite Resources

www.bls.gov/home.htm: career information from the Department of Labor, Bureau of Labor Statistics

www.bls.gov/oco: *The Occupational Outlook Handbook*

www.demographics.com: American demographics and trends

www.economist.com: weekly journal from England about world and national economics

www.fastcompany.com: career articles geared to the 20-something crowd

www.wfs.org: World Future Society

www.hotwired.com: from *Wired* magazine; information about technology

www.cnn.com: from the news station

www.npr.org: National Public Radio often carries features about careers

www.rileyguide.com: evaluates career sites and provides links to the good ones

www.salary.com: career information including salary by occupation and region

or read postings on a list for a while before participating in discussions. You can post questions and get responses from people working all over the world.

Before joining a discussion group or list, read the frequently asked questions (FAQs) to determine the etiquette rules for the group. Although most professional groups encourage student participation, some groups have specific requirements for membership and limit the discussion to specific topics.

You can find a list of Internet discussion groups at http://list-universe.com or www.topica.com

Many discussion groups maintain archives of past discussions, saving you time in gathering information. These archives save all of the e-mail discussions by topic and can be a good way to access information.

Ask people and professors for good discussion groups. Professional and trade magazines will often list appropriate groups. Once you've found an interesting discussion group, log on to the site. Each group provides instructions for subscribing to their list. Choose to receive e-mails in digest form; otherwise, you receive a separate e-mail from each participant in the discussion.

INFORMATION INTERVIEWING

Trends that seem obvious to one person may remain hidden from another. That's why it's best to use many sources to gather information. One of the best sources is real live people working in the field. Exploring print resources and Internet sites can be helpful, but they are limited. Visiting work sites and talking with someone doing the work gives you an insider's view of the profession. Research also involves feeling and sensing. Experiencing the work environment can help you decide if this career is for you.

Here's a tip from John Naisbett, leading trend-master, quoted in "Futurology Decoder Key": "All change is local and bottom up. And, what monitors local events? Local newspapers. If you keep track of local events, you can see the shifting pattern."

Alex is interested in the mass communication field and has zeroed in on journalism. Students usually enter journalism wanting to work as a reporter or publisher. Alex decided on reporting and conducted several research sessions at the library and on the Web. Although he gathered lots of information about the nature of the work, necessary skills, working conditions, employment outlook, earning potential, and related careers, he's still

Information Interviewing

Information interviewing allows you to:

- Learn about the profession beyond information gained through print and electronic resources
- Obtain information that is firsthand and up to date
- Gain a broader perspective of the work
- Develop a valuable network of professionals as potential contacts
- Visit different companies and compare work environments
- Gain confidence because you initiate the interview and ask the questions

not sure if this is an option for him. The information gave him some idea of what to expect, but it is one-dimensional and mostly generic. He still wants to know what it's really like to be a journalist. Work environments can range from fast-paced and frenzied to slow and calm. Would he enjoy working as a writer, researching in quiet calm places, or working under pressure in broadcasting, giving up-to-the-minute news updates? What is a typical day like in the life of a journalist? Is he better off getting a degree in communication or journalism, or would a liberal arts education be more valuable? How has the field grown? What technical competencies will he need? Only by gathering firsthand information, by talking to real people working in journalism, can Alex find the answers to these questions.

Scheduling Information Interviews

Identify people who are working in the professions or career fields you are interested in exploring. Is someone you know already working in the field? Does someone you know—a friend, relative, professor, manager, or community leader—know someone in the field? Ask friends, professional acquaintances, and teachers if they know someone working in the field you are researching who is willing to talk to students. Many professional associations keep resource lists of people willing to provide advice to students. Career centers often keep lists of alumni who are willing to grant interviews to students.

If you are unable to identify someone through your network, you can call companies directly. Ask the receptionist for the department where people in the field are likely to work. Use the following telephone script to schedule an interview. Another way to initiate contact when you don't have a name is to access a company's home page on the Internet. Usually you can send an e-mail, which will be routed to the appropriate department.

REAL-LIFE PERSPECTIVE

What Students Say About Information Interviews

"Imagine yourself being able to walk into your job and enjoy almost every moment of it. That's what came to mind when I interviewed someone at the Scottsdale Center for the Arts in Scottsdale, Arizona."

"Seeing the workplace firsthand makes the difference."

"After talking with someone in the profession, I'm questioning my decision to pursue physical therapy as the best career choice for me."

"I found the interview to be very interesting. Listening to someone else say 'you need a college education to get your foot in the door' confirmed my decision to pursue a business degree."

Questions for Information

- Would you describe a typical day?
- What kinds of skills are needed in your job? What new skills have you acquired recently?
- What trends do you see impacting this field?
- What are the most important personal satisfactions connected with your field?
- What do you like least about your job?
- What are some examples of current projects you are working on?
- How much travel is involved in your job?
- Would you describe the pressures and stress inherent in your work?
- What kinds of problems do you solve?
- What are the major skills, knowledge, and abilities necessary for success in this field?
- What type of experience is helpful for entering this field?
- What college courses helped you the most?
- How did you enter the profession?
- What did you do before entering this field? How did that experience help you?
- What is the best way to enter this profession?
- What advice would you give people entering this field?
- What is the starting salary in this field?
- Would you recommend other people I could talk to about careers in this field?
- What else about this field would be important for me to know?

When calling an interviewee, tell the person you are a student conducting a career study. Explain that you are gathering information about possible options and would like to gain further insight into the profession. Remember, most people like talking about themselves and the work they do and are willing to spend time with you.

Use the following script to schedule an interview:

"Hello my name is __________. I spoke with __________ about careers in __________. He (She) recommended I contact you because of your background in __________. I was wondering if I could spend 15 minutes talking to you about your profession. When would it be convenient to meet with you?"

or

"Hello my name is __________. I am a student at the __________. I'm researching careers in __________. I'd like to know if you could spend a few minutes with me to answer a few questions about the field. When would it be convenient to stop by?"

The following ideas will help you gain useful information:

- You may want to make contact through a letter or e-mail first and follow up with a phone call. If you choose this approach, follow the same thinking by explaining your intent and letting the person know you will be calling within a few days to set up an appointment.
- Plan the interview and review your list of questions.
- Practice. If you are uncomfortable speaking to people you don't know, practice asking questions to people you do know. Ask about their work, what they enjoy most about work, what they enjoy learn-

ing about, and other information you would like to know. Begin in low-risk situations and build your confidence. Soon, you'll be ready to talk to anyone you believe has information you can use.

- Record the answers to your questions and organize the information in a folder.
- Follow up with a thank-you note.

Interview several people in the field you are considering. Don't settle for just one or two interviews—you'd only have the opinions of one or two people on which to base your future decision. Prepare your list of questions before the interview and take them with you. If you take notes, people will form the impression that you are serious about planning your future.

The more people you talk to, the broader your information base is. The information interview can also be informal. Consider engaging people in conversation about their work at social gatherings, campus events, and other places where people gather. Remember, most people enjoy sharing information about their work. The more you know, the better informed you'll be in making career choices.

Top 10 Demand Occupations—Why They May Not Matter

For statistical projections, check out the *Occupational Outlook Handbook* at www.bls.gov/oco/.

What is the future demand for your career field? Many lists of the hot careers are published yearly. These projections are usually based on past statistical trends. Often, they don't consider new technologies that will be impacting the market. It's interesting to compare several lists and see how they differ. Remember, demand today is no guarantee for the future. Don't choose a career solely on projections because they may change. Hot careers inevitably cool off as quickly as they become hot. Look at investment banking in the early 1990s or aerospace engineering in the 1980s. Both of these high-demand careers have come and gone. Although IT professionals top the current list, we've seen their demand weaken as the economy tightens. Talking to people in the field can give you a more accurate picture of the demand for an occupation in your geographic area.

Don't dismiss a career option because demand seems low. People who choose occupations based on their passions and interests are often able to

Top 10 Fastest-Growing Occupations 2000–2010

1. Computer software engineers, applications
2. Computer support specialists
3. Computer software engineers, systems software
4. Network and computer systems administrators
5. Network systems and data communication analysts
6. Desktop publishers
7. Database administrators
8. Personal and home care aides
9. Computer systems analysts
10. Medical assistants

Source: 2000–2001 *Occupational Outlook Handbook.*

Occupations with the Largest Projected Job Growth, 2000–2010

1. Food preparation and servers
2. Customer service representatives
3. Registered nurses
4. Retail salespersons
5. Computer support specialists
6. Cashiers
7. Office clerks
8. Security guards
9. Computer software engineers, applications
10. Waiters and waitresses

Source: 2000–2001 *Occupational Outlook Handbook.*

discover a successful niche and develop work opportunities. You do need to be prepared, however, to work harder marketing your skills.

Determining Salary Potential

What is your earning potential? Even entry-level salaries can vary widely. Demand impacts the salary that employers offer and varies widely by geographic location. For example, Kate found that starting salaries for teachers in small rural areas of her home state were up to $5,000 per year more than teachers in the city. On the other hand, for many professions, salaries are much higher in urban areas to accommodate the higher cost of living.

The *Occupational Outlook Handbook* cites average salary information by occupation. Most professions also conduct salary surveys and publish this information in professional journals and on websites. These surveys often list average salaries in a career field by length of service, degree, region of the country, and size of the organization.

As you evaluate salary potential, remember that salaries, too, can be affected by outside events and trends. Medical doctors have seen their earning potential erode in recent years because of HMOs and the high cost of liability insurance. Thousands of middle managers have seen their earnings drop as new technology and self-directed work teams reduce the demand. Although it's important to have a realistic knowledge of your earning capabilities, it's also important not to base your career decision only on money.

www.salaryexpert.com/: excellent salary information with specific job descriptions by geographic area, including international information.

www.payscale.com: good resource to search for salary comparisons.

www.careerjournal.com/salaries/: this *Wall Street Journal* site lists salaries for several professions.

www.salary.com: this contains salary information on thousands of job titles by geographic location.

Using Scenarios to Make Career Decisions

Now that you've completed your research, you will put all the information together using a process called *scenario planning.* Scenarios are stories that take an imaginary leap into the future and allow you to see and feel what the future might hold. Well-developed scenarios paint pictures of the future that can trigger insight into your career decision. These stories, based on your research, include the facts and trends you discovered. This process is a good way to organize your research information so that you

REAL-LIFE PERSPECTIVE

ALICE

When Alice Tome decided to go back to school, she knew she wanted a career in the medical field. Her experience working as a lab technician before having a family generated that interest. So, in 1996 when she was choosing a field, it was easy to decide on pursuing a master's degree in occupational therapy. Occupational therapy was the number one occupation in demand that year. "Good Morning America" even featured interviews with new graduates as they evaluated 10 to 20 job offers with various recruiting bonuses and incentives. When Alice was accepted into the only occupational therapy master's degree program in her home state, she was on the road to career success.

However, when Alice graduated three years later, offers did not come pouring in. In fact, three months after graduation, most of her classmates were still looking for work. Although the predictions were accurately based on the medical needs of an aging population, they didn't predict that Medicare would reduce funding for occupational therapy. Studies projecting the demand also failed to predict the growth of occupational therapy aides, a position requiring only two years of education compared to six or seven years for a master's degree.

Alice's story has a happy ending, though. Through an internship and by volunteering, Alice developed many contacts and began to work on call at two progressive hospitals. Alice also volunteered to assist in a very exciting research project. Her expertise in this new technology led to a full-time position within a few months. Alice succeeded in a tight job market because her passion for the field led to her finding a successful niche. If she had entered the field simply to earn money in a high-demand occupation, she would have been disappointed before she even got started.

can make meaningful decisions about your career. This idea was developed at Shell Oil, where Peter Schwartz successfully used scenario planning to make strategic business decisions.

Scenario planning is based on this idea: since we won't know the future, let's look at a decision we're trying to make today and see how it would play out against several different futures.

Schwartz describes scenarios this way: "Scenarios comprise a tool for ordering one's perceptions. The point is not to pick one preferred future and hope for it to happen. Nor is the point to find the most probable future and adapt to it. Rather, the point is to make strategic decisions that will be sound for all plausible futures. No matter what future takes place, you are much more likely to be ready for it—and influential in it—if you have thought seriously about scenarios."

For more information about scenario planning, read *The Art of the Long View* by Peter Schwartz or check out his website at www.gbn.com.

KATE'S SCENARIOS

By using a futurist approach to her research, Kate learned many facts about the current status of education and about many future possibilities. Look at Kate's worksheet in Figure 5.2. All of the items listed under "Facts" are likely to happen so Kate will include them in her scenarios. Kate has prioritized the possibilities, and highlighted the ones she thinks are most likely to come true. She decided to write two scenarios so she could compare possible futures. Read Kate's scenarios on page 115.

Scenarios for Infotech Workers, 2010

Andy Hines is an associate with Coatis & Jaratt, Inc., a think tank and policy research organization specializing in the study of the future. He wrote the following scenarios to show how technology may impact four different careers.

The Farmer

Harry looks over the visual representation of his farm on the screen. "Show me the soil moisture map," he commands the farm-management system, which coordinates field sensors with the computer system. A barrage of colors comes up on his monitor. "Too much red," he observes. Red is the color representing dangerously low levels of moisture. He wistfully recalls last season's blue map, which resulted from record rainfalls.

Harry activates his expert-system assistant. "What are my options?" he asks. Three choices appear on the screen:

A. Divert water from purple areas (acceptable levels of moisture).
B. Borrow or purchase water from Johnson, who borrowed 1,000 gallons two years ago.
C. Purchase water from the municipal supply.

Harry dials up his weather forecasting service and asks for the next month's forecast. "More dry weather," he complains aloud. He decides that he will ask Johnson for some water and contract for the rest from the municipal water supply. He taps into the videotext service run by the county. It is an online bidding service. As Harry suspected, rates are up because of the drought. He winces and bids for the water he needs. The electronic data interchange service notifies him of the price and asks for his approval. Harry reluctantly adds his electronic signature.

The Police Officer

Testimony of Officer Nina Padula before the Seventh District Court, August 29, 2010: "My squad car's computer alerted me at 2:45 P.M. on May 7, 2010, that a QuickShop had been held up just two minutes previously. I was in the area and quickly spotted two young men running down the street with a bag. I ordered them to halt, apprehended them, advised them of their rights, and scanned their fingerprints into the computer. The computer searched the National Criminal Database and, within seconds, advised me to arrest the suspects because they were in violation of their electronic house arrest. I was warned that they had a history of violence and I took the appropriate safety procedures, stunning the suspects and fully activating my body armor."

The Scientist

A team of scientists headed by Lara Radinsky appears to be close to the breakthrough long sought by the bioremediation field: the demonstration of a new genetically engineered microorganism that will attack many of the plastics buried in landfills around the world. "Teamwork was the key," says Radinsky. "We had scientists in China, Germany, Indonesia, and Mexico working on the project around the clock." At first, some scientists had worried that the multinational team might have a hard time integrating its findings, but the interface problems were worked out. "The godsend was our new computer-supported, cooperative-work software," says Radinsky. "Findings from each team member were immediately available to the others. As a result, we never lost perspective of the project as a whole."

The Teacher

Samantha arrives at Shaker Elementary School and urgently advises her teacher Mr. Wheel that she is ready to move on to the next level of her geography program. Wheel smiles and brings the quiz up on Samantha's screen. He is amazed at how eager the kids are to learn since the new computer-assisted instruction programs arrived. Wheel has tailored the program to provide his students with varying degrees of help. Samantha completes the quiz in less than an hour. Meanwhile, Wheel is able to sit with Juan for half an hour and help him with his math program.

Wheel observes that Samantha called up the country screen six times and the pictures screen only once. He gives her the okay to move on to the next level and advises her to be ready for the science lesson in which a local scientist will give the students a tour of the lab by videoconference.

Source: From *Exploring Your Future: Living, Learning, and Working in the Information Age.*

FIGURE 5.2 *Kate's scenario research.*

CAREER FIELD: *TEACHING*

Facts

- The population of school-age children is increasing in the United States.
- Non-English-speaking or English-as-a-second language students are increasing as the United States becomes more culturally diverse.
- Many teachers are expected to retire in the next 10 years, creating openings.
- Teachers must know how to use the Internet and technology to help students access knowledge.
- Distance learning is growing and increasing.
- Interactive multimedia learning options are increasing. When the bandwidth becomes available to support video, online multimedia will explode.
- Average starting pay in my city is $23,000 per year.
- Teachers are required to update their education regularly. Typically, they go back to school about every other summer.
- Upon graduation, teachers will be required to pass a test to receive their teaching certificate. Graduates who fail may not teach.
- Teacher education requires students to spend time in the classroom as interns and student teachers prior to graduation.
- Teachers must graduate with a bachelor's degree to teach. Eventually, teachers must go back to school and complete their master's degree if they want to continue in the profession.

Possibilities

- The majority of students in your class don't speak English as their primary language.
- School is year-round.
- Support for teachers from parents varies widely—some schools receive no support from parents. In others, teachers work very hard to please parents.
- Teachers will increasingly be expected to facilitate learning, rather than give answers, as more information is easily accessible.
- Homeschooling will increase as more learning opportunities are offered on the Internet.
- Teacher evaluations and accountability for test scores will cause many teachers to upgrade their skills or lose their jobs.
- School vouchers will reduce enrollment and/or eliminate many public schools.
- Students will be entertained as they learn with well-known comedy actors teaching via satellite broadcasts. Classroom teachers will track student progress, facilitate learning, and maintain distance learning technology.
- Teaching will be conducted primarily online, as distance education becomes the norm.

When Kate contemplated her scenarios, she was very excited about certain elements. Kate could picture herself in that Chicago classroom really making a difference in children's lives. She also thought she would really enjoy helping students use online technology to facilitate their learning. Although she might miss being in a classroom, there were parts of "The Virtual Classroom" she found enticing.

To make a career choice, you don't have to be elated about all aspects of the scenarios. You do, however, have to be prepared to live with all potential futures. Often, students say, "Well, if that comes to pass, here's what I could do to adapt." That's the response we're looking for. Futurist planning through scenarios isn't a one-time event. With your ability to keep an eye on the

Kate's Scenarios for Bilingual Teacher

Satisfied in Chicago

I've graduated and obtained my bilingual teaching certificate. Even before I passed the state test, schools were calling me begging me to come to work. Bilingual teachers are in huge demand. Although school districts couldn't offer bilingual teachers more pay, they could offer educational opportunities and reimbursement. I chose to go to work at a school in the barrio in Chicago. I'm starting to work on my master's degree after school. With distance education and the support of my district, I won't have to attend any classes at the college campus.

My busy days are spent in a classroom brimming with children who don't know how to speak English. Most have been in the United States less than six months. Because of the shortage of bilingual teachers, I have all of the non-English-speaking children for three grade levels. It's a good thing that my teacher's aide, who speaks little English herself, can communicate well with the children; otherwise, I would have to spend all of my time disciplining children rather than teaching them.

Because of the growing population, my school operates year-round. Although I am often tired and overwhelmed by the amount of work, I also feel great satisfaction in helping these children learn to adapt to their new culture. I also enjoy learning more about the different cultures of Mexico and Latin America. Many of the families of my students share their customs with me. I would like to spend my vacation traveling in Central America, but that's not possible on $23,000 a year.

The Virtual Classroom

Most students today don't set foot in a classroom. When Congress passed legislation providing the funding to hook up every home with multimedia access, most parents and students chose to learn within their own homes. Every morning, I walk into my home office and log online to my classroom. Although I've never seen the 50 students assigned to me, I feel I know them well, as I communicate daily online. I spend my day talking to students, writing notes to students, guiding them to find resources to meet the curriculum requirements, scheduling online exams, scheduling interactive learning sessions with subject experts, and tracking those who are falling behind. Although I miss the camaraderie of other teachers, the flexibility of working at home has its advantages.

As a dedicated teacher, I don't really have a structured workday. I've made myself available to students 24/7. It's hard to believe that we used to be tied down to desktop computers. With voice recognition software commonplace, I can chat with my students and facilitate an information flow from anywhere. It paid off for me this year when my annual bonus was larger than my salary. I know I must be really making a difference when there's a waiting list for my teaching facilitation services.

My education as a bilingual teacher is no longer relevant. New software quickly translates any written or spoken materials into the student's primary language. However, I plan to use my Spanish this year, as I've rented a villa in Costa Rica for a year. It really is nice to be able to work from anywhere.

future, you can manage your future through flexible planning. You can make sure that your career stays on track, no matter which future occurs.

Refer back to your Career Kaleidoscope Elements. Compare the kaleidoscope elements with your scenario. Is there a match between them? Will this field really match your interests and allow you to use your preferred skills? How well does your scenario match your preferences? If you don't feel comfortable with the scenario you created, look at your mind map—it probably contains several related options you could explore.

Kate compared her career kaleidoscope to her scenarios. Both scenarios allow Kate to help children and make a difference in their lives. After

Activity 5.6 Creating Scenarios

Instructions: Create a scenario for your career field. Follow these six steps:

Step 1. *Include the facts* (the things you know will happen). You may not like some of the facts you've uncovered, but it's important to include them all.

Step 2. *Prioritize the possibilities.* Read through the trends and possibilities you've learned about. Include the ones you feel are very likely to come true. Choose three or four possibilities for each scenario.

Step 3. *Add details.* Now, it's time to turn the facts and possibilities into a story. Include details to make your story seem real and interesting.

Step 4. *Give it a title.* Give your scenario a descriptive title. Although this may seem unimportant, the title provides a way for you to easily discuss your potential future.

Step 5. *Sleep on it.* Sometimes new ideas and insights develop overnight. Add any new insights to your stories.

Step 6. *Evaluate your future options.* Through your scenarios, you've described what your future might be like. This future is based on your research—the more effort you took to uncover information, the more helpful your scenarios will be. As you imagine yourself living in this future, will you be happy if it arrives? Although it's unlikely that your scenarios will come true exactly as you've predicted, the future will most likely include some elements from it.

SCENARIO

____

____

____

____

____

____

Write two or more scenarios to compare possible futures.

examining all of the elements in her career kaleidoscope, Kate decided that no matter which scenario came true, it would fit well with her values and preferences.

You may discover that this career field is not for you. It's good to find that out now, before you've invested significant time and effort. If that happens, you should explore different career fields. Examine your other

Sample Scenarios for an Audiologist

Tired but Fulfilled

As an audiologist, my day is filled with attending to patients, keeping up with the latest technology, and studying continuously. Today, I will see patients of all ages with all types of hearing problems—those who were born with hearing loss, those who lost their hearing listening to loud music, and those who lost their hearing simply because of age. Working with all of these different people is both challenging and fulfilling. I am also very sad because I have to tell one of my patients today that complete deafness is in the near future. My own hearing loss helps me to be sensitive to my patients' needs. The technology of sound amplification and nerve reconstruction is constantly improving. I spend several hours a day learning the functions and uses of the newest technology. In addition to seeing patients all day and doing whatever work has to be performed on hearing aids, I also have a business to run. I'm always exhausted by the end of the day, but I know my effort is worthwhile when I see the face of a patient who is able to hear again.

The Technician

All health care, including that which assists those with hearing loss problems, is monitored and controlled through HMOs. Although HMOs have kept the cost of health care down for consumers, independent medical practitioners have been virtually eliminated. I work for an HMO, adjusting patients' hearing apparatus. Although I make a good salary and have a lot of flexibility in my schedule, I am responsible for a certain output every week. I spend my days alone in a small cubicle, programming hearing aids to correct different hearing problems. I follow the schematic to meet the prescription of the medical doctor. Sometimes, I feel that the prescription doesn't seem to fit the diagnosis. However, because I never see the patients and have little contact with the doctor, I assume that the hearing device must work OK or they would return it. Although I am disappointed that I don't get to see patients, I take pride in the fact that I work very hard to ensure that, technically, the hearing apparatus works.

career kaleidoscope patterns and choose a new field to research. Although the research process takes time, it's the only way to be prepared for whatever the future brings. Scenarios for different career options can be developed and compared to determine your career preferences.

Summary Points

- Think like a futurist to discover trends and possibilities that will impact your career field.
- Discover possibilities for the future by researching trends, evaluating assumptions, and focusing your research on the big picture.
- Excellent resources for career research include your college career center, print and online sources, and information interviewing.
- Good questions are the building blocks for scenarios. Scenarios describe potential futures based on detailed research. They provide a way to translate statistical and conflicting information into stories to help people make good career decisions.
- Thinking like a futurist means continually keeping an eye on the future so that the future doesn't catch you by surprise.

CHAPTER SIX

6

Learning

A LIFELONG INVESTMENT

What is the value of your college education in dollars?

How do you choose a major?

How do you get the most out of your education?

What are the skills employers want you to develop while in college?

Does graduate school make sense for you?

In the last chapter, you wrote scenarios and evaluated realistic career options, investigating the educational prerequisites and skills required. Now, it's time to begin creating your future. The word *create* means *you hold the keys to your future.*

As you think about your career and formulate plans, deciding how to continue your learning is an important part of the process. You are responsible for your own learning and have many choices and options as your learning continues beyond formal schooling and college.

The profession you choose and prepare for today is very likely to change dramatically in the future. The skills you need to succeed will surely change throughout your lifetime of work. Although no one can accurately predict what skills you'll need in 20 years, you will certainly need skills that weren't covered in your formal education today. The new skills you acquire are added to your career kaleidoscope—which allows you to create new work patterns. Through continuous learning, you will adapt and find new opportunities for work.

"There is nothing like a dream to create the future."

VICTOR HUGO

As participants in the knowledge-based economy of the United States, we depend more and more on the quality of our intellectual capital. Wealth increasingly comes from innovation. Some predict that the value of companies may be defined by *ideas* in the future. Everyone agrees that the current rate of technological change requires continual learning. Skills must be constantly updated just to keep up. Well-known futurists James Taylor and Watts Wacker (1997) say:

> Three decades ago, an aspiring junior executive was required to learn perhaps one new thing a *year*—a new skill, a new system of calculating, a new way of conducting the affairs of whatever business was at hand. Today, under the dual impacts of the speed and mass of change, that same aspiring junior executive at the same point in his/her job trajectory might have to learn one new thing a *day*. Change arrives too quickly, it piles up too high to do otherwise without being entirely left behind. By 2010, it is entirely conceivable that the same person at the same career point might have to learn one new thing an *hour* because, to survive and thrive, businesses, like ecosystems, will have to be subtly changing with their environment, subtly becoming different day by day, hour by hour, and minute by minute. There will be no other way to keep up.

"Knowledge is becoming the resource rather than a resource."

ARNOLD BROWN, *The Next Economy and What It Means for Education*

Today, regardless of the profession, people must continually learn new work approaches, skills, organizational techniques, and more to remain competitive. It means taking risks and seeking opportunities for growth. Continual learning doesn't just mean formal education or sitting in a classroom.

In this chapter, you will discover ways to make the most of your formal education to develop the skills that employers want. Critical-thinking skills and the ability to solve complex problems are crucial to career success and continued employability. You will set your own personal and professional learning development goals—goals that go beyond merely choosing a major—and make a commitment to continual learning.

"Education—continuing education, continually honing and expanding the mind—is vital mental renewal. Sometimes that involves the external discipline of the classroom or systematized study programs; more often it does not. Proactive people can figure out many, many ways to educate themselves."

STEVEN COVEY, *The Seven Habits of Highly Effective People*

You may be thinking, "If I'm expected to continuously learn, will I ever get out of the classroom?" Learning doesn't have to take place in a classroom. Tom Andriola, author of *Career Survival 101: Work in the Future*, advises: "There are many ways to learn, and *how* you do it isn't as important as *if* you do it. Community groups, professional societies, and coffee shops are all great places to learn. One thing that helped me is when I realized that every interaction I have is an opportunity to learn. It is amazing how your view of people and situations will change when you approach it in that manner."

"The whole way we do work has changed," observes John Challenger, Executive Vice President of Challenger, Gray & Christmas, a Chicago-based international outplacement firm. "Work requires more knowledge. The infusion of technology into the workplace is making for a much more educated work force that is much more comfortable with technology and one that is able to adapt to new technology."

Quoted in William O'Hare and Joseph Schwartz, *One Step Forward, Two Steps Back*

REAL-LIFE PERSPECTIVE

TERRI

"I started my life as a secretary, moved into typography and graphics production, added copywriting and, finally, became a corporate trainer working for a manufacturer of typography equipment. After a very short tenure as a trainer, I came to the conclusion that being a good typographer did not mean that I could necessarily teach others how to use typography equipment well. So, I resigned the position and enrolled in graduate school in instructional design. After a year of classes at one university, I transferred to Florida State University where there was a greater emphasis on learning theory. I appreciate the education I received at Florida State, but now that I have graduated and am working, I have found a few gaps in my knowledge. Probably the most glaring deficiencies I am now struggling to overcome are in the areas of technology and education policies.

"In my current position, I am involved in the development of a virtual university. With this project, I am finding another dimension has been added to the technology/education gap. I'm spending a lot of time figuring out and learning different processes.

"Instead of designing computer-based instruction, I'm helping instructors become computer-based instructors. In a relatively short time, I've had to become familiar with routers, multicasting, videoservers, network security issues, accreditation standards, workload policies, curriculum review processes, and more. It's very exciting work and I'm really enjoying it, but most of what I do wasn't addressed in my graduate work. Half of what I've learned wasn't addressed when I was taking courses three years ago."

What I've Learned — Activity 6.1

Instructions: List five things you've learned this week. Count what you've read in newspapers and magazines, watched on TV, and heard in conversations or in a college course, etc.

	WHAT I LEARNED	HOW/WHERE?
1.		
2.		
3.		
4.		
5.		

Whether you're learning on the job, in a classroom, in a coffee shop, at a seminar, or in an Internet chat room—the point is to *never* stop learning. You don't want to wake up one day to a world you no longer understand. The world won't wait for you to catch up. Realize that information is power—and absolutely necessary—for your career survival.

The Value of Education

"Don't go through life with a closed fist. Keep your palms open. It's like doors and windows to the world. Absorb everything . . . there will be a lesson."

FRANK LLOYD WRIGHT, architect

The ticket to a prosperous and rewarding career is often a college degree. Today, college is more important than ever. "Current and projected growth rates for professional careers out-distance the rates for semi-skilled labor by a wide margin, and, for the many types of work where a college education is optional, more and more employers are insisting on degreed job candidates," advises Nicholas Basta, author of *Major Options: The Student's Guide Linking College Majors and Career Opportunities During and After College.* The hard reality is that your earning power over your lifetime with a college degree is much greater than without one. The educational investment you make today will pay off in the long term with access to more work opportunities and salary earnings.

"I'm always getting ideas: by listening to talk shows on the radio, or just by driving around in the car, or by conversing with people . . . interesting things are always coming up."

CHARLES SCHULTZ, cartoonist

WHAT CAN I DO WITH A DEGREE IN VISUAL ARTS?

- Commercial artist
- Cinematographer
- Interior designer
- Computer programmer
- Film engineer

Earlier in U. S. history, college was pretty much reserved for the wealthy. If you could afford a college education, you chose the best university to attend and spent the next four years acquiring your degree and preparing for your future. If you weren't born wealthy, you would have to rely on *street smarts*—apprenticeships, on-the-job training, and community activities—for your education. Fortunately, that all changed at the end of World War II when the government introduced the GI Bill. Instantly, college was affordable for most young males in America. Despite the media clamor about rising education costs, college still remains affordable—and a viable option for most Americans. Scholarships, Pell grants, student loans, and corporate-sponsored tuition assistance programs have made a college education a possibility for millions. Acquiring a college education is a typical expectation in many households and is more of a necessity than a luxury today.

People with the most education report the highest average annual earnings according to the U. S. Census Bureau (see Figure 6.1). These are the

REAL-LIFE PERSPECTIVE

PHYLLIS HARPER-RISPOLI

PHR & Associates

"As an outplacement counselor, I see executives and professionals who often unexpectedly find themselves out of work. Sometimes, their skills are no longer needed because of new technology or a merger, or sometimes a downsizing just seems to help Wall Street. Whatever the reason, the clients I see are forced to find new work in the middle of their careers. The people who have the most difficulty are those without college degrees. Many times, they have some college, but they dropped out to go to work and progressed very well within the company. Their salaries mirrored those of college graduates until now, with many earning high salaries. It's difficult at 40 or 50 to start over and compete with recent graduates. These professionals consistently lose out to candidates with degrees who are infinitely more marketable."

Education and earnings: What's the link?

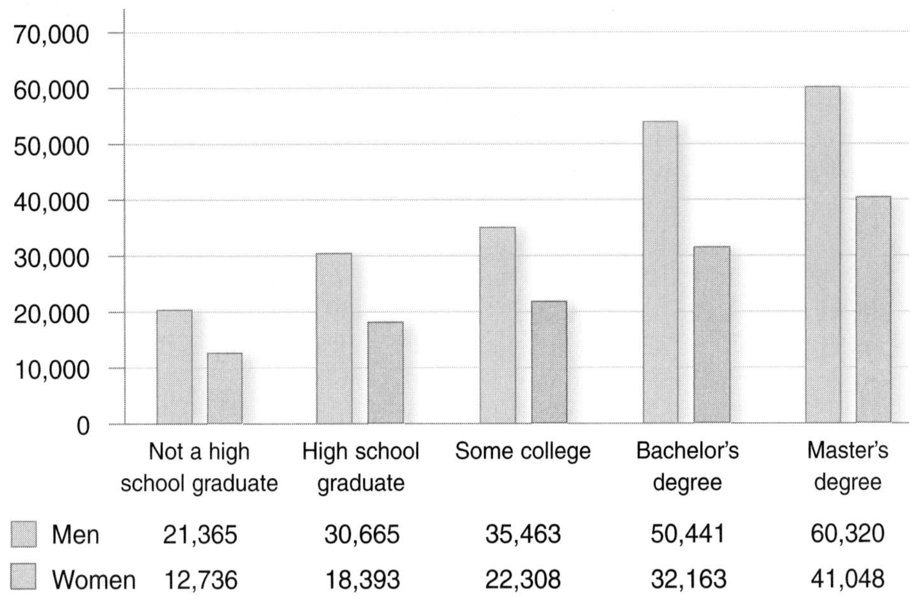

	Not a high school graduate	High school graduate	Some college	Bachelor's degree	Master's degree
Men	21,365	30,665	35,463	50,441	60,320
Women	12,736	18,393	22,308	32,163	41,048

Source: U. S. Bureau of the Census, 2002.

average earnings for men and women by highest level of education completed. The U. S. Bureau of the Census estimates lifetime earnings as follows:

TOTAL LIFETIME EARNINGS

Not a high school graduate	$608,810
High school graduate	$820,870
Some college	$992,890
Associate's degree	$1,062,130
Bachelor's degree	$1,420,850
Master's degree	$1,618,970
Doctoral degree	$2,142,440
Professional degree (law, medicine, etc.)	$3,012,530

"College graduates account for nearly 60 percent of labor-force growth and over half of the new jobs created since 1994."

GENE KORETZ in *U. S. Workers Get Smarter*

Education is more than imparting knowledge—it's preparing students for life and work success. Acquiring further education, whatever type you choose, will help you build the critical behaviors necessary for future success.

LINKING EDUCATION AND WORK

You may have recently graduated from high school and are wondering if you want to pursue a two-year, four-year, or higher-level degree. You may be a college sophomore deciding whether to continue pursuing a bachelor's degree. You may be an adult pursuing a career change and wondering if you should return to school. Today, there are many educational options. Choose the learning path that best fits with your career goals.

WHAT CAN I DO WITH A MAJOR IN SOCIOLOGY?

- Demographer
- Editor, magazine
- Journalist
- Public administrator
- Media planner

WHAT CAN I DO WITH A MAJOR IN PSYCHOLOGY?

- Business administrator
- Psychologist
- Marketing researcher
- Social worker
- Management consultant

"Don't just wait for information to come to you."

ROBERT H. WATERMAN, author and management consultant

In Chapter 5, you determined the type of college education and/or training necessary to attain your career aspirations. With most professions, your education determines the level of responsibility you can assume as well as the pay you can expect to earn. For example, if you are considering a position in social services, you could choose a two-year, four-year, or graduate degree. Completing a two-year occupational degree will prepare you to enter the social services field as a paraprofessional. The more education you complete, the more equipped you will be to work at the professional level. A master's degree in social work will qualify you to work as a social worker or in administrative positions, deciding social policy. Skills and knowledge can be acquired from a variety of sources. Different skills can enhance your employability. For instance, speaking Spanish fluently might increase your work options. Informal skills, however, don't usually substitute for degree requirements.

Different degrees and technical/vocational training prepare you for different fields of work and different levels of work within a field (see Table 6.1).

- **Apprenticeships**—includes training in the trades such as masonry, roofing, carpentry, plumbing, and electrical. Most apprenticeship programs are offered by unions and may be supplemented with course work at community colleges.
- **College**—includes an associate of arts, bachelor of arts, or bachelor of science degree.
- **Graduate**—includes taking one or more years of further educational studies. You could achieve a master's degree or a doctoral degree in many areas.

TABLE 6.1 *Examples of careers for various levels of education.*

TYPES OF DEGREES	EXAMPLES OF CAREERS
AA	social worker aide, library technician, accounting clerk, teaching assistant, engineer technician, dietetic technician, computer operator, human services worker, interior designer, fashion designer, assistant hotel manager
Technical	automotive technician, aircraft maintenance worker, licensed practical nurse, computer programmer, software analyst, graphic artist, court reporter, network administrator, paralegal assistant, medical technician, cosmetologist
Bachelor's	engineer, teacher, corporate trainer, stock broker, scientist, accountant, art director, journalist, technical salesperson, marketing executive, environmental planner, information systems manager, technical writer, sales manager
Master's	social worker, psychologist, librarian, counselor, architect, therapist, executive, consultant, curriculum designer, controller, educational administrator, speech pathologist, occupational therapist
Doctoral	psychiatrist, astronomer, veterinarian, doctor, lawyer, chemist, philosopher, college professor, educational administrator, research scientist

REAL-LIFE PERSPECTIVE

LILY

After her internship at a manufacturer, Lily decided that she would like to use her degree to help companies improve their purchasing and inventory control. She enjoyed working with vendors, and thought this type of work would offer an opportunity to use her negotiation and accounting skills. With a little research, Lily discovered APICS—The Educational Society for Resource Management, a nonprofit international educational organization promoting professional certification programs in manufacturing. She found that many manufacturing companies want APICS certifications and employees with credentials earned 15 to 23 percent more than non-certified professionals. After attending a meeting at her local chapter, Lily learned that she could receive college credit for her certification. Lily will increase her opportunities for manufacturing employment with both a degree and certification. For more information on APICS, go to www.apics.org.

- **Technical**—includes learning specific skills to prepare you for a specific occupation. You can earn a technical certification in six months, or, depending on the occupation, it may take two years. Technical certificates or degrees can be earned from a technical school, community college, and some four-year colleges.
- **Professional Certifications**—includes learning skills to enhance your marketability in such fields as information technology, health care, auditing, procurement, human resources, automotive, and childcare. Certifications are becoming more common as employers seek ways to measure and recruit for specific skills. Some manufacturers, such as Cisco and Microsoft, sponsor certifications as a way to promote loyalty to their brand. Professional associations also sponsor certifications to improve the professional stature of their members. College course work, technical schools, professional associations, and self-study programs prepare students to pass certification exams. Many certification requirements include college course work or years of work experience in the field. In some professions, certification is as important as a college degree. Before you invest in any certification tests, make sure that the certification is valued in your career field and that the certifying agency has credibility. Obtain advice from professional associations, professors, and people working in the field before investing money in a program.

WHAT LEARNING DO YOU NEED?

- Apprenticeship
- Associate of Arts Degree
- Technical Degree
- Bachelor's Degree
- Master's Degree
- Doctoral Degree
- Professional Certification

Sometimes, students eliminate careers because they are overwhelmed by the effort or time it will take to get their degree. Maria was discussing her career dream with an advisor. She said, "My dream has always been to be a doctor. But I'm 32 years old. By the time I complete my education, I'll be 42." The advisor replied, "You're going to be 42 in 10 years anyway. You'll either be 42 years old practicing medicine or 42 years old somewhere else, wishing you had pursued your dream." Like Maria, researching the type and amount of education you'll need may seem discouraging. The thought of spending 4 to 10 years preparing for your career may seem too long. But, as the advisor

REAL-LIFE PERSPECTIVE

JANA'S PATH

Even though Jana's favorite subjects were Latin and art history, she felt there was little opportunity in those esoteric fields. She decided to be practical and entered law school. During the first week of law school, Jana immediately knew this was not for her. She decided to stop by the College of Education to inquire about certification to teach Latin. When she found out that her state no longer offered certification in Latin, she decided she'd better stay in school and finish her law degree. Even though she hated the course work, her perseverance paid off; three years later, she graduated from law school. Jana soon discovered that she hated working as a lawyer just as much as she hated attending law school. After struggling for four or five years, unhappy in a job she disliked, Jana decided to pursue a master's degree in classical art. Jana is now an arts administrator for the City of Phoenix. She is the liaison between artists and government for public arts projects—a job she loves that allows her to blend her diverse professional and educational experiences and knowledge. For example, when citizens question the use of public dollars for highway sculptures and artwork, her legal expertise is a handy accompaniment to her aesthetic knowledge.

wisely said, the time will pass anyway—whether or not you realize your dream. Alternative education programs may reduce the time it takes to get your degree. Before you discard your dream, investigate accelerated programs and online learning options.

Is Online Learning for You?

- Do you like using computer technology as a learning aid? For online success, you'll have to understand basic hardware and software applications.
- Can you learn effectively without human interaction? As the primary means of communication, most online courses require the learner to read information and write responses.
- Are you self-motivated and self-disciplined? For learning success, you'll have to manage your own course of self-study through preparation and systematic self-regulation and time management.
- Do you have the right equipment? For starters, you'll need a computer and an Internet connection.

Online Learning

Universities have joined the ranks of many other competitive businesses and ventured into cyberspace. Online education is fast becoming a preferred learning alternative for many students. Initially, only a few courses were offered online. Now, entire degrees can be earned online. You can complete a bachelor's degree, a master's degree, or even a law degree and never enter a classroom.

Through your computer and an Internet connection, you can visit a virtual classroom; engage in a self-paced tutorial; interact with others in a Web-based, real-time conference; and participate in many other interactive learning environments.

Although the benefits of online learning include convenience (you can plan your learning around your schedule), cost (online courses are usually less expensive than traditional classroom courses), and diversity (opportunities abound to discuss issues with people around the world), online learning is not for everyone. Consider what it would mean to learn without face-to-face interaction with real human beings.

To Find Out More About Online Learning, Visit:

- Adult Learning Network: www.aln.org
- Careertips: www.careertips.com
- CyberEd: www3.umassd.edu
- Department of Labor: www.onet.org
- Distance Education Clearinghouse: www.uwex.edu
- Education & Career Center: www.petersons.com
- Electronic Career Center: www.wcc-eun.com
- Globewide Network Academy: www.gnacademy.org
- Google search engine: www.google.com
- Internet University: www.caso.com
- Lifelong Learning: www.geteducated.com
- Salary.com: www.salary.com
- Telecoop of Colorado: www.telecoop.org
- Yahoo! search engine: www.yahoo.com

Online learning can be a great alternative for many people. If distance learning interests you, but missing the human touch discourages you, consider other choices such as teleclasses that offer more human interaction. The scope of learning technologies continues to evolve, giving us ever more options as online learners.

The trend in online education will continue to rise as more and more people look for flexible learning options to meet their individual needs. Is online learning a good option for you? To answer this question, you'll have to assess the advantages and disadvantages in light of your personal situation. Also, talk to a college professor who teaches online and visit university Internet sites to help you learn more.

Going to College—What You Need to Know

People attend college for different reasons. *Careerists* attend college to prepare for a specific profession. The work they want to do requires a specific degree. Careerists begin college with very definite goals and ideas about what they want. Careerists major in fields such as engineering, architecture, or law—professions that require very specific courses of study. College is a great time to sample a career. If you decide on engineering, begin taking engineering courses. If you're not happy studying the course content, you probably won't like working as an engineer. Sometimes, careerists start out with definite ideas and later realize the field they chose is not for them. If you find yourself not enjoying your college course work, rather than sticking with your original career decision, go back to your kaleidoscope and define new career options. It's okay to change your mind.

Educationists value education for the learning. They love to learn. They believe they'll earn more money with an education and value work that offers the opportunity for intellectual growth. Educationists select courses of study based on their interests. With some planning, the accumulation of courses they enjoy learning about will ultimately end in a degree. The

A Look at Who Hires Liberal Arts Grads

Who hires liberal arts grads? The answer is: all types of employers. Here are the top five employment fields that made the most job offers to selected liberal arts disciplines.

COMMUNICATIONS

1. Merchandising
2. Communication services (broadcasting/ telecommunication)
3. Advertising
4. Educational services
5. Insurance

Nearly one in two offers to communications majors came from these five areas. Grads in this discipline were most likely to find sales, management trainee, customer service, and public relations positions.

HISTORY

1. Educational services
2. Federal government
3. Legal services

These fields accounted for more than half of the job offers reported for history majors. And what types of jobs did history majors get? In addition to teaching jobs, top jobs for history grads included salesperson, management trainee, paralegal, and military positions.

LETTERS (INCLUDING ENGLISH)

1. Educational services
2. Publishing

Grads in this discipline got most of their offers from these two fields. Besides teaching jobs, grads were most likely to find writing/editing, and management trainee positions.

POLITICAL SCIENCE/GOVERNMENT

1. Legal services
2. Local government
3. State government
4. Federal government

About half of the offers reported for this discipline came from these four areas. Management trainee and paralegal jobs were among the positions grads obtained.

PSYCHOLOGY

1. Educational services
2. Social services
3. Merchandising
4. Health care services (nonprofit)
5. State/local government

Fifty-five percent of the offers reported for psychology majors came from these areas; positions included salesperson, management trainee, counselor, social worker, social services administration, and teaching.

type of degree depends on their interests. Often, educationists graduate with liberal arts degrees. Although liberal arts students possess many desirable characteristics sought by employers, marketing their skills is essential. Marketing your liberal arts degree to employers means communicating what you've learned and how that learning transfers to the job.

The decisions you make as you begin college often change as you take courses, acquire more information about your chosen field, meet and talk to different people, and gain more experience. It's estimated that more than 70 percent of college students won't graduate in the major they choose as freshmen, and almost 60 percent of working people are doing something completely different from their college major.

Matching Majors

Activity 6.2

Guess what these famous people majored in at college? *Instructions:* Draw a line from the person to the major. (Tip: Harrison Ford majored in philosophy.)

Steve Martin	Art
Ellen Gilchrist	English
Tommy Lee Jones	Cultural geography
Andy Griffith	Philosophy
Charles Kuralt	Ph.D. (minus the dissertation in English literature)
Bob Newhart	Philosophy
Kate Capshaw	Music
Kevin Costner	Business administration
Garrison Keillor	U.S. Naval Academy
Harrison Ford	Education
Arnold Schwarzenegger	Double major: theater and communication
Bob Dole	History
Woody Allen	Political science
David Duchoveny	Accounting
Ross Perot	Radio and TV broadcasting
Jerry Seinfeld	Law degree
David Letterman	Philosophy, with minor in physics
Jane Pauley	English
Patrick Ewing (N.Y. Knicks)	Attended NYU (where he failed a course in motion picture production)
Michael Jordan	Designed his own major consisting of physical fitness, communications, and international marketing

Source: Ideas contributed by Marcia J. Eagleson, Assistant Director of Career Services, Georgia Southern University.

Choosing Your Major

When choosing a major, ask:

- Does the field I'm considering prefer or require a particular degree?
- What kinds of courses would I be required to take?
- Have I taken an introductory course in the major I'm considering?
- Did I like it?
- What are five things people could do with this degree?
- Have I met with faculty members and discussed the skills and knowledge I'll acquire in their course?
- What careers could this major prepare me for?

Answers to some of these questions were gained in Chapter 5; for the other questions, you'll want to continue to research for the answers.

WHAT CAN I DO WITH A MAJOR IN COMMUNICATION?

- Employee counselor
- Public relations
- Sales representative
- Director of volunteer services
- Events planner

Activity 6.3 Questionnaire for Deciding a College Major

Instructions: Read the following questions and determine if they are true (T) or false (F)

_____ 1. Before you can choose a career, you must choose a major.

_____ 2. Lifetime earnings for college graduates average one million dollars more than those for individuals without degrees.

_____ 3. A college major will develop the skills and specific knowledge that employers want.

_____ 4. Most accounting majors end up as CPAs.

_____ 5. Successful businesspeople have usually majored in finance or accounting.

_____ 6. Once you choose a degree/major field of study, you can't change your mind.

_____ 7. It's important to investigate careers that do not directly relate to your major.

_____ 8. Selecting a major is the same as selecting a career.

_____ 9. Employers hire candidates based on specific college majors.

_____ 10. You can major in psychology and work as a marketing researcher.

POSSIBLE RESPONSES:

1. **False.** You may ask yourself, "What kind of work can I do with a major in—?" But also ask, "What kind of work do I want to do, and where do I want to do it?" Setting out on a journey of self-discovery opens a wide range of options. Deciding the nature of the work you enjoy and identifying the work environment that fits you can lead to success in numerous professions. Remember that less than half of the people working are in a field that they majored in. Sometimes, your major isn't that important; it's the degree that counts.

2. **True.** College graduates do earn more than those without degrees.

3. **True.** College majors help develop a variety of skills, interests, abilities, and specific knowledge. These assets are elements to add to your kaleidoscope that will allow you to create new work patterns and opportunities. For example, a degree in English develops writing and speaking skills. English majors gain competence in communication. Communication skills can be applied to careers from sales and media to law, medicine, and business management. The skills you learn in a particular degree program may or may not match the expectations of employers. The owner of an instructional design company told us she recruits English majors, rather than instructional design majors, to write for her company. She finds that their writing skills are superior and that they're more open to following predetermined formats.

4. **False.** Many accounting majors don't opt to be CPAs, and some don't pass the exam. Other options for accounting majors include actuary,

bank administrator, business administrator, cost estimator, consultant, financial analyst, financial planner, financial software salesperson, public administrator, and stockbroker. Think beyond the title of the major to the work that uses accounting skills and knowledge.

5. **False.** People successful in business majored in all types of college disciplines. Certainly, finance and accounting are fields of study that prepare you for business professions. However, they're not the only disciplines that can prepare you. Many successful businesspeople majored in technical fields or liberal arts. Successful salespeople often have technical backgrounds. For example, a pharmaceutical salesperson might have majored in biological sciences, or a manufacturing equipment salesperson might have majored in mechanical engineering. Think of a particular discipline and how it appeals to you. Learn all of the career options that a major might prepare you for. Think beyond what's popular to the less obvious.

6. **False.** Research your interests and the world of work, and make the best decision that works for you. Changing your mind is OK. Remember, most people are working in a field other than their major.

7. **True.** Broaden your thinking to investigate alternative career options. Go beyond the obvious career choices within your major field of study; there are many work options within each major. Graduating with a degree in history has career opportunities other than teaching, such as editor, historian, journalist, lawyer, political scientist, and information specialist. Investigating careers you may not have thought of expands your range of choices.

8. **False.** It's important to understand the link between a college major and work. Majors will prepare you for the work you want and open up options for many different types of work. You may choose to major in journalism and decide to work in social services, creating newsletters for donors, or decide to write, self-publish, and market a niche publication. Selecting a major is not the same as selecting a career.

9. **False.** Employers don't hire majors; they hire people with the skills to be successful in the work. Skills in understanding logical structure and analytical thinking can be developed with a music or physics degree. These skills might land you work in the computer software industry. A technical vice president who took stock trades online told us he preferred to hire music majors with an interest in computers. He insisted that music majors made the best programmers.

10. **True.** A bachelor's degree is good preparation for a variety of professions. Majoring in psychology is a good base for understanding human behavior and the ways people think. These are important skills to use in a career in market research. When choosing a major, consider the skills you like using and/or want to develop, such as research, critical thinking, and understanding human behavior. It's important to link the skills and interests inherent in college majors to the skills and interests of careers.

WHAT CAN I DO WITH A MAJOR IN HISTORY?

- Reporter
- Producer of historical documentaries
- Vocational rehabilitation manager
- Director of public relations
- Bank manager
- Arts conservator
- Foreign service officer
- Library director
- Public analyst
- Consultant
- Product system leader
- Legislative aide
- Professor
- Research associate
- Attorney
- Television producer
- Kindergarten teacher
- EPA project manager
- Author/editor

Source: Based on jobs presently held by Washington University alumni; information supplied by the Career Center, Washington University, St. Louis, MO, careers@artsci.wustl.edu.

To generate ideas about different majors, pick up a college catalog and read through the course descriptions of various programs. Which courses do you get excited about taking? Which ones put you to sleep? As you read a description, look for the kinds of skills and knowledge that the course emphasizes. Which programs contain the most courses that seem interesting to you? Compare the skills and knowledge you'll learn in the course with interests and skills in your career kaleidoscope. Is there a match?

John, a college sophomore, investigated a major in communications. The courses emphasized learning about gender-related communication and cultural influences on communication, the exploration of communication issues in the development of personal relationships and the effects of new communication technology on society, organizations, and individuals. He thought all of these courses sounded interesting. When he compared what he would learn in this program of study to his interests and skills in his kaleidoscope, he found they matched his interests in communication, personal relationships, and cultural diversity. With a degree in organizational communication, John would have an opportunity to work with and influence people, develop technical skills, and become better skilled at interpersonal relationships.

Try this activity on your own. Select several majors you find interesting in a college catalog, read the program of study, and highlight the skills and knowledge you'd learn in the courses. For each major, compare the skills and knowledge with the interests and skills in your kaleidoscope. Is there a match between particular course descriptions and interests in your kaleidoscope? If so, this could be a good fit for you, and a good indication you would enjoy the learning.

Advice from College Seniors About Deciding Majors

- "Find your true self and true personality."
- "Be open-minded."
- "Research options and salaries."
- "Take different courses and explore lots of interests."
- "If you can, it's OK to quit part-time jobs. Try something else; get lots of part-time jobs. Doing different things can help you decide what you do and don't want to do."
- "Observe different cultures."
- "It's OK to drop out and take time off if you intend to go back."
- "Notice the world around you and study trends."
- "Have a plan of attack. When you first start taking general courses, research these areas and identify the opportunities, salary, is the field declining, etc. These general courses can lead to major areas of study—biology, zoology, math, accounting."

REAL-LIFE PERSPECTIVE

How I Selected My College Major

ANDREW PRICE, Sociology major, age 23

"I originally wanted to major in education, until I found out I would be teaching and working with kids! I know I want to work with adults. I enjoy and am good at explaining information and helping others understand concepts. I changed my focus after a year of college and didn't know what I wanted. I knew I liked studying science and humanities. I took the lower-level general courses at a local community college and transferred to Arizona State University with no idea of what I wanted and lots of panic! I needed to declare a major. I researched areas of interest and identified sociology, a discipline that encompasses science and humanities. The field looks at what functions our societal institutions provide for us. I based my decision on what I enjoy learning about. I think it's the perfect major for me. My first semester, I earned straight A's! I think that shows lots of interest."

KRIS FORST, Education major, age 23

"I decided to be a history teacher as a result of having great teachers in high school. I loved watching their enthusiasm and techniques in the classroom. It looked like a great job. I love teaching people. I'm good at history. I'm fascinated about the world and different cultures and enjoy learning about the past and what it has to teach us. I went to a community college right after high school and took courses but wasn't making the grades I wanted. I wasn't putting forth the effort needed. I dropped out for two years and worked construction jobs. I wasn't going anywhere and reminded myself of my dad whose work was construction. He always came home unhappy and grumpy. I decided I wouldn't be a grumpy old man! I went back to school and applied myself and, this time, I'm making the grades I want. I picked education because I want to work at work I enjoy, not because of the money. What's important to me is choosing something I know I enjoy."

BRIAN DANGEL, Multimedia major, age 23

"I followed my heart. I've always enjoyed art, and I chose this field because of my interest in art. I worked in ceramics and loved the design and creative aspects. A friend told me about a school where you could use your imagination and creativity and create Art in Motion. It sounded fascinating, so I checked it out. I applied and was accepted by the University of Advancing Computer Technology. I will graduate with a bachelor's degree in multimedia science. The program is three years long, going year-round with two months off during the year for Christmas, other holidays, and breaks. I'm excited about my future. I can go different ways with my degree, maybe freelancing. This field is so new, with limitless possibilities. You have to stay on your toes to keep up with the changing technology."

ROBERT MORRIS, Computer science major, age 30

"I was undecided between math and computer science until my senior year, when I decided to graduate with a computer science degree. I decided on computer science because of my interest in computer languages and applications. I'm earning a master's degree in the field and would like to eventually work in computer animation."

CHRISTY ALLINGTON, Biology major, age 23

"My parents were really into science as I was growing up, especially my dad. They nurtured my

(continued)

REAL-LIFE PERSPECTIVE

Continued

science interest. I've always been curious. Science is fascinating because it explains how we work and everyday life. I took lots of science courses in high school and general courses in college trying to figure out what field of science I wanted. I thought about anthropology but decided against it, realizing there isn't much money in the field. I enjoyed biology courses, especially studying genetics and disease, and got really excited about the field. Biology is a broad field. I'm environmentally conscious and think about studying in this area. I'm not sure of the work I'll do, but I'm sure that I'll like it. I also think about going on to graduate school and studying environmental biology."

WALKER HICKS, Computer animation major, age 22

"In high school, a friend got me interested in photography. I wanted to study photography and choose a photographic field. After high school, I enrolled in a community college and took a course called Digital Photographic Imaging and was hooked. I had a great teacher, and I really liked how the computer was used as a tool to make my photographs more interesting. Once I transferred to Arizona State University, I wanted a degree that combined photography with computers. I applied to the computer graphics program and was accepted. They accept only 12 students a year based on your portfolio of work, grades, and talent. What's amazing is that I move cameras in a virtual world instead of the real world. I never touch a camera. I broadened my focus in the field by taking an internship and working in a multimedia company creating multimedia presentations. As a result I'm interested in multimedia design work."

Choosing your major requires some investigation on your part. Ask good questions to find good answers. We interviewed college seniors and asked them how they chose their majors. The answers they gave varied and are as unique as each of them. You'll find that your own answers will make the best decision for you.

Getting the Most Out of Your Education

If you're just starting college, job hunting may be the furthest thing from your mind. You may be concentrating on what courses to take, making time to study, and passing your finals. It's often difficult for students to see the connection between their college careers and beginning work. Searching for work comes later, after graduation, right? Not necessarily. The time to begin thinking about what employers look for in job candidates is *now.* Employers consider the skills you learn in college as important as your major. Colleges and universities may not identify the skills and competencies you are developing in your course work. Taking the time to identify the skills you are acquiring through your courses will provide you with a wealth of qualifications to use later in your work search campaign.

Websites to Help You Find Out What to Do with a Major In . . .

- **www.monster.com**—At this site, tell the career doctor your major and find out all kinds of alternative careers, or tell the doctor your skills and find out ideas for majors.
- **www.usnews.com**—At this site, find out what *U. S. News & World Report* thinks is the hot career for your major, as well as some alternatives.
- **www.wustl.edu**—Use the site map to visit the online Career Center. Find out the job titles of Washington University alumni who graduated with specific college majors. Resources also include internship suggestions and additional sources.

What do you want to gain from your college experience? What skills and knowledge will you need for work success? What courses and extracurricular activities are important? Giving thought to the answers to these questions will help you make the connection between what you are doing in school and the work you'll seek after graduation. It will help you decide which courses to take, internships to pursue, and/or volunteer work to solicit. The more thought you can give to determining your college goals early, the more you can gain from your college years.

QUALITIES AND SKILLS EMPLOYERS SEEK

In 2002, employers responded to a survey conducted by the National Association of Colleges and Employers. They were asked to rate skills from 1 (not important) to 5 (extremely important). See Figure 6.2 for the survey results.

What skills are employers seeking? What should you be learning now to increase your employability? What skills should you continuously develop to attain career resiliency? During the mid-1980s through the early 1990s, the U. S. Secretary of Labor formed a commission to study the educational needs of U. S. business, industry, and government. The commission interviewed workers in 50 job classifications, including chefs, electricians, truck drivers, accounting analysts, programmers, dental hygienists, personnel specialists, and sales representatives. The commission's report, *What Work Requires of Schools: A SCANS Report for America 2000*, identified a three-part foundation (basic skills, thinking skills, and personal qualities) and five workplace competencies critical to effective job performance. These skills, personal qualities, and competencies were considered essential by employers, no matter what position a person held. Figure 6.3 summarizes the findings.

These skills that employers look for are gained from a wide variety of majors and experiences. You can begin right now, in school, to develop many of the characteristics employers look for in potential job candidates. Employers also expect students to have acquired some work experience and participated in extracurricular activities, campus organizations, and leadership opportunities while in school.

WHAT CAN I DO WITH A DEGREE IN COMPUTER SCIENCE?

- Artificial intelligence developer
- Computer systems analyst
- Corporate security specialist
- Information specialist
- Demographer

FIGURE 6.2 *The qualities and skills employers want.*

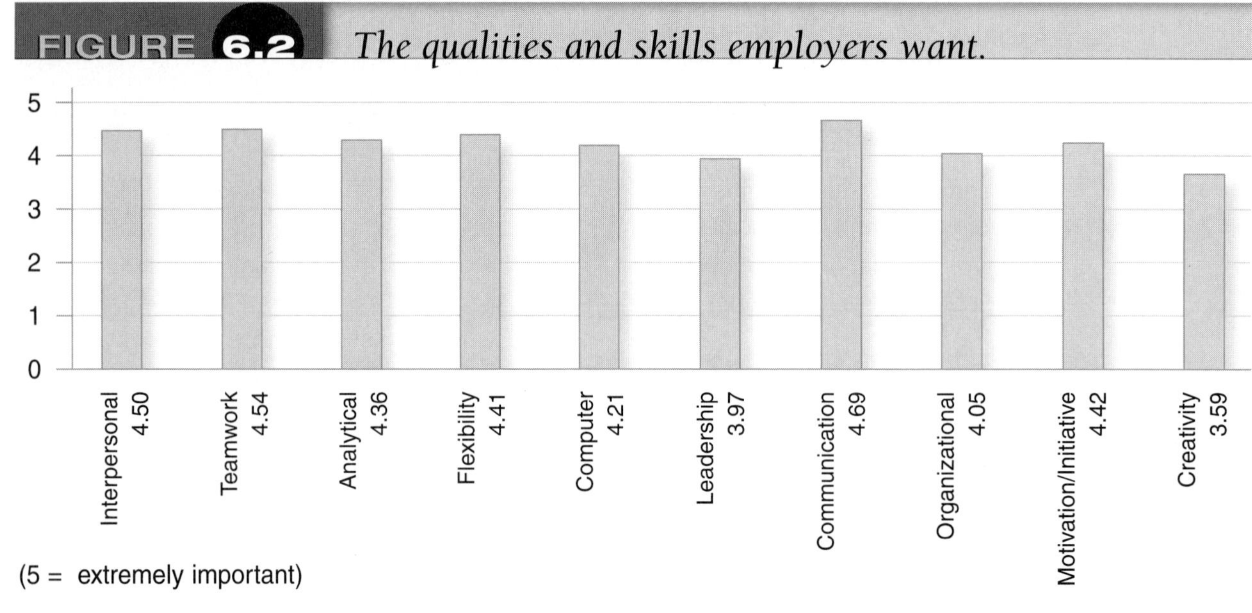

FIGURE 6.3 *The SCANS Report findings.*

THE FOUNDATION

BASIC SKILLS

- Reading
- Writing
- Arithmetic
- Mathematics
- Listening
- Speaking

THINKING SKILLS

- Able to learn and reason
- Think creatively
- Make decisions
- Solve problems

PERSONAL QUALITIES

- Effort and perseverance to attain goals
- Self-esteem
- Sociability
- Self-management
- Integrity

WORKPLACE COMPETENCIES

- Allocates resources
- Uses interpersonal skills
- Acquires and evaluates information
- Understands and improves systems
- Applies technology

Skills Employers Seek

Activity 6.4

Instructions: For each section, check (✓) the items preceded by circles that, in your opinion, best describe you. Ask others to evaluate your skill areas too. Then, on the bar above those items, check where you feel you fall on the continuum for that particular skill. There may be some skills you have not had an opportunity to develop. To develop these skills, look for ideas in the activities column and/or think of activities you can do to begin mastering the skill(s).

Interpersonal Skills—the ability to judge and engage in appropriate behavior. The ability to interact effectively with others. Notice and respond appropriately to the behavioral cues of others.

DEVELOPMENTAL NEED ——— STRENGTH

- ○ Appears unaware that others exist
- ○ Shows little recognition of the feelings of others
- ○ Demonstrates courtesy toward others
- ○ Only responds to obvious behavioral cues; more subtle cues are missed or ignored
- ○ Very high degree of courtesy and consideration
- ○ Recognizes the feelings of others

ACTIVITIES TO STRENGTHEN SKILLS

- ☐ Volunteer to work on group projects
- ☐ Work at a job that involves contact with the public
- ☐ Become skilled at solving problems for irate customers or upset people
- ☐ Improve listening skills—take a communication course
- ☐ ____________________
- ☐ ____________________
- ☐ ____________________
- ☐ ____________________

Teamwork—the ability to work effectively with others. Displays an appropriate balance between individual effort and team effort. Cooperates well with others.

DEVELOPMENTAL NEED ——— STRENGTH

- ○ Withdraws and does not actively participate
- ○ Takes individual credit for team accomplishments
- ○ Works well with others on team projects
- ○ Shares credit and opportunities
- ○ Works well with others and often assumes a leadership role
- ○ Shares credit and looks for ways to assist team members and offers assistance without being asked

ACTIVITIES TO STRENGTHEN SKILLS

- ☐ Volunteer to work on a team
- ☐ Coordinate a class project with others
- ☐ Seek out teaming opportunities at work
- ☐ Join a campus club
- ☐ ______
- ☐ ______
- ☐ ______
- ☐ ______

Analytical Skills—the ability to learn and reason. Identify, evaluate, and assimilate factors essential to analyzing a problem for a solution. Thinking creatively to analyze and solve problems.

DEVELOPMENTAL NEED ——— STRENGTH

- ○ Does not link sources of information to analyze a problem
- ○ Often defines the problem incorrectly because of not evaluating all of the facts
- ○ Generally links sources of information to analyze a problem
- ○ Rarely defines the problem incorrectly
- ○ Gathers information from many sources when analyzing a problem
- ○ Almost always is skillful when evaluating the most complex problems

ACTIVITIES TO STRENGTHEN SKILLS

- ☐ Develop a program of study
- ☐ Take a research methods course and/or a critical-thinking course
- ☐ At work, volunteer for opportunities to improve work methods
- ☐ ______
- ☐ ______
- ☐ ______
- ☐ ______

Oral Communication Skills—the ability to communicate ideas clearly, concisely, and persuasively.

DEVELOPMENTAL NEED ——— STRENGTH

- ○ Poor grammar and vocabulary
- ○ Ideas presented are confusing and misunderstood
- ○ Uses appropriate words
- ○ Ideas are presented clearly and understood
- ○ Articulate and precise use of language
- ○ Ideas are presented clearly and understood with enthusiasm and animation, generating interest in the subject

ACTIVITIES TO STRENGTHEN SKILLS

- ☐ Take a speech course
- ☐ Make oral presentations in class
- ☐ Make an oral presentation at work
- ☐ Join a toastmaster's club
- ☐ ____________________
- ☐ ____________________
- ☐ ____________________
- ☐ ____________________

Flexibility—the ability to modify behavior in order to reach a goal. Taking different approaches with people or problems.

DEVELOPMENTAL NEED ——— STRENGTH

- ○ Uses same approach in most situations
- ○ Demonstrates difficulty adjusting from one situation to another
- ○ Uses several approaches to accomplish tasks
- ○ Is able to revise priorities and plans when necessary
- ○ Uses varying approaches; adjusts behavior quickly to reach goals
- ○ Does not hesitate to switch to a better approach when necessary

ACTIVITIES TO STRENGTHEN SKILLS

- ☐ Seek out opportunities to work with people different from you
- ☐ Travel to a foreign country
- ☐ Study abroad
- ☐ Do a self-study project
- ☐ ____________________
- ☐ ____________________
- ☐ ____________________
- ☐ ____________________

Computer Skills—the ability to use a word processing program, a spreadsheet program, a database management program, the Internet, and e-mail.

DEVELOPMENTAL NEED ——— STRENGTH

- ○ Limited knowledge and use of a computer
- ○ Comfortable using computer technology
- ○ Proficient knowledge and skill in computer operation

ACTIVITIES TO STRENGTHEN SKILLS

- ☐ Take computer courses
- ☐ Visit the library and log on to the Internet
- ☐ Play video games

- [ ] Establish an e-mail address
- [ ] ______
- [ ] ______
- [ ] ______
- [ ] ______

Written Communication Skills—the ability to express ideas in writing (clarity and conciseness of thought, grammar, punctuation, and spelling).

DEVELOPMENTAL NEED — STRENGTH

- ○ Content of written material is confusing, incomplete, and difficult to understand
- ○ Spelling and grammar are unacceptable and distracting
- ○ Written material is clear and the message is understandable
- ○ Appropriate vocabulary, grammar, and spelling
- ○ Written material is clear, complete, and well organized
- ○ No errors in syntax and spelling

ACTIVITIES TO STRENGTHEN SKILLS

- [ ] Compose and write letters to other people
- [ ] Write term papers
- [ ] Write reports
- [ ] Take a creative or business writing course
- [ ] ______
- [ ] ______
- [ ] ______
- [ ] ______

Leadership Skills—the ability to influence a group or an individual to accomplish a task or accept an idea.

DEVELOPMENTAL NEED — STRENGTH

- ○ Does not attempt to exert influence on others
- ○ Rarely succeeds in getting ideas accepted
- ○ Is looked to for leadership by others
- ○ Ideas are generally accepted and acted upon by others
- ○ Is skillful at getting others to collaborate and work together
- ○ Ideas and suggestions are immediately accepted by others

ACTIVITIES TO STRENGTHEN SKILLS

- [ ] Volunteer to lead a team
- [ ] Run for a campus, community, or other board position
- [ ] Lead a study group

- [ ] Coach children's sports
- [ ] ______
- [ ] ______
- [ ] ______
- [ ] ______

Creativity Skills—the ability to creatively generate a wide variety of ideas, problem solutions, and alternatives. Uses resources imaginatively.

DEVELOPMENTAL NEED — STRENGTH

- ○ Displays a negative attitude fueled by fear and doubt
- ○ Unable to expand ideas and possibilities
- ○ Easily changes perspective and sees new possibilities
- ○ Sees problems as opportunities
- ○ Develops solutions to complex problems
- ○ Believes creativity dwells within every person

ACTIVITIES TO STRENGTHEN SKILLS

- [ ] Recognize negative thoughts and replace with positive thinking
- [ ] Learn and practice creative techniques (e.g., mind mapping)
- [ ] Believe you are creative and act as if you are creative
- [ ] Read to stimulate new thoughts and expand ideas
- [ ] ______
- [ ] ______
- [ ] ______
- [ ] ______

Motivation/Initiative Skills—the ability to work effectively in situations requiring a high level of sustained effort and commitment to accomplish tasks, meet goals, or overcome obstacles; a readiness and the ability to initiate action.

DEVELOPMENTAL NEED — STRENGTH

- ○ Waits for others to act first when problems happen
- ○ Responds only when an action seems necessary
- ○ Takes swift action to achieve goals beyond what is required
- ○ Implements new ideas or potential solutions without prompting
- ○ Takes the lead in initiating actions

ACTIVITIES TO STRENGTHEN SKILLS

- [ ] Initiate actions that go beyond task requirements
- [ ] Practice being proactive—prepare ahead
- [ ] Set a personal goal and achieve it

- [ ] ______
- [ ] ______
- [ ] ______
- [ ] ______

Organizational Skills—the ability to establish strategies for self and others to guarantee tasks are completed efficiently

DEVELOPMENTAL NEED — STRENGTH

- ○ Fails to meet project deadlines
- ○ Underestimates the amount of time to complete activities
- ○ Identifies between critical and less critical activities and assignments; prioritizes appropriately
- ○ Allocates appropriate time for completing activities and assignments
- ○ Uses time effectively
- ○ Avoids scheduling conflicts

ACTIVITIES TO STRENGTHEN SKILLS

- [ ] Take a Time Management class
- [ ] Invest in an electronic or paper organizer
- [ ] ______
- [ ] ______
- [ ] ______
- [ ] ______

WAYS TO EXPAND YOUR SKILLS WHILE IN COLLEGE:

- Gain career-related, hands-on experience—participate in internships, service learning, and co-op programs. Consider part-time and volunteer work in your field of interest. Some recruiters don't bother to interview students who haven't shown the effort to get real-world experience.
- Build teamwork skills through involvement in campus clubs and extracurricular activities.
- Develop communication skills with leadership roles and class projects. The ability to speak comfortably in front of a group is essential in today's team environments.
- Create a file on your computer or in a folder to track projects. Start now to track experiences that relate to the work you will do after graduation. Use academic and/or work projects, college activities, internships, and work experience to demonstrate you have used these skills. Create a form for yourself that makes it easy to summarize: (1) the goals of the project, (2) the skills you used to accomplish the results, and (3) the results you achieved. The NAB process explained in Chapter 7 will help you identify the results of your work.

Creative Ways to Obtain Marketable Skills—Student Views

- "Foreign Exchange programs. Study history in London for a semester. A great opportunity to learn different teaching methods if you're an education major. Are the teaching skills similar to those in the United States?"
- "Join a campus club, like the sociology club. An opportunity to network, develop skills, and make connections in school that could lead to work."
- "Enter your artwork for recognition and awards. When you win, it reinforces that you're good and keeps you going. It's also an opportunity to practice learning new software applications."
- "Take a summer trip to a foreign country to learn foreign language skills."

INTERNSHIPS

No question about it—internships provide opportunities to gain valuable work-related experience. It's a way for you to explore the real work world and decide if this truly is the career for you. With an internship, you are enhancing your academic education with practical career-related experience (see Figure 6.4). "Internships—paid or unpaid work-study experiences, often over a summer—have been around for generations, especially as a vehicle for engineers and business majors to get hands-on experience. But, the numbers have exploded since the 1990s." Jack had worked for four companies before he started his senior year. The exposure to different companies helped him learn about the workplace and the kind of career he wanted.

"We always select and offer first from our pool of co-ops or interns, then from the candidates that have worked during school to earn 50 percent of their way. We have found no correlation between GPA and subsequent performance, but have consistently found a substantial correlation between co-op/intern experience and performance in the first five years."

KENNETH R. PEDERSON, Global Process Leader for Staffing & Selection, Dow Chemical Company

Once thought of as optional, internships are beginning to blend with corporate recruiting. From the employer's point of view, an internship is a way of previewing candidates before hiring them. It's a win-win situation, both for the employer and the student. Get started *early*. Your freshman year is not too early to start!

ACTIVITIES TO DO IN SCHOOL THAT COULD CREATE WORK OPTIONS FOR YOU

- Internship
- Research assistant for teachers
- Cooperative learning (an education major hooks up with a high school and works as a student aid for a teacher)
- Volunteering
- Service learning
- Education abroad

SERVICE LEARNING

Richard was studying to become an engineer. He decided to volunteer for Habitat for Humanity, an organization devoted to building homes for the needy around the world. The experience gave him an opportunity to work side by side with engineers, architects, and craftsmen. He experienced first-hand the design and engineering of a shelter. The service learning connected him to the community and taught him valuable hands-on skills while he earned academic credit for his contribution. Service learning is a program at

FIGURE 6.4 *Employers rate importance of experiences.*

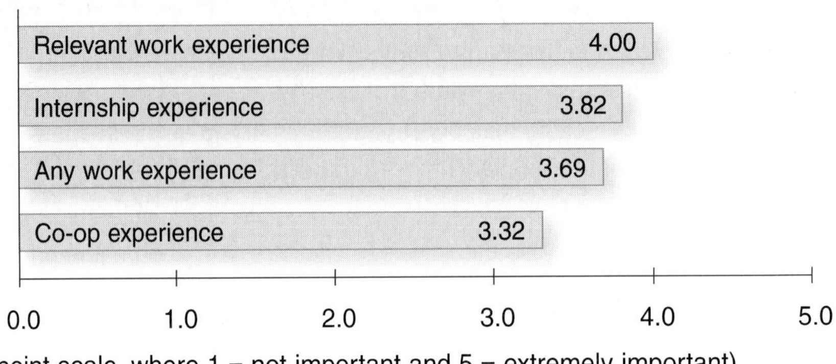

Reprinted from *Job Outlook 2002* with permission of the National Association of Colleges and Employers, copyright holder.

many colleges and universities designed to help students learn about themselves and the world through community involvement. Most often, students select an opportunity for learning connected to their major.

VOLUNTEER WORK

Volunteering is a great way to get a bird's-eye view of the work environment and the work you're thinking about doing. Opportunities to work as a volunteer are available in most professions. Check your campus career center or the Yellow Pages for volunteer listings. Internships often open the door to volunteer opportunities. Many professional associations have volunteer arms. This can be a good way to make contacts as well as learn while working alongside senior people in your field. Most cities have a volunteer bureau that will refer you to matching opportunities.

While pursuing her degree in communication, Lena Jong contacted her local volunteer bureau for information. She was interested in working

Finding a Good Internship and Getting the Most Out of It

- Completing a college internship is a great way to gain experience and make decisions about a career field. Think of it as short-term work where you get to try out particular skills, develop relationships, and gain work-related experience.
- Internships offer you practical work experience in government agencies, major corporations, nonprofit agencies, and even small businesses. Students may earn academic credit while participating in a partnership between the approved agency and the academic institution.
- Internships vary in length. Some employers are looking for short-term commitments, with interns working on short-term projects averaging six or seven months or less. Others may offer longer assignments, lasting 12 months or more.
- Do some research and find out if the college you're interested in or presently attending has internship programs. If not, you can create your own.

REAL-LIFE PERSPECTIVE

Advice Straight from the Recruiter's Mouth

- "My advice for those with little or no work experience is to get involved in something—volunteer, join interest groups, etc. Employers look for intellect, innovation, enterprise, good communication skills, and balanced confidence. Proactive involvement in activities can develop and help demonstrate these characteristics." Edward Ferris, President, Plus Ultra, Inc.
- "Find any way possible to get some practical experience in the field: summer jobs, volunteer work, etc." Grant Parks, V.P. of Strategic Relations, Skill Scape, Inc.
- "While in school, students should work. It's best to work or intern in an area related to their area of study and work goal. However, any job gives them the benefit of gaining a good work ethic. They should also take a few business courses along with whatever else they are studying. They should look to hone their skills—both oral and written. It's also important that they find a way to gain exposure to whatever state-of-the-art technologies they'll find in their career field (e.g., computer science grads must gain some experience with programming languages)." Marc Levine, Consultant.
- "When encountering students who have no work experience and are applying for management positions, I recommend that they try us part-time while still in school to see if this is an environment where they would thrive. Internships and work-study programs are very important for college students. They give students an opportunity to *try out* a company and also allow them to see the connection between what they are learning and the application to the work world." Ilana Austin, Human Resources Manager.
- "To close the gap on applicability, I would suggest that students focus on the behavioral and application skills they are learning rather than purely the knowledge they are gaining. Consequently, they can reflect on their learning skills, their research skills, their listening, writing, and speaking skills, their interpersonal skills, their resilience, their creativity, etc." Edward Ferris, President, Plus Ultra, Inc.
- "Internships and meaningful summer jobs are important to prospective employers. It means you have some real-world experience and know what to expect from a real job. Even if you don't need the money, *work,* and not as a lifeguard or camp counselor if you can avoid it." Susan Lamb, Human Resource Director.

in an environment using some of the knowledge and skills she was learning in her program of study. With her knowledge of group dynamics, facilitating of group learning, design of learning activities, intercultural communication, and human behavior, Lena went to work as a volunteer for a nonprofit agency and spent several hours a week working with groups. The practical, hands-on work experience helped her link what she was learning in college to the real work world. She gained confidence in her skills and reinforced her career choice.

Max Martinez is a journalist for a large newspaper in southern California who started as a volunteer—preparing page proofs, running errands, and performing small editing jobs. All through his senior year in

REAL-LIFE PERSPECTIVE

NIK HARRIS

Nik Harris entered college thinking she didn't want to work for a large corporation. During a year off from school, she worked full-time for an insurance company, which confirmed her belief that big business wasn't for her.

When she returned to school, she had three career ideas in mind: teaching, working in a community organization, and working for a nonprofit organization. She began working part-time in a YWCA after-school program. She enjoyed working with the children and could see positions within this community organization that she would enjoy.

This experience increased her interest but didn't help her narrow her options. Then, she took her first political science course and loved it. She realized that you can have a broader influence on social issues by working in the political arena rather than providing direct services in one organization. Soon after, she walked up to a kiosk on campus where college Republicans were recruiting volunteers to work for Senator John McCain's reelection campaign. She worked one morning a week and some Saturdays, passing out literature and talking to voters.

During the victory celebration on election night, she met the manager of Senator McCain's Arizona office. She applied for a position as a full-time intern and was accepted. This position did not pay money, but she learned it could lead to an internship in his Washington, D.C., office. At the same time, Nik decided to major in political science and work to improve education.

During her senior year, Nik spent one semester in Washington, D.C., working as an assistant to a legislative aide. The position paid a stipend, which covered room and board at Thomson Markward Hall, a lodging hall for women across the street from the Hart Building where the Senate meets.

Nik came back home for graduation and then returned to job-hunt in Washington, D.C. Today, she is the membership coordinator for Educom, a national association that brings together high-tech companies and colleges. Its mission is to help colleges make the best use of technology. She thinks this job helps her fulfill her personal mission—to improve education. Someday, she plans to return to college to get a master's degree in education and teach. Nik has found a calling and plans to work for that cause in a variety of ways.

college, he worked at the paper. Shortly after graduating with his degree, a position with the paper became available, and Max was hired.

Volunteering in your field has many advantages. Often, like what happened to Max, volunteer positions can turn into paid positions. People get to know you and your work; as a result of volunteering, you have first-hand knowledge about the workplace that can help you in an interview.

GRADUATE SCHOOL RESOURCES

- www.gradschool.com
- Peterson's Education Center—www.petersons.com

CONTINUAL LEARNING OPTIONS

By now, you know the importance of an education and the need to continually learn to maintain your lifetime employability. Having completed your assessments and research, you should have a fairly clear idea of your career goals and the educational requirements. Do your career goals include going on to graduate school? If so, there are some things you should know. Complete Activity 6.5 to get you thinking about the advan-

REAL-LIFE PERSPECTIVE

BILL BRESNAHAN

The ideal internship couples valuable practical training with the development of relationships that can have unexpected future benefits. Bill Bresnahan experienced such a rewarding internship when he was selected to intern in the state's attorney's office of a major city. Not only would his own abilities be developed and tested, but he was the first representative of his university to be chosen for an internship after an earlier disastrous one. His performance was under particular scrutiny by both the state's attorney's staff and the university.

Bill's role was to act as ombudsman for senior citizens who were experiencing fraudulent treatment by unscrupulous service providers. It was a job he thoroughly enjoyed, especially with the prestige of the state's attorney's office behind him as he challenged tradesmen, lawyers, and business managers who were cheating the elderly.

His work was particularly noticed and valued by an assistant to the state's attorney who became his mentor and role model. When his internship ended, the ombudsman position became permanent. Bill was hired to fill it and remained during the rest of his university education.

This experience convinced him to choose a career path in law enforcement. He joined the police force and attended law school, earning his law degree and passing the bar examination. During these years, the state's attorney had been elected mayor of the city, and his assistant became commissioner of a large city department. Bill and the commissioner had met infrequently during this time, but she always asked to be updated on his progress with the police department and his promotion to detective.

One day, he received a call from the commissioner with an amazing offer to join her staff as an assistant. It meant citywide responsibilities, the title of assistant commissioner, and a significant increase in salary. So, at the age of 34, Bill was given a leading position in one of the country's largest municipalities. By his outstanding performance as an intern, earning the respect and support of an influential mentor, and his own continuous professional growth, Bill was able to reach impressive career heights.

Internship Resources

- *The National Dictionary of Internships,* published by the National Society of Internships and Experiential Education, Suite 207, 3509 Haworth Drive, Raleigh, NC 27609
- *Peterson's Internships,* 800-338-3202, an annual directory of job training opportunities for many types of careers
- *The Princeton Review Internship Bible 2002,* Random House, Mark Oldman and Samer Hamadeh
- Rising Star Internships—www.rsinternships.com/
- Washington Internship Foundation—http://interns.org/
- Best Bets for Internships Abroad—www.uci.edu/~cie/iop/internsh.html
- Intern.net—www.intern.net/
- Mission Possible: Finding an Internship—www.washingtonpost.com/wpsrv/scoop/interns/intern.htm
- National Internships—www.internships.com/

REAL-LIFE PERSPECTIVE

TERRY LONG

"As a child, I aspired to be an elementary school teacher. As an undergraduate, I attended the University of California at Santa Barbara, a former teacher's college, with this intention. When I received my B.A. in 1973, however, the prospects of finding a teaching position were pretty grim: The country was in recession, elementary schools were being closed in response to declining enrollment, and teaching jobs were scarce. This trend was expected to continue, so I went on to other occupations.

"I've always liked analyzing information and communicating it to others. I started my career as a technical trainer, writer, and editor. At Visa U.S.A., Inc., I worked my way up to vice president and editor-in-chief of the *Visa Business Review,* a family of monthly publications. I also acquired an MBA in marketing. Then, in the mid-1990s, I saw a big opportunity to expand my technical skills and my contribution to the organization by putting my publication online. I continually read, talk to colleagues, take classes, and attend technology conferences to keep up with the requirements of new communication channels. I think I'm very good at looking ahead and preparing myself to take advantage of new technology in such a way that it benefits and enhances corporate goals.

"Two years ago, my husband was presented with a lucrative employment offer from a Washington state firm. We jumped at the chance to explore the Pacific Northwest and its unique opportunities. My career goals have again changed. I'm eager to put my considerable success as a trainer, writer, editor, and manager to work and give something back to my community. With over 15 years of experience in computer applications and marketing management, I can be particularly effective teaching secondary school students in the professional/technical area. I started substitute teaching last fall. I have acquired a vocational education certificate and developed a professional growth plan.

"It's ironic that after all this time, my current career goal is similar to my original one! What I like about my choice is that I'll be teaching (my original passion), and I'll be using the technical skills I acquired during my career at Visa. I believe almost any position becomes uniquely yours with the particular skill set you bring to the job. I've continued to learn and create new facets in all of my jobs. It's what keeps them challenging."

tages and disadvantages of graduate school at this time. The decision to go to graduate school requires careful thought and planning.

If you're thinking about continuing your education, complete Activity 6.6, Checklist for Graduate School. This will help you reflect on the reasons you want to apply. The more information you have to consider, the more informed you'll be about continuing your education in graduate school.

Graduate school is one way to continue your education and higher learning. As mentioned earlier in the chapter, there are many ways to learn—we are always learning. As you read Janet's story (p. 151), you realize how much she has learned through all of the experiences she's had. Some of her learning has come from formal education, but she's acquired many adventures in learning through life experiences. Like Janet, we all have a story. Our lives and our careers are always developing through what we learn. Sometimes, we're not aware of all we have done and all we know until we think about it and write it down. What kinds of things do you want to learn about and experience? What learning is related to your career goal? To help you create ideas, complete Activity 6.7, Continuous Learning Plan.

Graduate School: Asset or Liability?

Activity 6.5

1. Does the career you are planning require an advanced degree?
2. What level of education do entry-level employees have in this field?
3. Do you see yourself as a researcher who wants to add to the body of knowledge in your field?
4. Will a graduate degree earn you more money?
5. Do you thoroughly enjoy studying about a subject you love?
6. Do you believe a graduate degree earns you more money?

SOME ANSWERS:

1. You probably already know what fields require advanced degrees, and you should have a plan to continue your education.

2. Normally, getting an advanced degree can make you less marketable for entry-level positions because employers will see bachelor's-level individuals as being a better *fit* and better satisfied with a lower salary. They may also believe training and work experience are more beneficial than an advanced degree. Sometimes, too much education can make it difficult to get hired. After graduating with his bachelor's degree, Carlo went right on to graduate school and even completed his doctorate without stopping to work and gain experience in his field. Carlo wanted to be an administrator in a public school. Teaching experience in elementary and secondary schools is a requirement to obtain certification as a school administrator. Carlo had a difficult time finding employment to gain this necessary experience because his degree priced him out of the market. In school districts, pay is directly related to education. School administrators were more likely to hire teachers with a bachelor's degree whom they could pay considerably less than Carlo.

3. Academic research like this requires further education. However, explore opportunities before heavily investing in higher education. College professor positions that pay for this type of research are getting harder and harder to secure. It's crucial that you do your homework before investing in a degree where you plan on researching and teaching. Dreams are never impossible, but they may require more effort.

4. Don't assume that you will be a preferred candidate because you have a graduate degree. Find out who is being hired. Sometimes, fear of rejection is the motivator for pursuing graduate school. The inevitable day will come when you must plunge into the job market. Most employers prefer hiring candidates with viable work experience, rather than those with advanced degrees who lack experience in the field.

5. You may not be satisfied until you are immersed in your field of study, so go for it and get as many degrees as you want.

6. A graduate degree can bring you more money. Teachers' salaries are based on their continuing education. However, an advanced degree is *not* a guarantee that you will earn more money; as noted above, it can actually be a liability in some cases. If you decide a graduate degree is for you, begin planning in your junior year for admittance to the schools of your choice.

Activity 6.6 Checklist for Graduate School

(advanced degrees; both graduate and professional study)

EVALUATION	YES	NO	NOTES
Is it a requirement for your chosen career field?	☐	☐	____________
Will the degree create greater salary potential?	☐	☐	____________
Are you more marketable with an advanced degree?	☐	☐	____________
Are your career goals clear?	☐	☐	____________
Have you researched graduate school programs and faculty?	☐	☐	____________
Does the program of study interestyou?	☐	☐	____________
Have you made an appointment with an advisor for assistance?	☐	☐	____________
Have you considered costs/ financial aid?	☐	☐	____________
Have you researched required entrance exams (GRE, MAT)?	☐	☐	____________
Are you ready to make the commitment?	☐	☐	____________

- Graduate study means post-baccalaureate education in a given academic field—history, literature, foreign language, etc.
- Professional study stresses the practical application of knowledge and skills in business, law, and medicine (i.e., Doctor of Medicine—MD or DO).
- Use the reference *Peterson's Guide to Graduate & Professional Programs* to learn more about the distinctions between graduate academic programs and professional programs.

Learning is your responsibility—not that of the organization you work for or the college you attend. Take responsibility for your learning, and you'll end up with the knowledge you'll need to sustain your career. The patterns in your kaleidoscope will change as you add new skills. Your work views and options will increase as you continually add knowledge. Outdated elements will be replaced with a continual renewal of information. Your future employability requires a relentless motivation to learn new skills and remain on top of trends and changes in your field. Remember, *your education is never finished!*

Different Goals—Different Choices

When Sarah graduated from college with a degree in education, her father insisted that she go right on to graduate school. Sarah had a very clear career goal: She wanted to become a university dean. However, she was debating whether to get classroom experience and accumulate some savings before continuing her education. Sarah's father feared that by postponing the education that would qualify her for a university career, she could lose sight of her goal.

On the other hand, her brother Bob also graduated with a degree in education but was eager to experience classroom teaching. His dream was to make a difference in children's lives. Dad agreed that Bob should start interviewing with schools and begin his desired work with children.

Both Sarah and Bob were fortunate in having the encouragement of an astute parent and followed his advice to pursue their dreams. Sarah went immediately to graduate school and did become a university dean. Bob went into the classroom and on to a career as a high school coach and teacher. He eventually earned his master's degree many years later. Both agree today, after 25 years, that they made the right decisions.

"You should think of yourself as a set of skills or a tool set that you are continuously developing. You should not stop learning when you get out of college. If possible, continue to take classes, take advantage of training programs at your company, and always try to be learning new skills that are marketable from the job you're in. Each time you change jobs, you become more marketable because you have acquired new skills and experiences. Computers and technology are opening up the world so it's vital that you keep up with technology. Many people recognize that technology changes, but they don't really pay attention to it."

JEFF TAYLOR, founder of the Monster Board, in *First Job, Great Job*

REAL-LIFE PERSPECTIVE

JANET

"This is a chronological listing of learning and experiences I've had in my life, starting with high school.

WAYS I'VE LEARNED IN MY LIFE

- Studied math, biology, art, English, and German in high school
- Received an art certificate, majoring in ceramics, including design, drawing, and printmaking
- Waitressed in cafes
- Received a bachelor of arts degree in design
- Learned visual communication, design, typography, business management, history, drawing, printmaking, and illustration
- Worked as a manager of a boardinghouse
- Was employed as a governess on a Northern Territory cattle station
- Worked as a shop assistant (bookshop/art gallery)
- Freelanced for a design partnership
- Worked as a graphic designer at the Adelaide University Student Union, for the Elizabeth Munno Para Project, and for the Department of Housing and Urban Development
- Designed multimedia projects for the University of South Australia
- Was employed as a part-time instructor in a photo shop
- Designed educational materials
- Studied Japanese
- Learned Macintosh and PC software
- There's still more to learn and do!"

Activity 6.7 Continuous Learning Plan

My current career goal: ____________________

ACTIVITY	WHERE	COMPLETION DATE
Degree or certificate desired		
____	____	____
____	____	____
Additional schools (if needed)		
____	____	____
____	____	____
Internships		
____	____	____
____	____	____
Training/apprenticeship		
____	____	____
____	____	____
Volunteer/service work		
____	____	____
____	____	____
Extracurricular activities related to my goal		
____	____	____
____	____	____
____	____	____
Leadership roles I'll seek		
____	____	____
____	____	____
____	____	____
Graduate school		
____	____	____
____	____	____

Summary Points

- Continuous learning is part of the lifelong career process and is essential for career competitiveness.
- Acquiring a college education used to be considered a luxury; today, it's essential. Those with college degrees earn more and have more work opportunities available than those without a degree.
- There are many ways to learn; not all learning takes place in a classroom.
- Today, there are many educational options. Choose the path that fits best for you and your career goal.
- Your college major/education is an essential part of your career preparation.
- Employers consider the skills you learn in college as important as your major. Identify and track the skills you are developing in school. Seek out internships, service learning, volunteer positions, and part-time work to gain real-world experience.
- Graduate school may or may not be the best choice right out of college. Identify the advantages and disadvantages of going on to school before enrolling in a program.
- Continuous learning is *your* responsibility.

CHAPTER SEVEN

7 Communicating Your Value

MARKETING YOU

How do employers decide whom to hire?

How can you communicate your value in an interview?

What kinds of questions do interviewers ask?

How can you translate academics, internships, and work experience into skills that matter to employers?

How does communicating value sustain your career?

Wouldn't it be convenient if employers recognized the contributions you can make? Unfortunately, they don't automatically know your capabilities. You may be thinking, "I'm completing my education, so I'll have a diploma to get my foot in the door." Your education, although important, won't bring employers to you. It's up to you to let people know what you have to offer.

The good news for recent graduates is that success is based on what you know, not on years of experience. Joan Farrell, Vice President of Human Resources for Lawson Mardon Wheaton, Inc., a supplier of packaging for pharmaceutical and cosmetic markets, gives this advice: "Demonstrate your ability to THINK. That's right . . . ask appropriate questions, explore relevant issues, develop good, solid data that yields its own conclusions. Bring a good brain in the door, show that you can use it, and the rest is no big deal. It's easier to find people with experience than it is to find people who can think. Experience isn't always useful, particularly in times of great change, so give me a good brain anytime!"

Exciting choices are available for those who can communicate ideas and solutions. By using your imagination, solving problems, and sharing ideas, you will be able to open doors and create work opportunities tailored to your particular skills.

This chapter presents strategies on how to demonstrate your good brain—whether you're looking for a job, beginning a new project, or starting a business.

Tuning In to the Marketplace

TUNE IN TO THE MARKETPLACE

Use a marketing approach

Develop your one-minute commercial

Learn how candidates are selected

NAB the interview with memorable stories

Maintain your marketability

Converging economic factors have fundamentally changed the way organizations operate internally and in the marketplace. These factors include:

- Increased competition among suppliers of products and services
- Increased demand for more profits and financial growth
- Increased global competition
- Shorter lead times in the development of new products
- Increased demand for innovative products and services
- Emergence of niche markets and customized products and services
- Faster adaptation to changes in the marketplace
- Greater reliance on information, technology, and teamwork to improve productivity

As a result, companies are focusing more on the bottom line than ever before. After all, the number one goal of any company is to stay in business. Every employer wants workers who can find ways to make or save the company money. You must offer employers a package of knowledge and skills that contributes to their bottom line, either through increasing revenue or saving costs. Your mission as a job hunter is to communicate how you can contribute to the bottom line.

If you're looking for work in the public sector, be aware that government institutions are driven by the same economic factors as private industry. The public expects the same level of service from government agencies as they receive from business.

Old Business Maxim—It's not what you know, but who you know.

New Reality—In the Information Age, it's what you know and how well you can communicate it. And, who you know is still important!

Even nonprofit organizations are bottom-line oriented. Funding for nonprofits is often unstable and fluctuates with government and society priorities. As a result, most nonprofits are continuously looking for new sources of money to support them. Funding sources expect agencies to be able to justify their programs and budgets. Agencies challenge employees to find innovative ways to improve services and reduce expenditures. Successful job candidates communicate how they can contribute to these efforts.

Savvy careerists know that communicating how their work benefits the company (i.e., contributes to the bottom line) is not just for the upwardly mobile—it's an essential skill for everyone. The ability to talk about yourself so others understand what you do and appreciate the value of your work separates the successful from the less successful. The best skills in the world won't do you any good if no one knows about them.

You will have many employers and working relationships over the course of your career. How quickly you are able to move from one work setting to another depends on your ability to search out new opportunities and communicate your value to the person in charge. Whether you're an employee, free agent, or entrepreneur, you have to sharpen your communication skills to stay employed. The days of depending on the company to take care of your career are long past. Performing good work is no longer enough. Today, it's essential to communicate your value, whatever your profession.

USE AN APPROACH BORROWED FROM MARKETING 101

Like it or not, getting a job consists of marketing and selling yourself to a company. It's the same thing as a company's marketing and selling products to customers.

Every product or service exists in the marketplace to fulfill a need or desire. If it didn't meet someone's need, no one would buy it. Company experts market products in terms of features and benefits. A product's features are its physical qualities—the bells and whistles. For example, the features of a diamond necklace are the number of stones it contains, the color and clarity of the stones, and its 14-carat gold setting. However, people really buy a product not merely for its features, but for its benefits. The benefits of a diamond necklace might be that it makes you feel special, it commemorates your anniversary, or you love showing it off. Effective advertising evokes the benefits of the product by appealing to the customer's hidden needs—such as status, time savings, or emotional satisfaction. We buy a car, software, or CD when the advertiser convinces us the benefits outweigh the cost. To borrow from current advertising, we buy a truck not for its weight, horsepower, or cup holders (its features), but because it appeals to our image of being a rugged outdoorsman (its benefits). As an employee, you want to convince your customer (an employer) that the benefits of your work more than justify the cost (your pay).

Job Hunting Tips

Consider potential employers as your customers. What does the employer need? What problems need solving?

- Describe how you can fill those needs.
- Explain the benefits of your particular skills.

It's easy to recognize your features as a worker: You are efficient, hardworking, computer-literate, and/or have people skills. But, by themselves, your features won't convince the employer that you are worth your price. Think like a marketing professional. Identify the *needs* of your potential employer, and then communicate to him or her the *benefits* of your work. If you know the work requires tight deadlines, you can turn your features—efficient and hardworking—into benefits by emphasizing that you can be counted on to consistently meet deadlines, and that you have no problem working on weekends or evenings, if necessary. The more you know about the company and its needs, the easier it is to sell your benefits. Applicants with solutions to real company needs will be the successful candidates.

To identify the benefits of your skills and knowledge, think of yourself from the customer's perspective. Your current boss, the company you are pursuing, and the person interviewing you for a new position are your customers. Each of them has needs and will hire the person who is perceived as best meeting those needs.

What is the need that you can help fill?

What problems can you help solve?

What can you do to improve customer satisfaction?

How can you reduce costs?

What can you do to improve sales or speed service?

What new product, service, or creative twist can you offer that would help increase the company's ability to meet its goals?

Go beyond the obvious—think in terms of customers and how your work impacts them. For example, Disney is well-known for its view that all employees are cast members who are onstage from the minute they come to work. Groundskeepers at Disneyland spend their first four days in training not because pushing a broom is a complex task, but because visitors to the park ask anyone in uniform for directions. A groundskeeper contributes to Disneyland's success by keeping the grounds neat (feature) and by helping visitors have a pleasant experience (benefit). Disney groundskeepers contribute to the bottom line by solving customer problems and ensuring customer satisfaction.

WHAT IF YOU'RE AN ENTREPRENEUR, CONTRACT EMPLOYEE, OR CONSULTANT?

If you choose to work as an independent contractor or free agent, you may be wondering how the information in this chapter relates to you. As a free agent, communicating your value is the strategy you'll use to keep working.

All of your satisfied customers offer potential for referrals. The people you work with during a project, as well as the person who originally hired you, can give you referrals. As a free agent, you must continuously scan for new opportunities and develop new relationships. Otherwise, you will experience dead time (read as NO INCOME) between projects.

Experienced free agents always think in terms of the bottom line—and the benefit their work brings to it. This is how they sell their services to new clients. When bidding a project or negotiating a contract, do more than describe your skills. Describe how the results you intend to achieve will benefit your customer in terms of time or money. Use the ideas in this chapter to help you communicate more effectively. Many of the ideas in Chapter 10 about how to access the hidden job market can be successfully used by free agents when looking for new projects.

As a working adult, you will be asked many times to explain what you do. Whether you are job hunting, networking at a professional association meeting, looking for a new contract, or trying to find a new project team at work, it helps to be able to communicate your value positively and distinctively in a brief statement—the one-minute commercial. Your commercial in Activity 7.1 should clearly summarize your accomplishments and sell your benefits.

One-Minute Commercial — Activity 7.1

Example:

1. **What need can I fill?**

   I can design and maintain webpages to sell products and services. I can use my creative skills to inform, persuade, or amuse people in innovative ways.

2. **My features:**

   I can use HTML, graphic design, and a variety of database programs.

3. **My benefits:**

   The pages I create help market and sell products and services in unique ways.

WRITE YOUR COMMERCIAL BELOW:

As a Webmaster, I create visual images and content for companies that want to use the Internet to expand their markets. I design creative, user-friendly webpages that link information and technology to consumers worldwide.

Your Turn:

My One-Minute Commercial

1. What need can I fill?

2. My features:

(continued)

3. My benefits:

____

____

____

WRITE YOUR COMMERCIAL BELOW:

____

____

____

____

____

____

____

Practice your commercial until you can say it with confidence. Now, air your commercial to a few classmates and friends. Ask them for feedback on how you could improve it. If you like their suggestions, alter your commercial.

How the Selection Process Works

Interviewing for a professional position, even an entry-level one, is more complex than interviewing for a part-time job. Many companies interview candidates three or four times and may take several weeks to extend an offer.

1. Screening interview. Your first interview may be over the phone with a personnel analyst in human resources. This is a screening interview to determine whether you meet the basic qualifications for the job. If you do, you will be asked to interview in person.

2. Company-fit interview. The first in-person interview determines whether your personality, skills, and attitudes match the company culture. It may take place on campus or at the company's place of business. Usually, a recruiter or human resources representative conducts the interview and screens out candidates who don't fit. For example, a company may be looking for people who work well in teams, deliver excellent customer service, or solve problems independently. Successful candidates are referred to the hiring manager.

3. Hiring manager interview. Your second in-person interview will probably be with the hiring manager—the person for whom you will work. Usually, the hiring manager interviews 6 to 10 candidates to evaluate technical skills and experience related to the specific work that has to be done.

REAL-LIFE PERSPECTIVE

CARRIE

Carrie worked hard in her job as marketing director for a national chain bookstore. She worked long hours and developed many creative ways to publicize the bookstore and increase sales. When the corporate office eliminated all local marketing positions, Carrie was out of a job. Her job search was slow and difficult because she hadn't taken the time to create a network of colleagues or join professional organizations. She thought her hard work and strong resume would be enough to get a new job, but it wasn't. She had to learn how to market herself as effectively as she had promoted the bookstore.

4. Final selection interview. The top two or three candidates are asked to come back for another interview, which might be a panel interview with several people. Companies with a team environment may also schedule an interview with the team that has the opening. Making a good impression with the team is just as important as impressing the manager. Many managers will reject a candidate if coworkers don't think the person will fit in.

Interviewing and selecting candidates is not a science. You will be interviewed by experienced people who know how to make you comfortable and ask questions that bring out your best. You will also meet interviewers who are inexperienced and end up doing most of the talking. Preparation and practice will help you find ways to interject relevant information to sell yourself. If an interview goes poorly, it might have more to do with the interviewer than yourself.

Human resources professionals and hiring managers know that resumes and interviews are only two ways to evaluate candidates. In addition, many companies administer tests, request work samples, and examine portfolios.

SELECTION TESTS

Many employers, ranging from consulting firms to manufacturers, use pre-employment tests to help decide which candidates to hire. Current estimates suggest as many as 30 percent of Fortune 500 companies use some type of testing to match candidates to openings. Testing job candidates is not new. For the past 50 years, companies have used typing tests and other basic skills tests to evaluate candidates' abilities. Many companies use personality tests to measure characteristics such as motivation and extroversion in candidates for sales positions.

In competitive fields where finding enough qualified candidates is difficult (e.g., health care, engineering, technical positions), professional certification is used instead of testing. At the same time, in industries where customer service is critical (e.g., retail and hospitality), the use of tests is increasing. You may not encounter pre-employment testing as you enter your profession, but you are likely to face testing sometime during your career.

Testing is controversial. Because many people are concerned that tests are culturally biased, federal and state legislation has been enacted to ensure that tests are administered equally to all candidates. Any company using tests for selection must show that the criteria used to evaluate test results are relevant to the job.

Tests allow employers to ask more questions in a shorter amount of time and to ensure consistency among all applicants. Several types of pre-employment tests are frequently used: personality tests, task-oriented tests, and problem-solving tests.

Personality Tests

Gary Behrens, Manager of Assessment Systems for NCS Workforce Development Group, suggests you should remember that a test is just one element of the hiring process: "Don't put too much emphasis on a test or worry about it because organizations don't use them exclusively to select a candidate." He says to think of a test as a written interview: "Too often, people try to ace the test, but this may create a false impression. You may do yourself a disservice by presenting yourself inaccurately. The employer may, for example, expect you to be more outgoing than you are, if that's how you responded to the test. Honesty is the best policy. Be yourself and be realistic about your strengths. People should remember that the employer is not expecting to find a perfect person." The goal of personality tests is to help identify candidates who match the corporate culture. If you present yourself as someone you are not, you may be selected for the position and find yourself in a job that doesn't fit your personality. Personality tests do not diagnose psychological problems such as clinical depression or personality disorders. There are no right or wrong answers to the questions on a personality test, so answer what is true for you regarding your beliefs and attitudes about work.

Task-Oriented Tests

Task-oriented interviews or tests evaluate your technical knowledge and skills. You may be asked to demonstrate computer literacy, programming, or other technical skills required in the position. Your scores will be compared to those employees currently working in the position. Like personality tests, these scores are only part of the selection process. A company will often hire candidates with lower test scores if, overall, their response to questions is more positive.

Problem-Solving Tests

Problem-solving assessments present a variety of situations that the candidate may encounter on the job. You may be asked to role-play a situation (like dealing with a difficult customer) or solve a particular problem. Some companies use assessment centers where an observer watches you complete a variety of tasks. In both of these situations, your analysis of the problem and the way you go about solving it are more important than whether you arrive at a perfect solution.

Employers who hire people for work that involves direct access to money often administer honesty tests to help screen out applicants who may be dishonest. These multiple-choice tests ask the same questions several times to test the consistency of your answers and your honesty. They are often worded in a way that makes it sound as if everyone is dishonest. Don't be offended. Again, there is no way to prepare for these exams. Just answer them truthfully.

Demonstrating the Personal Characteristics Employers Want

Sometimes, you will be asked direct questions about personal characteristics such as honesty, self-confidence, and teamwork skills. Following are 10 characteristics employers look for, as well as some tips and suggestions from recruiters.

Honesty/Integrity

Kenneth R. Pederson explains how the Dow Chemical Company assesses honesty and integrity: "We ask for examples of situations or projects where applicants have faced what they considered to be personal dilemmas on the job or in project work and then ask for details on how they handled the situation and the outcome. We look for the level of match between what the interviewee described and what we would expect of an employee confronting a parallel situation. Candidates who are disingenuous or perhaps painfully naive will be more expensive to develop and will convey that in the interview."

Recruiters we interviewed said that even if they don't ask direct questions about honesty, they rate candidates as honest who can back up information on their resumes with more detailed data. Marc D. Levine, Director of Technology Staffing Applications for Compunnel Software Group, Inc., states, "I always measure my hearing with my gut. I structure questions to confirm suspicions and probe for more detail. I also use past employment references—the best I can—to validate applicant information and to gain more insight into a person's story." Double-check the accuracy of your dates and resume information. Most employers confirm dates, employers, and degrees listed on your resume. Dishonest people often stretch the truth. Some employers conduct extensive background checks, including researching criminal records and credit ratings.

What Do Employers Look For?

1. Communication skills (verbal & written)
2. Honesty/integrity
3. Teamwork skills (works well with others)
4. Interpersonal skills (relates well to others)
5. Strong work ethic
6. Motivation/initiative
7. Flexibility/adaptability
8. Analytical skills
9. Computer skills
10. Organizational skills

Each year, the National Association of Colleges and Employers conducts an employer survey. In 2002, employers rated these personal characteristics as the top ten they are seeking in job candidates.

Reprinted from *Job Outlook 2002* with permission of NACE, copyright holder.

Motivation/Initiative

Employers want candidates who have demonstrated initiative by gaining experience in the industry while in college. Daniel Bonsick, senior human resources representative for a Fortune 500 electronics company, stresses the importance of relevant work: "I speak to college groups and high school students and give one message: Internships are key! We do not consider candidates without intern or co-op experience. Part of the reason is that they are so widely available that it demonstrates a possible lack of motivation."

Show motivation and initiative in the interview by being prepared. Research the company and ask good questions. Show the interviewer that you have invested the time to learn about the company and this position.

Did you work to help pay your way through college? Did you work in a related field? Share stories about projects you completed for extra credit, or give examples of times at work when you solved a problem on your own or suggested a solution to your manager.

Communication Skills

Interviewers look for written, verbal, and electronic communication skills. Your resume and cover letter demonstrate your writing ability. The interview shows whether you can clearly express your ideas verbally. One recruiter told us, "I look for communication skills—are they able to get their thoughts and ideas across verbally? I also study the candidate's body language. It may say, *I don't really want to be here.* I want their nonverbal behavior to communicate their interest."

Interviewers expect you to be somewhat nervous and aren't looking for the slickest responses. Marc D. Levine, who recruits for Compunnel Software Group, Inc., offers this advice: "Applicants should be themselves and be honest. Their thinking must be structured, focused, and organized. They shouldn't ramble. They need to talk in action terms not only about what they've done, but what they will do for my company." Remember, practice helps!

Talk like a professional. Know your industry, learn the right language, and use the right buzzwords. Don't use academic jargon and talk in generalities. Discover the key words or phrases used by insiders in your industry. If you don't understand an acronym or what the interviewer is asking, don't be afraid to ask questions for clarification. It is much better to ask than to assume incorrectly.

Self-Confidence

Sound self-confident. Speak with enthusiasm—no monotones. Build your confidence through interviewing practice. Videotape yourself and practice answering the sample questions in this chapter. Read books on interviewing and/or attend workshops in your campus career center. Self-confidence comes when you are comfortable and knowledgeable about the subjects you are talking about. Do your company research and practice, practice, practice.

Many inexperienced workers feel that they should already know how to do everything the job requires. Listen to the advice from one recruiter: "To be qualified for the position, you should be comfortable with 25 percent of the work, able to learn 50 percent of the work fairly quickly, and the other 25 percent should scare the pants off of you. If it doesn't, you're not seriously growing."

Flexibility/Adaptability

Interviewers say flexibility is important in today's workplace as organizations continuously strive to improve the way they do things. Daniel Bonsick, who recruits for a Fortune 500 electronics company, says, "We are looking for flexibility and the ability to remain calm under pressure. We evaluate this through a variety of interviews of different styles. We look at how the candidates mesh with people of different levels and positions and how they react when out of their comfort zones."

Share experiences that demonstrate your ability to manage change—moving to a new city, changing colleges with good reason, adapting to a new boss, taking on new responsibilities at work, trying different approaches to solve a problem, and so on.

Interpersonal Skills

Do you get along with a variety of personality types and styles? Do you adjust your communication style to that of other people? Do you resolve conflicts or create them? You will be asked questions to assess your ability to get along with others. Saying you are a people person is not adequate. Employers want work-related examples that show how you successfully worked with a difficult teammate or calmed an angry customer.

Strong Work Ethic

Employers want workers who will do more than simply show up on time. They want employees who will complete their projects on time and care about the quality of their work. Pointing out that you worked or interned while attending school and maintained a high grade point average are two ways to show evidence of a strong work ethic.

Teamwork Skills

Most companies use teams to complete projects or solve problems. Whether they're looking for computer programmers, accountants, or customer service reps, they want people who can work with others. One recruiter told us, "I look for a person who can bring balance to our team. I discuss their skills and accomplishments to find what value they can add." Describe how you participated in study groups, student activity committees, and work teams. What did you contribute? What was your role? What did you do to help the team stay focused on the task?

Leadership Skills

Even if you don't aspire to hold a management position, you will be expected to lead teams and influence others throughout your career. Share experiences about your leadership opportunities in extracurricular activities, in volunteer positions, or at work. How have you led others to successfully reach a goal or meet a deadline? What were the results? What role did you play?

Success Strategy

In Chapter 5, you conducted information interviews to gain information about potential careers. Now, it's time for more interviews! This time, identify some companies where you would like to work. Find someone in each company doing the work you want to do, and ask for an information interview. Find out the direction of the company, the type of person who does well in the company, and the kinds of skills the company looks for in a candidate. Ask about the company's hiring process—do they use a recruiting firm, temp agency, or a human resources department?

Enthusiasm

"If you show tremendous energy, excitement, and enthusiasm, interviewers will remember you and talk about you. Practice showing it, until everybody comments on how enthusiastic you are." This can be a real edge for a new graduate, says Dr. John Sullivan, as many experienced people have lost their passion. "Ignorant enthusiasm is not attractive, however. You must know the company and its products to the point that your interviewers are literally in disbelief."

Talk about experiences when you were excited—you'll show enthusiasm when you tell these stories. Rita Bresnahan, Program Director for Parents Anonymous, interviews candidates for management and supervisory positions in this statewide nonprofit agency. Rita says she looks for "a sparkle in the eye, and real interest when describing your work." She's looking for candidates who have a commitment to their missions. Candidates who light up win out over candidates who have good answers but lack enthusiasm.

Looking Experienced Straight Out of College

Like other new graduates, you may feel caught in a catch-22 situation: You need experience to get work, but how do you get experience if you can't find work? What do employers really want when they ask for experience? They want a self-starter who can solve their problems and begin working independently right away. One of the best strategies is to participate in an internship while earning your degree. Another strategy is to take the experience you do have and translate it into skills that employers need.

PROVIDE THE PROOF

- **Research papers.** Your experience writing a research paper demonstrates that you know how to find and organize information, summarize the research findings, and discuss the implications. You also know how to estimate a project time line and keep it.
- **Study groups.** Participating in a study group to pass a course or prepare a project is evidence of teamwork. Discuss your role in the group. Were you the leader, the person the team could count on to dig up resources and information, or the person who resolved conflicts? Every team needs people who serve these functions. Talk about how you contributed to the group and the results of your actions.
- **Special class projects.** Some projects you completed might directly relate to the work you will be doing. You could discuss business case studies or computer programs you developed for a class.

Interviewing Basics

An astonishing thing often happens when searching for work—people who are normally articulate start to falter and stammer the minute they hear those famous four words: "Tell me about yourself." It even happens to experienced people!

People have trouble talking about themselves because as children they often heard, "Don't brag about yourself. It isn't nice." Bragging is saying you are better than everyone else. You were bragging when you came home from school and said you were the smartest, strongest, or fastest in your class. When you communicate your value, don't compare yourself to others. Just say what you can do and describe the benefits. Become comfortable talking about yourself—the solution is practice, practice, and more practice!

Before the Interview

- Research the company so you can relate your skills and experience to its products or services. Ask for a job description, if available. Find the company's home page on the Internet. Go to your college career center to research companies that interview on your campus.
- Analyze the job description and the information you gathered about the company. If you were doing the hiring, what skills, attitudes, and characteristics would you be looking for?
- Practice your answers to questions out loud. If you've ever given a speech without practicing, you know there can be a big difference between what your mind thinks and what your mouth says.
- Develop questions you will ask.
- Dress professionally. If the workplace is casual, dress one step above. Expensive clothes are unnecessary, but clothes that are neat and that fit well are a must. Don't forget to polish your shoes!
- Arrive a few minutes before the interview is scheduled to begin. This allows you to relax (try deep breathing) and review the information you want to emphasize.

During the Interview

- Greet the interviewer with a smile and a firm handshake.
- Express a positive attitude and show enthusiasm in your responses.
- Consider the interview a 50/50 exchange—evaluate how well the company fits you.
- Ask good questions.
- Ask for the job!

After the Interview

- Follow up by sending a thank-you note to everyone who interviewed you. Mention a topic that you discussed so the person can connect your note with you.
- Call one week after the interview to check on progress. Often, the decision process gets delayed for business reasons. It is better to know where you stand than to keep wondering.
- Remember, every *no* gets you closer to *yes.*

Things New Graduates Do Better

1. Relate to college students
2. Travel
3. Do activities others dislike
4. Perform routine tasks—they aren't boring yet
5. Spend more time researching and preparing for interviews
6. Provide a fresh perspective
7. Know latest technology
8. Bring a flexible approach
9. Cost less
10. Show enthusiasm

How to Look Experienced Right Out of School!

by Dr. John Sullivan

Can you tell an experienced person from a rookie by their looks? (No, not even the gray hair shows experience because you can be old and inexperienced in this job or industry.) The *most important factor* in looking experienced is having solutions to their problems.

> "The number one secret to differentiate yourself from other college grads is developing detailed answers to employers' complex problems."

Experienced professionals can do things rookies can't. If you can solve their complex problems, you are NOT a rookie. Many college grads are a mile wide and an inch deep in their ability to identify and solve real business problems. In fact, the reason want ads specify experience is that companies cannot afford to hire people who can't solve their complex problems. Rookies often make more costly mistakes, ask thousands of time-consuming questions, and take too much time and training to get up to speed. If you are a rookie but don't act like one, you are a great hire because rookies are cheaper than XPros! Rookie players who win games get to start!

HOW DO I IDENTIFY THEIR TOP PROBLEMS/OPPORTUNITIES?

- Review expensive seminar offerings (even XPros need answers, and seminar pros can only sell seminars on the top problems with few answers).
- Look at the professional association annual meeting topics.
- Look for financial/industry analysts' reports on company strengths and weaknesses.
- Post the question on a discussion list or chat room.
- Ask industry consultants.
- Conduct information interviews, student or university class-sponsored surveys, or ask your contacts and mentors.
- Review professional journals' tables of contents and indexes to see what is hot and what is getting cold.
- Read annual reports.
- Visit anti-company websites that are critical of a specific company.
- Look at the want ads over time to see where and what companies are hiring.
- Evaluate the product and those of the competitors. Ask employees after work in the restaurant bar across the street from the company.
- Ask business reporters, or read the business section and business magazines.

HOW CAN I LEARN HOW TO SOLVE THEIR COMPLEX PROBLEMS SO I CAN BE EXPERIENCED?

Solving complex business problems is difficult for everyone, but in some ways, college students actually have an edge getting help and information because:

1. Students have a lot of free time to focus on one issue.
2. Students have access to professors, computers, and libraries that others might not have access to.
3. Students have access to guest lecturers, internships, projects, other students, student organizations, and mentors for help.
4. XPros are often sympathetic to college students and will help them and give them information they might not be willing to share with others. Student enthusiasm, charm, or even naiveté can bring down barriers.

HOW CAN I PROVIDE PROOF TO THE HIRING MANAGER/RECRUITER THAT I CAN SOLVE THE SAME PROBLEMS THAT XPROS CAN?

- Write an actual solution to the problem in a brief executive summary format.

(continued)

- Propose a detailed, step-by-step time line on which steps you would (did) take to solve the problem.
- Develop a solution as a company intern for a special project, and ask your supervisor to write a letter of praise for your ideas.
- Ask for an assessment of your solution by your mentors, other experienced professionals, consultants, or even your professor.
- Compare your solution to those in use by superior competitor firms, and use it as a benchmark. Bring it to the interview as part of your portfolio to show that the level of your work meets experienced professional standards.
- Co-write an article with an XPro for a magazine, journal, or newsletter.
- Give a presentation to a professional association group.
- Post a summary of your solution on a discussion list and solicit comments.
- Place your solutions on your own portfolio webpage.
- Ask your instructor to assign the problem as a class project, and invite XPros to visit as outside evaluators of your presentations.
- Hold a student project contest, and ask a professional association to evaluate the entries.
- Have an employee submit it as an idea (or in the suggestion box) to gauge its value.
- List it on your resume as a *consulting project,* and describe its projected value if it is implemented.
- Send executive summaries to key executives (especially the college/community relations leaders), and ask for constructive criticism (especially from alumni of your school) as part of a student assignment.

In summary, being experienced involves much more than the number of years on the job. You could have had many years of unsuccessful experience, or the experience could be out-of-date because of the speed of change in today's business environment. If you fail to grow on the job, you might really have 1 year of experience 10 times rather than 10 years of experience.

So, if the recruiter wants to reject you because of a lack of experience, it's probably because you don't talk or act like an experienced person. But, more importantly, your lack of focus and no proof that you can solve their problem are the biggest barriers to getting the recruiter to pass your resume along. So the answer is: *Great answers, maturity, and knowing the language CAN be substituted on a year-by-year basis for the numbers of years of experience suggested in the want ad!*

Available online at johns@sfsu.edu.

Communicating Your Value: The NAB Process

The NAB (need, action, benefit) process will help you focus on the employer's needs and show you how to communicate effectively, whether you want to interview for a job or write a dynamic resume.

1. Need—What does the employer need or want? Identify an employer's needs or problems that you can solve. Look at job descriptions, talk to employers, read trade journals, and visit websites. For example, using a job description, underline or highlight the skills, knowledge, and capabilities the employer needs.

2. Action—How have you demonstrated each skill? Write down a time when you used each skill or knowledge. Include who, what, where, and why.

3. Benefit—What was the result? Describe the results you achieved—the benefit of your skills in the situation. Use numbers, dollars, and percentages whenever you can.

A job description like the one shown in Activity 7.2 can help you identify what an employer is seeking. A student highlighted an employer's needs and then transferred them to the "*Need*" column on the NAB worksheet. Next, she thought of times when she had demonstrated these skills and wrote them in the "*Action*" column. She thought about the results she achieved and how they benefited others. She wrote these ideas in the "*Benefit*" column.

NAB the Interview with Memorable Stories

Interviewers want to know about your accomplishments and the results you achieved. Many applicants respond to interview questions by listing personal skills and characteristics. After listening to five applicants in a row say they're dependable, hardworking, flexible, and a team player, the interviewer's eyes begin to glaze over—everyone sounds the same. These adjectives are not action words. They don't sound convincing and don't show your potential benefit to the company.

How can you stand out from the other applicants? How can you convince the interviewer you can solve their problems? By telling memorable stories that illustrate what you can do.

It's always story time.

"Don't take an interviewing course—take a storytelling course. Sit down and write your story. Write about the times when you've felt great about yourself, the times when you've made a difference." EUNICE AZZANI, V.P., Korn/Ferry International

Personal, real-life stories will be remembered by the interviewer. Your stories provide the context in which you used skills and show that you're a person who takes action to achieve results. A positive side effect of telling stories is that you take yourself back to a time when you were with people you like and accomplishing something important. The retelling will relax you and at least temporarily take your mind away from the stress of the interview.

To create your memorable stories, use the NAB worksheet (Activity 7.2). Look at your *Action* column. For each entry, create a story that explains the situation. The story should focus on the interviewer's need. Be sure to clearly describe what you did and emphasize the results you achieved. You might want to write the story first. Practice telling your story until it rolls out easily. The final step is to look at the Frequently Asked Questions in the next section and decide which of your stories would be a good answer for each question.

NAB—Need, Action, Benefit

Activity 7.2

Job Description:

MARKETING ASSISTANT

We're Optico Corporation, a leading supplier of optics, photonics instruments and components, opto-mechanical components, positioning equipment, and vibration control. We are currently seeking a detail-oriented and highly motivated marketing assistant. Selected candidate will assist in the development and implementation of promotional marketing activities in our vibration control group. This will include: forecasting marketing trends of new/existing products; developing catalogs, brochures, and other collateral material; tracking and reporting advertising/collateral budget expenditures; implementing trade show efforts; and supporting product management processes. Requires a bachelor's degree in marketing or 3+ years' applicable marketing experience. Knowledge of MS Excel is essential. Optico offers an excellent compensation and benefits package, a leading-edge work environment, and opportunities for professional growth. We invite qualified candidates to send or fax a resume to: . . . .

NAB—NEED, ACTION, BENEFIT (EXAMPLE)

Need What does the employer need or want?	**Action** How have you demonstrated each skill?	**Benefit** What was the result?
detail-oriented	accounting clerk	maintained accounts receivable—reduced delinquent accounts by 20%
highly motivated	grade point average while working	3.8 GPA while working
forecast market trends	marketing class	wrote paper forecasting marketing trends in publishing
develop brochure	fund-raiser	helped write fund-raiser flyer, raised $1,800 for local candidates
track budget	treasurer, Young Republicans	my reports helped club raise 20% more money than ever before
trade show	canvassed local residents for reelection campaign	learned to be comfortable informing and persuading public
Excel	accounting job	created new reports that improved tracking of accounts receivable
develop materials	term papers	excellent comments on PowerPoint visuals
communication skills	speech class club treasurer	A in speech class; Treasurer's report helped us set goals
teamwork	study group	kept group on track by facilitating discussions—received an A on project

Your Turn:

Instructions: Complete the worksheet below using a job description in your field. You can find hundreds of job descriptions on the Internet at www.monster.com.

Use your own experiences in school, work, internships, or volunteer activities to fill in the "Action" column. Describe the benefits of your actions in the last column.

Need What does the employer need or want?	**Action** How have you demonstrated each skill?	**Benefit** What was the result?

Sample Stories

HOW WOULD YOU HANDLE WORKING AT A TRADE SHOW?

"I think I would be good at representing your products at trade shows—I like talking to people and giving them information. When I was a member of the Young Republicans Club, we went door-to-door asking people to vote for local candidates. As a group, we decided which neighborhoods were the most critical. I helped write the script we used and kept everyone's motivation up on the days we canvassed. We met our goals in less time than we expected. I enjoyed talking to people about our candidates' views on the issues—I think I convinced a number of people to vote for them. I'm sure these are the same skills you would need to talk to potential customers at a trade show."

TELL ME ABOUT A TIME WHEN YOU WORKED ON A TEAM.

"One of my favorite classes was a class on market trends and research. One of our assignments was to form a group to write and present a market research project. Our group chose online education. In the beginning, we had so many ideas about how we could do this that we couldn't focus very well. I volunteered to lead our discussions so we could decide on a plan of action and get busy on the project. People in the group seemed relieved that someone took charge. I made sure everyone had input into our decisions, but I didn't allow the group to waste time either. We had one member who wasn't contributing much at first, but I talked to him privately, and we found a part that he was interested in doing. In the end, he developed all the visuals, which really added to our presentation. We developed some innovative ways to research our topic, and we gathered comprehensive information. There was a lot of interest from the class when we made our presentation—and we got an A on our project!"

How to Handle Behavioral Interviews

Most recruiters use an interviewing approach called *behavioral interviewing*. It is based on the premise that past behavior most likely predicts future behavior. Thus, if you've demonstrated the skill or knowledge in the past, you will do it at this company, too. Recruiters are looking for positive behaviors—real-time examples, not traits or personality characteristics.

Behavioral interviewing questions start with "Tell me about a time when . . ." or "Give me an example of . . ." Recruiters then continue to probe and ask questions about this particular experience until they have a clear, realistic picture of the event. Choose situations with positive outcomes. If you describe a stressful experience, talk about the event in a positive, upbeat manner. If possible, find a way to transition into one of your prepared answers, using your NAB experiences to paint a picture of your accomplishments. Always describe the results you achieved and their benefit.

With this style of interviewing, the recruiter strives to create a comfortable environment, encouraging the applicant to describe and tell more. Beware of becoming too comfortable and saying things you will regret later. We've heard stories of people who described how they told off their last boss or went over the heads of their teachers to get their grades improved. Even though recruiters may seem very friendly, they are evaluating your responses. Give a favorable impression.

REAL-LIFE PERSPECTIVE

Advice Straight from the Recruiter's Mouth

- "Can I work with this person? Do they fit in with our corporate culture? These are the two questions that are in my mind when I interview. I use scenarios to see how the person responds to actual events. I select candidates who show enthusiasm, strong interpersonal skills, and good judgment when answering questions." Rita Bresnahan, recruiter for a statewide nonprofit organization
- "I look for a person's ability to solve logical problems. I want real-world experience (just school experience isn't enough). The person must be good at verbal and written communications and be able to work independently because I'm a hands-off manager." Anonymous manager
- "(1) Seriously assess yourself—strengths, weaknesses, and preferences; (2) Research prospective employers; (3) Don't put on an act you can't sustain day in and day out, if hired." Kenneth D. Pederson, Ph.D., Global Process Leader for Staffing and Selection, Dow Chemical Company
- "Learn how to dress, speak, WRITE! Know themselves and begin improving their counterproductive behaviors. Listen more, speak less. Let the interviewer do the talking. Many times interviewers just love to talk and see applicants who listen as more qualified." Robert F. Gately, PE, MBA, President, Gately Consulting
- "Be sincere, ask questions when you are confused, don't play hardball, and read a book on interview tips. Don't talk about drinking or sex habits, and keep clean the night before an interview. I have had people come in late and hung over. They think because I am young that I would laugh. They were wrong." Daniel Bonsick, Senior Human Resources Representative of Fortune 500 electronics company

Take time to organize your thoughts before answering a question. You don't want to ramble or appear off track. It's okay to say, "Let me think about that for a minute." It is okay to ask a question if you don't understand something. You may be asked to describe the situation you choose in greater detail, as the interviewer looks for examples of specific behaviors.

Frequently Asked Questions (FAQs)

Although it's impossible to predict the questions you'll be asked, practice answers to these typical questions. The secret to good interviewing is to be prepared to discuss your skills and past performance. Your NAB stories will do this for you. Remember to practice your answers out loud. Practice until you can say them with enthusiasm and confidence.

Check this site for FAQs in specific career fields: www.job-interview.net/sample/demosamp.htm

- **Tell me about yourself.** Interviewers often ask this broad question to build rapport and begin the interview. Launch your one-minute commercial. Focus your answer on your skills and interest in the field, giving a brief chronological overview. Avoid discussing personal or family information.
- **Tell me about a time when you achieved more than was expected.** The interviewer wants to know about your personal commitment to a task. Are you results-oriented? Do you inspire others? Are you motivated? How

have you shown initiative in the past? Use examples from your education or work experience. The recruiter is most interested in what behaviors you exhibited to achieve a particular goal.

- **Describe a time when you had a conflict with someone.** What happened and how did you react? What was the result of the conflict? Recruiters want to know how you handle and resolve conflict. Are you the kind of person who blows up and adds fuel to the fire, tries different ways to keep the peace, or avoids conflict and walks away? Your answer should describe a time when you successfully resolved conflict in a reasonable and appropriate way. Choose a small conflict at work or school, and focus on what you did to fix the problem.

When asked this question, the most recent or important conflict you've experienced pops into your head. Don't talk about these situations or any issues that you feel emotional about—eliminate discussions about parents, roommates, and spouses. You want to appear rational and even-tempered. Stay away from blaming or berating anyone. Instead, discuss how differences in work styles can cause conflict, and describe how you resolved it. Don't pick a situation you walked away from, such as dropping a class or quitting a job. You can't avoid this question by saying you have never been involved in a conflict. Interviewers are trained to continue probing until they get a response.

- **Give me an example of a time when you had to work under pressure.** The recruiter wants to know how you handle stress and deadlines. What do you consider stressful? Can you meet deadlines? Do you thrive under pressure or buckle under deadlines? Describe a situation with pressure that has to do with deadlines rather than personalities of coworkers. Talk about strategies you successfully used to stay calm.

- **Tell me about a time when you dealt with an angry customer.** The recruiter wants to know how you react to angry people. Do you use different strategies to calm irate people? Do you do everything you can to make sure customers walk away happy? Do you strictly enforce company policies or often bend them to keep customers coming back? Talk about an exchange that ended positively—a time when you successfully calmed an angry customer and resolved the situation. Don't use examples when you referred an angry customer to others.

- **Describe a situation when you analyzed a problem and arrived at a solution.** The recruiter wants to evaluate your decision-making skills. Did you use a systematic approach or intuition? Were you impulsive, or did you delay and overstudy the problem? Choose a problem that you systematically analyzed, and describe how you resolved it.

- **What are your strengths?** The interviewer looks to see if your strengths match the skills needed in this position. Use this opportunity to talk about your strengths that are related to the job. Give examples of times when you demonstrated them. Describe skills by using one or two of your NAB experiences.

- **What are your weaknesses?** The interviewer uses this question to assess your self-confidence. Don't talk about conflicts with past bosses, coworkers, or roommates. Pick a weakness, and then describe how you overcame it. "I sometimes volunteer to take on too many tasks because I see they need to be done. When this happens, I may ask my supervisor to help me prioritize them."

True Stories—Real-Life Interview Disasters

"The woman who explained a lost job by telling me she was right to have punched her boss—he needed to realize how frustrating he was as a manager."

"This guy came in for an interview at our corporate office in jeans and a T-shirt. He said he forgot to pack his suit."

"I asked a student what he liked to do as hobbies—this is important to me because it helps round out the impression of an individual. He responded: 'I like to pick up chicks in bars.' Although at his age, I found this healthy and relatively normal, I had to laugh at his judgment in sharing this tidbit with me!"

"I received a great resume, the person seemed to be just what I was looking for, but he forgot to include his phone number or address."

"This woman had so much perfume on that her aroma lingered the entire day, despite turning on the air conditioning in February. Little did she know that the vice president was allergic to perfume."

"I was interviewing applicants on campus. I was very impressed by this woman engineering student, but she was dressed a bit bizarre in an Aladdin costume. She looked like she had stepped right out of "I Dream of Jeannie." It wasn't until I got home that night that I realized it was Halloween and the outfit was really a costume."

- **Why do you want to work for this company?** The interviewer wants to know what you know about the company. This question gives you the opportunity to show you have done your research. Don't just say it's a great company that's growing. Instead, look the interviewer in the eye and say, "I really want to work for your company because . . ." Talk about what you can do to solve a problem or add value to the team. One recruiter told us, "We asked an applicant why she wanted to work for our company. Her reply, 'It must be a good company to work for,' wasn't enough and I didn't hire her. I think anyone should be able to express why they want the job they are applying for."

- **Why should I hire you?** Tell specifically how you can be an asset to this organization, and let the interviewer know that you want to work there. You would be surprised how many applicants never ask directly for the job.

- **What did you like best about your last job?** Focus on similarities between that job and this one. Share another NAB experience.

- **What did you like least about your last job?** The interviewer is hoping you will reveal conflicts—don't do it. Beware of complaining! Focus on your readiness for new challenges, no matter what happened at your last job.

- **Where do you see yourself in five years?** The interviewer wants to know if you set goals and plan to keep learning. Talk about skills you can reasonably learn in this position and responsibilities you could meet as a result. Don't talk about promotions within the company or long-term employment—that may not be in the cards. Don't mention returning to school full-time or any plans that might indicate a short commitment to the employer.

- **What was your favorite class in college?** Describe a class related to the type of work you are interviewing for. Tell about relevant class activities, assignments, and group projects you enjoyed.

Test Your Interviewing Savvy

Activity 7.3

Instructions: Read each question and circle the letter of the best interview response. Be prepared to discuss your answers.

1. Tell me about yourself.
   A. I am, like, 23 years old and I was born in Chicago. When I was three, we moved to California. I really liked living near the beach, and I spent every second I had surfing while in high school. I was really good. Then I went to college, and here I am looking for a job.
   B. I will graduate in May with a business degree in accounting. I have always liked math. I have worked on campus for the last two years in the accounting office as an accounting clerk and am currently looking for an entry-level position with an accounting firm.
   C. I'm single and ready to go to work. I'm the best programmer around.
2. What are your strengths?
   A. Communication skills.
   B. My written communication skills—I majored in English and really enjoy writing. I consistently received A grades on college papers and have been told by many teachers that my writing skills are excellent. I seem to have the knack for putting concepts into writing in a way that makes it easy for others to understand.
   C. One of my biggest strengths is my ability to simplify complex instructions and write easy-to-understand directions that novice users can understand. In my last job, I wrote the training manual we used to convert to a new system. Everyone in the office found it easy to use, even those who normally have difficulty with the computer. We were able to make the transition to the new system much more quickly than we had anticipated.
3. What are your weaknesses?
   A. I can get very frustrated with coworkers who just don't care. I work very hard and I don't tolerate slackers. I've learned to control my temper and keep these thoughts to myself.
   B. The fact that I don't have any direct work experience in human relations is probably my greatest weakness. However, my five years of experience as a manufacturing supervisor taught me the kinds of problems human relations professionals experience in this environment and gave me an ability to relate well to employees of all levels. This experience, combined with my degree, gives me an understanding that many new graduates lack.
   C. I'm often late. I really try to be on time, but sometimes life gets in the way.
4. Why do you want to work for this company?
   A. I have a friend who works here, and she says really good things about XYZ Company. It would be fun for us to have the opportunity to work together.
   B. I know XYZ is looking to expand into the Latin American market, which I find really exciting. My fluent Spanish could be a real asset here.

C. XYZ Company seems to offer good opportunities for growth and good benefits. That's what I am looking for.

5. Why should I hire you?

A. I'm the best person for the job.

B. It sounds like you are looking for a person with the ability to quickly adapt as priorities change. That's something I had to demonstrate daily as a team leader in my last job. I feel my skills are a great match for this position. Give me a chance and I'll do a great job for you.

C. Throughout this interview, I've told you how I'm qualified. I have the right degree, the right experience, and the right attitude. I'm the right person for the job.

6. What did you like best about your last job?

A. When calls weren't coming in, I could study and get my homework done.

B. My boss was really rad.

C. I had the opportunity to serve on a team to improve our work process. We made suggestions on changing the paperwork that reduced the amount of process time for new orders. I was selected as team leader and was involved in implementing the new process. It was satisfying to see our ideas implemented.

7. What did you like least about your last job?

A. As a part-time employee only working on weekends, I was unable to become involved in marketing projects. There wasn't a mechanism for me to share my ideas for increasing sales, as I seldom saw my department manager.

B. My boss—he was this student who wasn't very serious about work and tended to goof off a lot. Any one of us workers could have done a better job. He would just go in his office and goof off, call his girlfriend, or study while we did all the work.

C. Lack of variety—the work was boring, boring, boring!

8. Where do you see yourself in five years?

A. I'm not sure what I will be doing because technology changes, but I will be working in a team environment with people who value my contributions and skills. I want to be on the leading edge.

B. After I get several years of experience behind me, I would like to go it on my own. That's the way to really make money and have control of your destiny.

C. I would like to move up and progress with this company.

9. Describe a time when you had a conflict with someone. Tell me what happened and how you dealt with the conflict.

A. In my biology class, we were assigned to groups to do a semester-long project. One of the students in my group was a real pain. She would promise to do some of the work and never get it done. She would come to our next meeting with these unbelievable excuses. I had been working really hard on this project, and I didn't want her screwing around to impact my grade. So I went to the teacher and told her how impossible it was to work with Lisa. She assigned me to a new group, and we got an A on our project.

B. Last summer, I coached my little brother's Little League team. One of the parents was a real case. She was always on me for something. Her kid didn't get to play enough, or he had to play a position she didn't like. Well, finally, I had enough—it was after a practice where the kids had all been acting up and I had made them run laps. She came over and told me that I was too young to be an effective coach and needed to get the boys' respect. I lost it and started yelling at her. It worked; I never saw her or her kid again.

C. When I was working as a technician for a temporary service, there was an opportunity for one person in our work group to become permanent. I was sure it would be me—I was the only one attending college, and I had the most education. When Jill was made permanent instead of me, I was really upset. It seemed so unfair. I thought about it and decided the best thing to do was talk to my boss. When I talked to him, he told me that he had something better in mind for me and that it was really important that I maintain my good attitude. It really worked out better for me, as I was promoted to senior technician three months later and made permanent at the same time. Jill ended up reporting to me.

10. Describe a situation when you encountered a problem. Tell me what you did.

A. When I was the assistant manager of Sirloin Stockade, we had six tour buses pull into our parking lot at the same time. We had a quick meeting, and I was able to organize everyone's work so that all customers were efficiently served. We met this huge challenge by getting everyone to work together. We were able to serve everyone quickly. It was our biggest night of sales ever!

B. My manager sold a system to a customer and told him I would install it tomorrow. He neglected to check the stock, and the item had been discontinued. I called the customer and told him that he couldn't get the item. He was really mad. I explained that it wasn't my fault, and that I couldn't do anything about it if the manufacturer wasn't making any more of them. I explained that new models would be available in six weeks and that he could call back then. Then I talked to my manager and told him to make sure to check the stock levels in the future to avoid any other customer problems.

C. One day when I was a receptionist, I got three angry callers in a row. I thought that was unusual so I asked the third caller if something was wrong. He said, "Why aren't you answering your phone? It just rings and rings and rings." I knew something was wrong, as I was answering the phone as usual. I told the office supervisor, who immediately had the line checked out. Something had happened when they changed a voice mail box that caused many calls to ring into never-never land. They were able to fix the problem quickly in response to my actions.

What Questions Do Successful People Recommend You Ask in the Interview?

"What could I do as an applicant to get a better understanding of the company?" Loren J. Hulber, President and CEO of Day Timers, Inc.

"Why do you think I should come to work for ___________? What type of work environment could I expect if I accept this job?" Bill DeVries, President and CEO, Foot Locker

"What are the three things that you most like about working for your company? What are the three things you like least about working for this company?" Dr. Amar Bose, founder, Chairman, and Technical Director, Bose Corporation

"Please describe exactly what I'll be doing if I accept this position." Jerry Yang, Cofounder and Chief Yahoo of Yahoo! Inc.

To find out more hints from 25 of today's top business leaders on getting started in your first professional job, read Mr. Rich's book.

Source: Jason Rich, *First Job, Great Job: America's Hottest Business Leaders Share Their Secrets* (Macmillan Spectrum, 1996).

Questions You Can Ask

Chapter 10 offers more information about comparing job offers.

During the interview, you will be asked if you have any questions. Remember that the interview is a 50/50 exchange—as much an opportunity for you to find out about the employer as it is for the employer to find out about you. If you don't have good questions, the interviewer will see you as unmotivated.

Don't ask about benefits at any point prior to a job offer. Asking questions about what they have to offer you, before you have convinced them you are the best candidate, gives the impression you are just here to see what's in it for you.

- **Ask questions to demonstrate your knowledge of the company and the industry.** Do research, read annual reports, and develop specific questions that show you know and can talk the language of the industry. What trends do you think will impact this business most?
- **Find out if the company's values match yours.** Develop questions based on what you want.
- **Clarify the type of employee they are seeking—so you can sell yourself better.** What is the biggest challenge the person selected for this position will face? What kind of person would do well in this position? Follow the interviewer's answer with examples that show you are that kind of person. If your previous answers were on target, just briefly summarize yours skills. Ask, "Is there anything else you'd like to know about my qualifications? I have brought some samples of my work. Would you be interested in seeing them?"

Questions That Count

Activity 7.4

Instructions: List your top five values from Chapter 3. Develop a question you can ask in an interview for each one.

MY TOP VALUES **QUESTION**

1. ________________________________
2. ________________________________
3. ________________________________
4. ________________________________
5. ________________________________

- If a collegiate atmosphere is important to you, ask what it is like to work at the company. Also ask the interviewer to describe the people with whom you will be working.
- If you value training or advanced education, ask what the company's policy is regarding training and tuition reimbursement. Ask what opportunities you will have to learn new things.

- **Determine the company culture.** How would you describe your management style? How would you describe the company culture? Could you tell me about the people I would be working with?
- **Find out the next step in the hiring process.** What is the next step in the hiring process? May I call you to follow up? Always, always ask for the job (even if you're not sure you want it). End the interview by saying (enthusiastically or passionately) that you want to work for this company.

Maintaining Your Marketability

As you learned in the beginning of this chapter, communicating your value doesn't end when you accept a job. Following are four strategies that will help you stay enthusiastic about your work and boost your value in the marketplace.

MAINTAIN YOUR MARKETABILITY

1. Determine what the company values
2. Look for ways to add value
3. Track your achievements
4. Boost your market value

1. DETERMINE WHAT THE COMPANY VALUES

Once you are working in your professional field, find out where the industry (in general) and your company (in particular) are headed. Ask to see the company's strategic plan—a projection of the goals the company wants to achieve. It defines the priorities of upper management and gives an indication of how resources will be allocated. As the company changes, anticipate the skills that will be relevant in the future and map

Listening Skills in Interviews

Many recruiters say that one of the most important aspects of interviewing is to see if you can carry on an intelligent conversation. Conversation is a two-way process that requires you to listen as well as speak. Here are the basics for good listening anytime—be sure to use them when you interview!

1. Allow the other person to finish speaking. No matter how enthusiastic you may be, interrupting is not only rude—it may cause you to miss the speaker's intent.
2. Use cues to let the speaker know you are listening. Use expressions such as "I see," "umm-hmmm," and "oh."
3. Pause before answering a question to be sure the speaker is finished.
4. Use body language to show you are listening: Sit upright in your seat and lean forward slightly; face the person and look directly at him or her. If the interviewer is speaking for a long time and you become uncomfortable, shift your gaze to his or her forehead.
5. Analyze the questions you are being asked. What skills are they trying to assess? For example, a candidate for a firefighter position was asked the following question: "If you entered a burning house occupied by a woman and child, which one would you save first?" There is no right or wrong answer to this question. The interviewer was assessing the applicant's decision-making skills.

out a strategy to develop them. Even if you're the very best at your profession, your job may be replaced by technology or eliminated by outsourcing. Prepare for future changes that may affect your job security. Seek answers to the following questions, knowing that the answers are continuously changing:

What primary business will the company be in five years from now?

What should you do to prepare for the changes?

How does the company plan to achieve its goals?

Which company goals are most interesting to you?

How can you contribute to these goals?

REAL-LIFE PERSPECTIVE

JOSH WILLIAMS

Josh Williams works as the corporate training manager for an insurance company. In the past six years, the company has been bought, sold, or merged four times. After the latest sale, Josh investigated the values of the new owners. He adjusted his duties to fit their priorities. He's not entirely thrilled with his new tasks, but he still has his job. Meanwhile, 27 of the department's 30 employees have been laid off.

Tip: Read Chapter 9, Developing Relationships, for ideas about how to build a network and develop a mentoring relationship.

2. LOOK FOR WAYS TO ADD VALUE

What's the connection between your work and the company's goals? Sometimes it's obvious. If you're in sales, it's easy to quantify your value: "I increased sales in my territory by 10 percent," or "I developed a new territory and exceeded first-year goals by 40 percent." A computer programmer who writes code for a software development company contributes to the bottom line by helping develop a product to sell. Writing a program to help fellow employees deliver better customer service is another way programmers can add value.

Other work may be harder to describe and measure, but if you think about the goals of the organization, you can find ways to show how your work contributes to the bottom line. For example, if you pursue a career in social services, your value may be how you create a fresh approach to solving a social problem that is a focus of the organization. As a teacher, you may demonstrate your ability to manage a classroom when children come to school with multiple behavioral and family problems.

Look for ways to align your work with your employer's strategic goals. If your company uses cross-functional teams to solve problems, volunteer to work on a team. If you discover recurring problems that affect deadlines and profitability, ask your manager if you can form a team to find solutions.

REAL-LIFE PERSPECTIVE

MARTIN SMITH

HOW DO YOU LET OTHERS KNOW YOUR VALUE?

- I send e-mail to managers and other key people about things that are happening. I try not to brag about myself; instead, I tell them about something someone else has accomplished. I copy the e-mail and also send it to the person I am discussing. They appreciate my praise and, in turn, have good things to say about me.
- I volunteer for assignments, such as leading a team.
- I participate in corporate-sponsored community service projects. I get to work side by side with people I might not otherwise come in contact with. After the project, I can continue developing the relationship. For example, I work with Habitat for Humanity to build homes for the needy in the community. The person next to me pounding nails might be a VP, and I wouldn't even know it unless I asked.

Martin Smith works in supply management at Honeywell Air Transportation Systems. He started as a production planner and was promoted to buyer. Early in his career, he volunteered for teams and learned how to lead them. He says changing a large organization is like turning around a battleship—it takes lots of people and moves slowly. He has found a way to be part of turning the ship. Martin survived a major restructuring and downsizing. For the past 18 months, he has had a special assignment to solve global supply problems.

3. TRACK YOUR ACHIEVEMENTS

Keep a record of the quantity and quality of your work whenever possible. Quantify your accomplishments. Ask your manager what he reports regarding department performance. Then, track all activities you perform that contribute to those results and forward the information to your manager. Don't assume that your boss knows what you're doing. Although she may know your assignment, she may not know how well you are performing or the results of your work. If your manager writes a monthly report, send your information in time for inclusion in the report. You'll be helping your manager by supplying data and helping yourself by creating greater visibility.

While working on a project, send progress reports about information you have gathered and the direction you or the team is taking. Use e-mail to let your manager and key people in the organization know what you're doing. It's an easy way to share information, ask advice, and praise others. Many people we talked to say that e-mail allows them to increase their visibility and develop more relationships than ever before.

4. BOOST YOUR MARKET VALUE

By now, you should be able to see yourself as a product in the employment marketplace. In any market, few products survive by staying the same. Companies continuously find ways to boost their products' value. One way to boost a product's value is to find new markets. When Levi Strauss extended its line of blue jeans from work gear to leisure wear, it attracted many new customers. You can find new markets for your skills and knowledge by researching future developments in your profession or industry.

Another way to increase the value of a product is to reengineer it. Technology is constantly being reinvented for new applications—the modern computer chip has many more applications than did the first circuit boards. You can reengineer your skills through continuous learning.

Summary Points

- Communicating your value is a skill. It involves the ability to talk about yourself so others understand what you do and the value of your work.
- Use the NAB (need, action, benefit) process to create memorable stories to use in an interview. Illustrate how you can add value to the organization.
- Communicating in an employment interview involves a two-way dialogue with the interviewer, exchanging information and evaluating whether this is the right work for you.
- Succeeding in today's workplace means continuously contributing your value.

CHAPTER EIGHT

Getting Noticed 8

WRITING A RESUME THAT COUNTS

How do you write an effective resume?

How do you get your resume noticed by employers?

Will your resume work with electronic scanning systems?

How do you write a cover letter?

Should you use a portfolio?

Imagine describing yourself to someone you've never met or spoken with—someone who hasn't a clue as to who you are as a person. All the interviewer knows about you is written on one or two sheets of paper. This piece of paper tells your name, where you live, and (hopefully) enough information about your skills, abilities, and education to determine whether they want to know you better! This written piece of communication screens you in or out—opening up or limiting your work opportunities; your resume communicates your value—beginning the job search process. Although a resume won't get you a job, it is necessary to help you land the interview.

Myth: A well-written resume gets you a good job.

Reality: A well-written resume hopefully helps you get your foot in the door and gains you an interview. Employers never hire people based only on their resume.

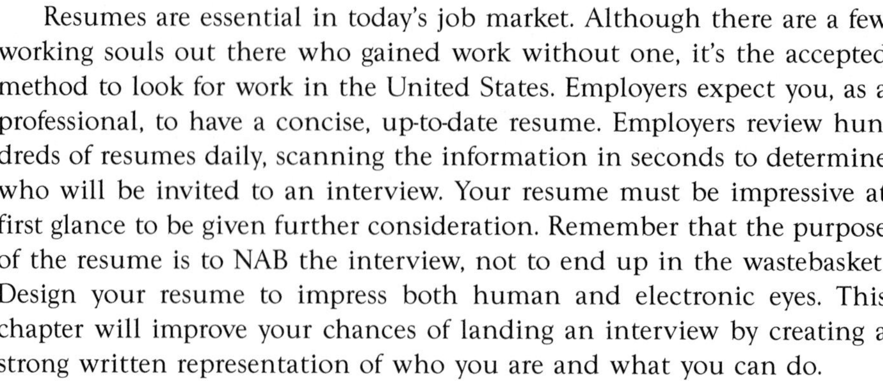

Resumes are essential in today's job market. Although there are a few working souls out there who gained work without one, it's the accepted method to look for work in the United States. Employers expect you, as a professional, to have a concise, up-to-date resume. Employers review hundreds of resumes daily, scanning the information in seconds to determine who will be invited to an interview. Your resume must be impressive at first glance to be given further consideration. Remember that the purpose of the resume is to NAB the interview, not to end up in the wastebasket. Design your resume to impress both human and electronic eyes. This chapter will improve your chances of landing an interview by creating a strong written representation of who you are and what you can do.

> **"Most people gear their resume toward getting another job just like their last one. The secret to advancing your career is to focus on the needs of your next employer."**
>
> **PHYLLIS HARPER-RISPOLI, PHR & Associates**

Writing a resume is often a dreaded task. Most of us find it difficult to write about our accomplishments and don't feel comfortable advertising our skills on paper. It's hard to tell when you've crossed the boundary from selling your skills to boasting and bragging. Knowing that this piece of paper is determining your future opportunities doesn't add comfort. Even people who write resumes for a living, as outplacement counselors, find it difficult when it's time to write their own resumes. Go into any bookstore, and you will see row after row of resume-writing books—evidence of the difficulty people have in transferring their skills and abilities onto a piece of paper. Resume writing doesn't have to be difficult.

Resist the urge to hire a resume-writing service. You know yourself best. You've already learned to communicate your value in Chapter 7, and that's at least half of the work. In this chapter, you will write a concise resume, following a specific format. You'll be able to build on this resume as you go to work, continually updating it throughout your career. Articulating your skills on paper in the format of a resume and cover letter is an essential skill that you will use over and over again to obtain new work. Although it's unlikely that anyone would describe writing a resume as fun, the format in this chapter makes the process as painless as possible.

Using NAB for Your Resume

With the NAB process, your resume focuses on the needs of the employer. Most people gear their resume toward getting another job just like their last one. The secret to advancing your career is to focus on the needs of your *next* employer, not just describing what you've done in the past. In Chapter 7, you created personal stories, using the NAB process, to help you in the interview. If you haven't completed this activity, go back and do it now. You will use the NAB process to formulate action statements for your resume.

In Activity 8.1, there is an example of a NAB worksheet for a marketing assistant position. Catherine Bolivia thought of several ways that she could demonstrate each of the needs listed. You may have needs that you are unable to demonstrate. That's to be expected. Employers seldom find applicants who meet all of their needs. After reading the example, complete the blank worksheet.

Catherine Bolivia's resume in Figure 8.1 was constructed using the NAB process; it reflects her NAB worksheet example. Note how she tailored her skills to the needs of this employer. Remember, your resume has to be intriguing enough so you'll be called for an interview. A clear explanation of relevant achievements demonstrates to the employer that hiring you will solve the company's problem.

The NAB Process

Need—What does the employer need or want?

Action—How have you demonstrated that you can fulfill the employer's needs?

Benefit—What's the result?

1. **Need.** Find out what the employer needs or wants. Read job descriptions and advertisements, conduct research, and talk to employees to identify the specific needs or wants of the employer. Examples of employee skills an employer needs:

   Is detail oriented

   Knows how to troubleshoot Microsoft Office products

   Communicates well with others

2. **Action.** Select from your past experience, endeavors, accomplishments, and education the skills that demonstrate your ability to meet these needs. As you record past accomplishments, ask yourself, "What needed to be done? What action did I take?" List accomplishments that demonstrate your ability to meet the needed skill. Use action verbs; refer to page 201 for a list of action verbs. Your examples may come from your education, work experience, or volunteer activities. Don't forget to include examples from your internships, college club activities, community service projects, and class projects. Examples of actions include:

   Developed PowerPoint presentations

   Led team to complete report on time

   Organized fund-raising activity

3. **Benefit.** "What was the benefit of your action?" Examine each of your actions; when possible, quantify the result using percentages, dollars, numbers, and time. For example:

   Developed a new filing system *for faster access to information.*

   Created a marketing plan that *increased profits by 10 percent.*

   Designed a new office procedure *that is more responsive to customers.*

   Also, indicate in your resume where you demonstrated the skills. List the employer, volunteer activity, school project, internship, and so on.

Getting Organized—Building the Framework

Through the NAB process, you have identified the major content of your resume. You will put this content into a format that works for you. There are many different ways to write a resume. You will find that recruiters and job-hunting books have their own opinions. Although format and content can vary, your resume has to personally represent you. Every resume also contains common elements. Employers expect to find out your qualifications—what skills, abilities, and competencies you offer. Presenting a resume that is neat, concise, and easy to read helps you stand out from the crowd and create a lasting impression.

Don't worry about being the most qualified. Often, very qualified people write poorly designed resumes, limiting their chances for interviews. The reverse is also true—applicants whose qualifications are not as strong can make the interview list with a well-designed resume.

The categories in your resume can vary, depending upon your experience. The resume of a recent college graduate should be structured differently than that of someone who has several years of relevant work

RESUME ESSENTIALS

- Identifying information
- Job objective or career summary
- Education
- Work experience

Activity 8.1 NAB Worksheet

Catherine's Example:

Need	Action (use action verbs)	Benefit	Where
Detail-oriented	Maintained accounts receivable	Reduced delinquent accounts by 20%	Accounting clerk
Excel	Created reports	Improved tracking of accounts receivable	Accounting clerk
Tracking budget & expenditures	Managed spreadsheet database in Lotus 1-2-3 As Treasurer of Young Republicans Club, tracked & wrote budget reports Calculated daily sales	Accurate reports Helped raise 20% more dollars Sales information reports were accurate	Accounting clerk YR club Sales associate
Develop brochures	Created fund-raiser flyer	Raised $1,800 for association	Intern
Implement trade show	Canvassed local residents for reelection campaign	Persuading the public	YR club
Trade show	Coordinated marketing plan	Successful trade show—developed new partnerships	Intern
Support product management process	Initiated marketing strategy Developed marketing display	Identified new markets Increased jean sales by 50%	Sales associate
Highly motivated	Developed monthly plans to increase sales Implemented new accounting procedure Worked full-time while in school with high GPA	Increased sales and profits; often exceeded quota Increased process efficiency Graduated with honors	All jobs & school
Communication skills	Presented monthly treasurer reports	Updated membership on financial status	Speech club treasurer
Forecast market trends	Wrote paper forecasting market trends in publishing	Received an A	Marketing class
Teamwork	Facilitated group discussions; kept group focused	Received an A on class project	Marketing class

Instructions: Using a job description and other information, write in the needs and wants of the employer in the column labeled NEED. In the column labeled ACTION, write down how you demonstrated each skill or knowledge. In the column labeled BENEFIT, describe the results you achieved—the benefit of using your skill. Last, write down where you demonstrated the skill, so you can include it on your resume.

Your Turn:

Need	**Action** (use action verbs)	**Benefit**	**Where**

FIGURE 8.1 *Catherine Bolivia's resume.*

Catherine Bolivia
120 Stapley Street
San Francisco, California 94105
(415) 352-6834/cbolivia@hotmail.com

Career Objective Marketing Assistant position involving market research and analysis

Education
2002
B.S. in Business Administration, emphasis in Marketing, Golden Gate University, San Francisco, CA
- Cumulative GPA 3.8
- Course work focused on market research, forecasting market trends, and market analysis

Catherine emphasizes her education and course work related to her career objective.

Work Experience

3/2001–Present
Gap, Inc., San Francisco, CA
Sales Associate
- Developed marketing strategy and identified new markets
- Designed marketing display that increased jean sales by 50%
- Developed monthly plans to increase sales, resulting in increased profits
- Calculated daily sales and created accurate sales reports

8/2001–12/2001
American Heart Association, San Francisco, CA
Intern
- Created fund-raiser publicity, raising $1,800
- Coordinated trade show marketing plan, resulting in new corporate sponsors
- Assisted in research and prepared data and figures for reports to Board of Directors

3/1998–2000
Crate and Barrel, San Francisco, CA
Accounting Clerk
- Maintained accounts receivable, reduced delinquent accounts by 20%
- Improved tracking of accounts receivable by creating reports using Excel software
- Implemented new accounting procedure, increasing accounting process efficiency

In her descriptions, Catherine tells what she did and the results or benefits.

Computer Skills Microsoft Word, Excel, PowerPoint

Honors and Activities
National Honor Society, 2000, 2001
Speech Club Treasurer, 1999
Peer Tutor in Accounting Principles, 1999–2000
Young Republicans Club Treasurer, 1998

REAL-LIFE PERSPECTIVE

What Recruiters Agree On About Resumes

1. Use correct grammar and spelling—they are a MUST for employers.
2. Include accurate telephone number and address information.
3. Include dates of employment, including months as well as years.
4. Include a cover letter that tells how you heard about the position and why you are a good choice.
5. Be honest. Recruiters are very adept at reading between the lines.
6. Target your resume to the position for which you are applying.
7. Keep your resume to no more than two pages, preferably one.
8. *Don't* write an objective that tells what *you* want from the employer.
9. Describe actual achievements instead of listing lots of job responsibilities. Employers want to know about your accomplishments—what have you done and how well you did it.
10. "References Available upon Request" can be eliminated.

experience. Review these resume samples, noting the differences. These are just a few of the different types of formats you might use for your resume.

The sample resume in Figure 8.2 belongs to a person who already has related work experience. Michael Jones returned to school and obtained his degree while working in the accounting field. He used a summary to highlight his accounting skills, followed by his work experience that emphasized his ability to impact business processes. His education and computer training came last.

As a college student, Jerome Blakesley chose to begin his resume with a career summary, immediately followed by his experience (see Figure 8.3). Jerome has not graduated from college yet, so he listed his anticipated date of graduation and included his high school education. Although Jerome has worked at other jobs for short amounts of time, he has chosen to only list work that is relevant to his job search. He included activities, both in high school and college, that demonstrate his skills. Near the end of his resume is a special category, "Activities and Awards," where he listed his professional memberships and special achievements.

As a recent technical graduate, Kesha Moore began her resume with a job objective, followed by her education (see Figure 8.4). Because her work experience in electronics is very limited, she chose to highlight the skills she learned in school.

Jennifer DiCarlo is a graduating senior. As she has very limited work experience, she chose to use her resume to highlight her skills (see Figure 8.5). Jennifer listed the projects she completed in college, grouping them by types of engineering work. This allows an employer to easily see that she gained practical experience in these specific engineering areas while in school.

Websites to Help You Write a Resume

www.resume-place.com/jobs/

www.damngood.com

www.eresumes.com (online advice)

www.stetson.edu/hauser/writing.html

FIGURE 8.2 *Michael Jones's resume.*

Michael E. Jones

3438 East Monroe
Portland, Oregon 97231
503-888-5909/meg99@aol.com

You can use key words in a summary. It tells more about you than an objective.

Summary

Accounting professional with five years of experience in the manufacturing and service industries. Proficient in financial reporting, budgeting, and variance analysis for public corporations. Proven leadership and management skills.

Experience

He describes relevant skills and explains the benefits.

2002–present **Senior Accountant**

Metramex, Inc. Phoenix, AZ

Responsible for monthly financial reporting analysis and consolidating for 15 branch offices with total revenue of $50 million. Coordinated accounting staff in Phoenix, Arizona, and Fairfax, Virginia. Implemented and supervised accounting procedures for new acquisitions and branches.

- Organized accounting systems during an aggressive growth period, improving access to accounting information.
- Increased communication between branch management and corporate office, increasing efficiency and decreasing the length of the closing process by four hours per week.
- Assisted with transition to new payroll system.
- Provided accurate and on-time accounting reports to meet due diligence requirements for purchase of eight corporations.

2000–2002 **Senior Accountant**

Jackson Controls, Inc. Phoenix, AZ

Assisted in financial statement preparation, planning, and variance analysis. Controlled administration of accounting system. Trained and supervised accounting staff. Prepared property tax and sales tax returns.

- Created and implemented new system for accounting and consolidation of information from manufacturing plant in Ensenada, Mexico.
- Organized and administrated duties related to financial statements audits, decreasing the length of audits by improving the organization and filing system.

1997–2000 **Consultant**

Robert A. Jones, CPA Phoenix, AZ

Prepared personal and corporate income tax forms, financial reports, and advised a variety of clients to improve their financial position.

1996–1997 **Beverage Controller**

Marriott Corporation Scottsdale, AZ

Supervised beverage service teams. Provided training for all resort staff. Monitored and controlled resort beverage inventory. Responsible for departmental budgeting and variance analysis.

Education

CPA Candidate, November 2002

2001 **Bachelor of Science in Accounting**

Arizona State University Tempe, AZ

Here's another place to put key words.

Computer Training

IBM-compatible PC and client/server systems, Great Plains Dynamics, Microsoft Windows NT, Excel, Word, PowerPoint, Quicken, Peachtree, Lotus, Lacert, Cyma

Jerome L. Blakesley's resume. FIGURE 8.3

Jerome L. Blakesley

32 S. Dorsey Lake Road (480) 657-9000
Tempe, AZ 85002 jblakesley@amug.org

Jerome describes relevant skills.

CAREER SUMMARY

Broadcasting professional experienced in hosting daily radio show and weekly television talk show. Proven ability to increase viewership through program development. Strengths include:

- Extemporary speaking abilities
- Fluent in Spanish
- Outstanding written and oral communication skills

PROFESSIONAL EXPERIENCE

Disc Jockey, KASR 1260 AM 2/2002–present
Arizona State University, Tempe, AZ
Followed station music format. Trained disc jockeys. Promoted station and advertisers.

- Produced short promotion clips.
- Assisted in development of new format for morning show, increasing audience by 15%.

Floor Manager, Grady Gammage Auditorium 12/2001–present
Arizona State University, Tempe, AZ
Assisted in managing activities in theater. Supervised ushers and greeted patrons.

Host/Producer, The Forum-Live Campus Talk Show 9/2000–5/2001
Arizona State University, Tempe, AZ
Organized and directed interviews, discussions, and debates for weekly show. Served as liaison with guests and specialists. Developed schedules, setting future interviews and determining content.

- Increased viewership by 20%.

Features Editor/Staff Reporter, Ashes Newspaper 9/1998–6/2000
Chaparral High School, Scottsdale, AZ
Researched, interviewed, and wrote stories on relevant topics. Edited copy for the Features Section. Conducted opinion polls.

- Received state award for outstanding feature article, 1999.

EDUCATION

Bachelor of Arts, Broadcasting Anticipated, May 2004
Walter Cronkite School of Journalism and Telecommunications, Arizona State University, Tempe, AZ

Because some jobs didn't last long, he puts dates on the right side so they are less noticeable.

ACTIVITIES AND AWARDS

National Academy of Television Arts & Sciences, member, 2000–present
Gamma Beta Phi, Honor Society, member, 2002
Speech and Debate, award winner for dramatic interpretations, 2001, 2002
National Thespian Society, active member, 2000–present
Dean's list, 2001, 2002
Sophomore Star Award, academic excellence at ASU

He highlights his education achievements

SKILLS

Language: Fluent in Spanish, familiar with Hebrew
Computer: Windows, MAC, DOS, MS Word, and Excel

FIGURE 8.4 *Kesha Moore's resume.*

430 North Monroe
Southridge, SC 45701

Home 415 893-7800
Cell 415 667-9870
kesha.moore@scnet.com

Kesha Moore

Objective To obtain a technical position in the electronics industry.

Education May 2003

Associate in Computer Technology

Alpha Technical Institute

Southridge, SC

GPA 4.0

Kesha highlights the skills she learned in her technical training program.

Technical Skills **Circuit configuration and troubleshooting:**

Analog and digital circuitry

Reading schematics

Network operating systems and networking protocols: LAN/WAN, TCP/IP, ATM

Operating Systems: Linux, Sun Solaris, and Windows

A+ certification

CCNA-Certified Cisco Network Analyst

Work History 8/2002–present

Tech Assistant

AML Cable Electronics Southridge, SC

- Assisted technicians in troubleshooting cable converter boxes operating DMM, oscilloscope, and Spectrum analyzer.
- Accurately repaired units following technician instructions.
- Secured parts in place by solder, bolts, crimps, epoxy, and similar methods.

3/2001–8/2002

Cashier

Taco Bell Southridge, SC

- Greeted customers and filled orders.
- Operated cash register.

Jennifer DiCarlo's resume. FIGURE 8.5

JENNIFER DICARLO

OBJECTIVE

To obtain a civil or environmental engineering position.

EDUCATION

B.S. in Engineering, Civil & Environmental Engineering, May 2000
Arizona State University, Tempe, AZ
GPA 3.26/4.0, Dean's List 3 semesters

SKILLS

- Software—MS Word, Excel, PowerPoint, FileMaker Pro, Aldus PageMaker, Kaleidograph, NetScape, and Word Perfect
- Languages—WWW hypertext language and BASIC

Jennifer describes engineering projects she completed in college.

PROJECTS

Steel Structures—Designed various angles, channels, columns, and frames under given design criteria.

Structural Analysis—Designed a truss and frame bridge to span 18-foot gulch supporting a load of 5,000 lb/ft 2. GS-USA software utilized for final checks.

Senior Design Project—"College Avenue Traffic Calming and Pedestrian Bridge Improvement Plan" to solve parking congestion, increase safety, improve aesthetics, and reduce volume and speed on actual road in Tempe. Plan included modifications to pedestrian bridge to meet ADA specifications. Completed cost estimations, proposal, and AUTO CAD drawings.

Surveying—Performed a building layout, including elevations, contours, location of trees, lines, and sidewalks, submitting project as blueprint with title block and legal description.

Highway—Designed a 2-lane highway section with an intersection. Design included critical and horizontal curves, drainage culverts, and cut/fill calculations.

Geotechnical/Foundations—Designed a retaining wall, including wall profile, back-fill properties, lateral earth pressure, and cost estimates.

WORK EXPERIENCE

Administrative Assistant
2/2002 to present
Industrial Associates Program, Arizona State University, Tempe, AZ

- Created and updated Internet home page.
- Designed PowerPoint presentations for papers and conferences.
- Assisted in collection, tabulation, and presentation of data.

12345 MAIN STREET • TEMPE, ARIZONA 12345-6789 • PHONE (123) 456-7890
FAX (123) 098-7654 • E-MAIL JENN@MYCOMPANY.ORG

Writing Your Resume

IDENTIFYING INFORMATION

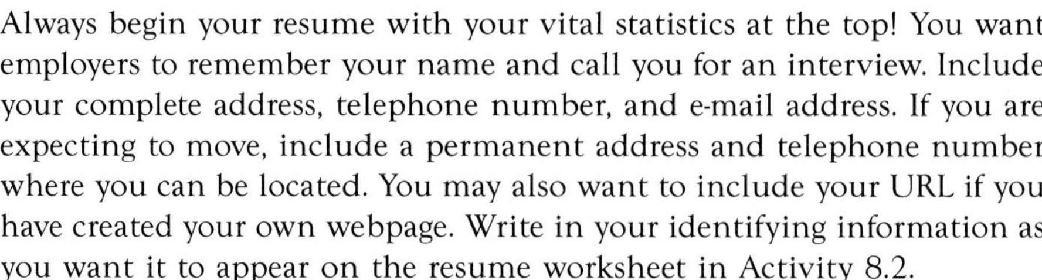

Always begin your resume with your vital statistics at the top! You want employers to remember your name and call you for an interview. Include your complete address, telephone number, and e-mail address. If you are expecting to move, include a permanent address and telephone number where you can be located. You may also want to include your URL if you have created your own webpage. Write in your identifying information as you want it to appear on the resume worksheet in Activity 8.2.

JOB OBJECTIVE OR CAREER SUMMARY

Your objective is the career goal you are pursuing. The body of your resume will prove your ability to meet this goal.

Your resume will start with a job objective or career summary. Most recent graduates use job objectives to begin their resumes. However, once you have a few years of relevant work experience, a career summary highlights your strengths more effectively.

Many people don't bother to write job objectives or career summaries. Imagine that you're an employer needing to hire an accountant who will manage the accounts payable department. You're comparing two resumes to decide who to interview. Both are recent college graduates with a similar work history. One resume begins, "Job Objective: A position in accounting where I can use my accounts payable experience." The other resume doesn't list a job objective. Which resume are you most likely to toss aside? Certainly, a job objective or career summary is not essential to gain an interview; however, a well-written objective or summary sends the message that you know what type of work you are looking for. Candidates who articulate clear job goals win out over people who say they'll do anything—every time.

USE A JOB OBJECTIVE IF:

- You don't have two or three years of experience directly relating to the position
- You are changing careers and your work experience doesn't match

Job objective. Describe the position, profession, or field of work you are looking for. Identifying your career interest immediately shows employers that there's a match between your objectives and their need. Often, people write objectives describing what they want: "Desire a position that allows me to utilize my strengths and offers challenging opportunities for growth." Every candidate wants an exciting, challenging, growth-oriented position. There are few applicants for stagnant, boring, dead-end positions. Employers aren't interested in what you want from them. Instead, focus on what *you* can offer to the employer.

USE A CAREER SUMMARY IF:

- You have relevant work experience, even if it's from working part-time while in college

Career summary. The career summary briefly describes, in one or two sentences, your strengths and experience. A recruiter can read the top of your resume and immediately see your strengths and abilities. Because your career summary does not describe specific jobs, skills that you cannot list under work experience can be highlighted here. For example, Meiko has learned how to read schematics as part of her education; however, she has not had the opportunity to read schematics at work or in an internship. By including "skilled at reading schematics" in her summary, Meiko can make sure employers know immediately that she can demonstrate that skill. Often, summaries describe the number of years of experience you have in the field; however, it's not necessary if you have less than three years of experience.

Tip: Refer back to Chapter 7 to your one-minute commercial to write your career summary.

Go to Activity 8.2 and write your job objective or career summary. *Tip:* If you're targeting two very different career options, you may have to write two different resumes with different job objectives or career summaries to match each goal.

EDUCATION

If you are a recent graduate without relevant work experience, your education should follow your job objective or career summary. It's always a good idea to start with your most important qualifications. Usually, job hunters with relevant job experience will list their education after their work history. Resumes for professions that require specific degrees or certifications, like a teacher or CPA, usually start off with education at the top of the resume, regardless of years of experience.

Begin your education description with your most recent college degree and work backward. Include your degree, major, date of graduation or expected date of graduation, school, and location. You may wish to include information about specific course work if it's specifically relevant to the position you are seeking. Don't just list classes; instead, cite what you learned or achieved.

It's optional whether to include your GPA. If you have a 4.0 or are on the Dean's list, that's an accomplishment to include. Otherwise, it won't matter much from an employer's point of view. Employers are much more interested in what you learned in school that will apply toward the work you're looking for.

It is no longer necessary to include your high school education, once you have completed your college degree, unless it is highly relevant. For instance, if you attended a high school magnet program specializing in the arts and are now looking for a job in theater, your high school education should be included.

Objective Examples

Objective: An entry-level marketing position in retailing.

Job Goal: Graphic designer with strong skills in PhotoShop and Adobe Illustrator.

Job Objective: Sales representative in the pharmaceutical industry.

Job Goal: To obtain an entry-level engineering position that will utilize my technical education and my ability to contribute to a team.

Employment Objective: An entry-level finance position in the oil and gas industry.

Career Summary Examples

- Over three years of accounting experience in the retail and hotel industries. Skilled at accounts receivable and accounts payable. Strengths include:
  - Attention to detail
  - Adaptable and flexible
  - Excellent work ethic
  - Knowledge of Great Plains and SAP systems
- Over four years of electronics experience in manufacturing, assembly, and service. Demonstrated aptitude for resolving technical problems and establishing employee relations. Highly skilled in the following areas:
  - Troubleshooting
  - Customer relations
  - Basic electronics
  - Ability to learn independently
  - Test equipment operations
  - Organizational skills
  - Reading blueprints
  - Reading schematics
- Webpage designer, skilled at creating innovative, user-friendly sites to expand sales of products or services. Strengths include knowledge of HTML, graphic design, and database programs.

If you haven't completed your college degree yet, it's important to show your high school education. If you're beginning to look for work prior to graduation, it's fine to list your anticipated date of graduation. If you are over 40 years old, you may wish to omit the date you graduated from high school. Dates automatically show your age and may encourage age discrimination.

If you have attended specialized training, this may also be included under education. Expand the label of this section to "Education and Training." Include any relevant employer-sponsored training, courses in computer training, certifications, and so on. Include the title of the training, the location, and the date.

List your education and training in Activity 8.2.

WORK EXPERIENCE

This category gives you the opportunity to discuss real-world experience. Begin with your most recent work experience and work backward, describing each type of work. Include all types of employment, including part-time work, volunteer positions, and internships.

For each position, include:

- Dates of employment (month and year)
- Name of employer and location (city and state)
- Your position title

Review your NAB worksheet and list your accomplishments for each position in Activity 8.2.

Use action verb statements to describe the skills and competencies you used, emphasizing the results; refer to the action verb list that follows. Begin each statement with a verb, describing for the reader what you can do. For example, *motivated* students to improve reading skills, *organized* and *taught* educational seminars, *designed* and *implemented* accounting process. Describe your experience with concrete words rather than vague descriptions. For example, it's better to use *researched environmental issues* than *responsible for researching, organizing . . .* Remember, the person or computer reading your resume doesn't know you (most likely) and can't easily make assumptions about your resume. Provide detailed evidence of your accomplishments to help the employer better understand your experience.

Education Examples

CURRENTLY ATTENDING SCHOOL, WITH ANTICIPATED GRADUATION

2002–Present	Currently attending Rio Salado College, Phoenix, AZ AAS in Computer Electronics anticipated in September 2004 Currently maintaining 4.0 GPA and perfect attendance while working full-time
2001	Graduated Moosehead Senior High, Moosehead, AK

COLLEGE GRADUATE (DOESN'T INCLUDE HIGH SCHOOL)

2003	BS in Biology, Kansas State University, Manhattan, KS Specialized studies in genetic applications

ADDITIONAL INFORMATION

This optional category can be titled in many different ways. Once you have described your education or work experience, you may want to include other information you believe would strengthen your resume. Are there any accomplishments on your NAB worksheet that you haven't included? If so, use this section to describe honors and activities, technical skills, volunteer work, and/or membership in professional associations. Do not include personal interests and religious or political affiliations.

Action Verb List

Accomplish
Achieve
Adapt
Administer
Advertise
Advise
Affect
Analyze
Anticipate
Apply
Approach
Approve
Arrange
Assemble
Assess
Assign
Assist
Budget
Build
Calculate
Catalog
Chair
Clarify
Collaborate
Communicate
Compare
Conceive
Conceptualize
Conduct
Construct
Consult
Contract
Contribute
Control
Coordinate
Counsel
Create
Decide
Define
Delegate
Demonstrate
Design
Detail
Determine
Develop
Devise
Direct
Distribute
Draft
Edit
Educate
Employ
Encourage
Enlarge
Enlist
Establish
Estimate
Evaluate
Examine
Exchange
Execute
Expand
Expedite
Facilitate
Familiarize
Forecast
Formulate
Generate
Govern
Guide
Handle
Hire
Identify
Implement
Improve
Increase
Index
Influence
Inform
Initiate
Innovate
Inspect
Install
Institute
Instruct
Integrate
Interpret
Interview
Invent
Investigate
Lead
Maintain
Manage
Manipulate
Market
Mediate
Merchandise
Moderate
Modify
Monitor
Motivate
Negotiate
Obtain
Operate
Organize
Originate
Participate
Perceive
Perform
Persuade
Plan
Prepare
Present
Preside
Problem solve
Process
Produce
Program
Project
Promote
Prompt
Propose
Provide
Publicize
Publish
Recommend
Reconcile
Recruit
Rectify
Redesign
Relate
Renew
Report
Represent
Research
Reshape
Resolve
Review
Revise
Scan
Schedule
Screen
Secure
Select
Serve
Staff
Standardize
Stimulate
Strengthen
Suggest
Summarize
Supervise
Survey
Systematize
Taught
Team build
Train
Update
Utilize
Verify
Write

What Gets Noticed by Employers—Resume Writing Do's and Don'ts

DO'S

Begin sentences with action verbs. Use words such as created, designed, directed, implemented, and managed.

Keep your sentences short and concise. Use simple phrases that can be easily understood. For example, instead of *engaged in problem-solving strategies,* use *solved problems.*

Be truthful. Represent yourself accurately, resisting any temptation to exaggerate your experience. Employers often verify resume information. If you stretch the truth on your resume, they assume dishonesty in other matters also.

Tailor your resume to the job you're seeking. Employers want to know if you fit their position. Show how your education and experience relate.

Emphasize your accomplishments. Employers want to know how well you accomplished a task, not a list of your responsibilities.

Include skills and knowledge that you can demonstrate in your new work, even if you have not been paid to perform the skill. Employers want to know what you can do, not just what you've been paid to do in the past.

DON'TS

Avoid using the first-person pronoun I. The reader already knows whom you are talking about.

Avoid professional jargon. Don't assume your reader will automatically understand words, phrases, and acronyms that are common to your work but not to people outside the industry. Be careful about using abbreviations and words that are too trendy.

Don't include your picture.

Don't include experience that is over 10 years old. Unless the experience is directly relevant (such as if you worked for the company you're applying to more than 10 years ago), leave it off.

Don't emphasize your past experience if it doesn't relate. Instead, highlight your skills that apply to the position you're seeking.

Omit job responsibilities that you've had in the past that you no longer want to perform. For example, Mary no longer wants to supervise others, so she doesn't mention that she supervised three people in her last position.

Looks Count

There's no need to buy a resume-writing word processing program. It's easy to make your resume professional using any word processing program. Many word processing programs include resume templates. Although these may provide a distinctive graphic look, they are often inflexible. Most people are better off using a plain, professional format. Follow these guidelines for an attractive, winning look.

- **Choose standard bond paper.** Use ivory, white, or light gray paper; stay away from exotic colors. Use the same stationery for your cover letter and references.
- **Use lots of white space.** Make your resume easy to read. Use consistent margins throughout for a clean look; set all margins for at least one inch.

Additional Information Examples

Honors—What awards have you received that are relevant to your work goal?

Employee of the Month, June 2002, Avnet

National Merit Scholar, 2001

Volunteer Achievement Award, Big Brothers, 2001

Captain of National Championship Team, 2000

Technical Skills—What technical skill sets are relevant to your work goal? You can group your skills by category.

Computer Skills	*Languages*
MS Office	Perl
Goldmine	HTML
MS Access	Basic

Troubleshooting

LAN/WAN environments

Component level electronics

Volunteer Activities—What volunteer activities would employers be interested in knowing about? (Avoid religious and ethnic affiliations).

Member of City Planning Committee, 2002

Big Brother volunteer, 1999, 2000–2002

Valley Youth Soccer League, coach 1999–2001

Professional Associations—What professional groups do you belong to?

American Society for Training and Development

AIESEC (The International Association of Students in Economics and Management)

Activities and Interests—What interests do you have that are relevant to your work goal?

Strong understanding of Latin American cultural issues

Exchange Student, Lima, Peru, 2002

- **Stick to basic fonts.** Use two fonts—one sans serif font, like Arial or Helvetica, that can be used for your name and category titles, and one easy-to-read serif font, like Garamond or Times. Either 10-point or 12-point type is fine. Bold your headings and your name, but avoid italics and underlining.
- **Check to see if you addressed key skills and knowledge.** The employer emphasized certain skills and knowledge in the job description; make use of them in your resume.
- **Proofread, proofread, proofread!!!** Pay careful attention to spelling, punctuation, grammar, and writing style. Don't send the message that you don't pay attention to details by including misspellings and grammatical errors.
- **Invite other people to proofread your resume.** The more eyes you have reading your resume and identifying any mistakes before it goes out to employers, the better. We've found that there's almost always at least one mistake you don't find until much later.

UPDATING YOUR RESUME

Every time you change jobs, inquire about opportunities, or update your accomplishments, you'll have to update your resume. It's recommended that you update your resume every six months. Keeping track of new knowledge, new skills, and recent accomplishments can seem over-

REAL-LIFE PERSPECTIVE

LOOKS COUNT

"I was sitting on an airplane next to a recruiter who was hiring managers for a rapidly expanding healthy fast-food chain. He had received a Fed Ex package of resumes that he was reviewing on this one-hour flight. The stack was at least three inches thick. As he started to flip through these resumes and quickly decide who to weed out, it became apparent how many people rely on Microsoft Word templates to do their resumes. At least two-thirds of the resumes looked exactly the same—which makes it very difficult to stand out from the crowd."

whelming, especially when the most difficult part of writing your resume is remembering and organizing the information.

WRITING A SCANNABLE RESUME

When you write a resume for the computer to read, you want it to be *scannable.* With the latest in technology, companies are turning more and more to the electronic process of scanning resumes. Here's how it works. Your resume is scanned into the computer as an image. Then, optical character recognition software examines the image to distinguish every letter and number (characters) and creates a text file. Artificial intelligence then "reads" the text and extracts the important information about you, such as your name, address, telephone number, work experience, education, and skills. The information is stored in databases organized by particular occupations and retrieved when an opening

Tips for Resume Scanning

The computer is programmed to search for nouns instead of verbs. It will search for degrees, titles, organizations, and other information specific to a particular job. For example, if you are applying for a position in software sales, the computer may scan resumes looking for particular software systems (SAP, Great Plains) and job titles (software salesperson, account representative).

- Use white paper printed on one side only.
- Don't condense spacing between letters or lines.
- Use standard typefaces and fonts between 12 and 14 points in size.
- Mail flat—creases from folding make it difficult to scan clearly.
- Place your name, address, and telephone number at the top of the first page, and your name should appear as the first text on subsequent pages.
- Avoid fancy italics, underlines, and shadows. Unlike a human, the computer becomes confused with an eye-catching resume.
- Shoot for simplicity.
- Avoid vertical and horizontal lines, graphics, and boxes.

To E-mail Your Resume

- Save your resume in your word processing program as a *text only* document. Then, open the file to view what your e-mail will look like. Correct any odd spacing by removing unwanted paragraph returns, etc.
- To emphasize your name and headings, use CAPS, as bolding and italics won't show up in e-mail.
- Find out if they will accept attachments. If not, copy and paste your resume into the body of the e-mail.
- Don't forget to include a cover letter with your e-mailed resume.

becomes available. The computer searches the database for *hits.* These are *keywords* it has been programmed to search for and *match* to a certain position. The chance of your resume appearing on a screen read by human eyes depends on the number of keywords the scanner hits. To maximize your chances for computer hits, use many keywords to define your skills and abilities, work experience, education, and academic achievements. Savvy people create two versions of their resumes: one with a scannable format the computer can read, and one that is more graphically appealing for human readers.

REAL-LIFE PERSPECTIVE

RESUME BLUNDERS

- "I have learnt Word Perfect 6.0 computer and spreadsheet programs."
- "Received a plague for Salesperson of the Year."
- "Wholly responsible for two (2) failed financial institutions."
- "Reason for leaving last job: maturity leave."
- "Failed bar exam with relatively high scores."
- "It's best for employers that I not work with people."
- "Let's meet, so you can 'ooh' and 'aah' over my experience."
- "You will want me to be Head Honcho in no time."
- "Am a perfectionist and rarely if ever forget details."
- "I was working with my mom until she decided to move."
- "I have an excellent track record, although I am not a horse."
- "I have become completely paranoid, trusting completely no one and absolutely nothing."
- "My goal is meteorology. But since I possess no training in meteorology, I suppose I should try stock brokerage."
- "I procrastinate, especially when the task is unpleasant."
- "Instrumental in ruining entire operation for a Midwest chain store."

Source: Samples come from real resumes and cover letters. Reprinted from the July 21, 1997, issue of *Fortune* by special permission.

Activity 8.2 Resume Worksheet

IDENTIFYING INFORMATION

Name ______________________________

Mailing address

____

____

____

Permanent mailing address

____

____

____

E-mail ______________________________

URL ______________________________

Home telephone ______________________________

Message phone ______________________________

Work phone ______________________________

JOB OBJECTIVE

____

____

____

CAREER SUMMARY

____

____

____

____

____

____

EDUCATION

College ______________________________ City, state ______________________________

Degree ______________________________ Graduation date ______________________________

Honors ______________________________

Specialized studies ______________________________

College ______________________________ City, state ______________________________

Degree ______________________________ Graduation date ______________________________

Honors ______________________________

Specialized studies ______________________________

High School ______ City, state ______

Degree ______ Graduation date ______

Honors ______

Specialized studies ______

SPECIALIZED TRAINING

Course ______

City, state ______ Date ______

Certifications ______

Course ______

City, state ______ Date ______

Certifications ______

Course ______

City, state ______ Date ______

Certifications ______

Course ______

City, state ______ Date ______

Certifications ______

Course ______

City, state ______ Date ______

Certifications ______

WORK EXPERIENCE (START WITH MOST CURRENT EMPLOYER.)

Job title ______ Employer ______

City, state ______ Dates of employment ______

Accomplishments (Use action verbs and show results. Quantify whenever possible.)

______

______

______

______

______

Job title ______ Employer ______

City, state ______ Dates of employment ______

Accomplishments (Use action verbs and show results. Quantify whenever possible.)

Job title ______________________ Employer ______________________

City, state ______________________ Dates of employment ______________________

Accomplishments (Use action verbs and show results. Quantify whenever possible.)

Job title ______________________ Employer ______________________

City, state ______________________ Dates of employment ______________________

Accomplishments (Use action verbs and show results. Quantify whenever possible.)

ADDITIONAL INFORMATION

Professional affiliations ______________________

Specialized skills ______________________

Other ______________________

Writing a Cover Letter That Works

Whenever you send a resume, include a cover letter. A well-constructed cover letter allows you to sell yourself to a specific employer. Cover letters include details that you can't put on your resume. In your cover letter, write about what you know about this company, what you find interesting about this position, and how your background and experience specifically fit. Describe to the employer specific ways that hiring you will benefit the company.

"I look for a well-written cover letter that is not simply a re-hash of the resume. It's the opportunity for the individual to show a little personality and demonstrate that they know a little bit about my organization, or at least that they read my ad."

SUSAN KENNEDY, Director of Human Resources, New York Academy of Science

If you are mailing a cover letter, always use high-quality paper, the same color as your resume. Don't forget to include a cover letter even if you're e-mailing or faxing your resume. If you are faxing your resume, the cover letter may be typed on the cover sheet. In all cases, your letter should be typed, using a standard format, with proper headings, with correct spelling and grammar, and with paragraphs that are brief and concise.

Find out where to send your letter and to whom. If you're answering an ad, you may not know the name of the person or the company. Then, the letter may be addressed to "To Whom It May Concern." Otherwise, if you don't know the person's name, call the company and ask. You're more likely to get results if you send your letter directly to the person doing the hiring. Make sure you get the correct spelling of the person's name, title, and address.

Using these steps to write your cover letter will increase your chances of getting the interview opportunities.

PARAGRAPH ONE—THE INTRODUCTION

The introduction provides your chance to grab readers and entice them to read on. Most cover letters are very boring reading. Find something interesting to say, and your letter will leap out from the stack recruiters are reviewing. This is not necessarily easy, but it's worth the extra effort. Some career counselors estimate that applicants can expect 1 interview for every 60 resumes they mail out. You can beat these odds by investing time and effort in a good cover letter. Fortunately, because so many cover letters are so poorly written, it's not too difficult to stand out from the crowd. Talk about the position you are seeking, how you learned about the position, and whatever it is that interests you most about the position.

Catherine Bolivia wrote the cover letter in Figure 8.6 to reply to a specific ad in the newspaper. Note how she researched the company on the Internet to find a good way to open her letter and gain the reader's attention. A colleague referred Jennifer DiCarlo to Ms. Owens, so she gets the reader's attention by mentioning the mutual contact in the first paragraph (see Figure 8.7).

Ideas to Start Off Cover Letters

- Drop names—who do you know that they know?
- Let them know you've done your homework. Say something specific about the company that you've found out from your research.
- Share your approach to work. Describe how you fit in with their work environment.
- State specifically why you want to work for this company.
- Go back and review the NAB process. Choose a story that directly relates to this position.
- Describe how your skills fit with their needs.

PARAGRAPH TWO—THE BODY OF THE LETTER

Use the body of the letter to emphasize your experience and its relevancy to the specific position. Repeat the qualifications that the employer is looking for, demonstrating that you are a good fit for this position. Cite accomplishments as they relate to the desired characteristics. List particular skills and academic achievements that demonstrate you are a good match for the job.

In her cover letter, Catherine Bolivia discusses her degree and experience as it relates to the marketing position she wants. She describes how her internship specifically prepared her with the necessary skills the employer is looking for.

Although Kesha Moore (see Figure 8.8) is a recent graduate with minimal work experience, she is able to show how her skills relate to the job and write a strong letter demonstrating the job fit.

PARAGRAPH THREE—THE CLOSING

End your cover letter with an active strategy to get the interview. Tell the reader that you will call to set up a convenient time to meet and discuss your qualifications further. Thank the reader for the time and consideration. Remember to follow up with a telephone call!

RESPONDING TO BLIND ADS

Ads in the newspaper often do not divulge the name of the employer. Some of these ads may not be bona fide job openings. They may be from companies trying to determine a salary range for a position. A company may be replacing a person who has not yet been notified. It's risky to apply for a position when you don't know the company. If you decide to apply, you obviously can't write a dynamic cover letter.

Developing a Portfolio

A portfolio is a portable collection of your best work samples, project summaries, articles about you, articles you've written, videos, diskettes, and personal performance evaluations. Although portfolios are required for visual arts and graphic design positions, they may be an option you want to consider for other types of positions. A portfolio might be contained in a zippered case, a notebook, or a presentation book. The key is to organize the material so that you can quickly find relevant examples to show an interviewer.

Portfolios should be used judiciously. In the limited time interviewers have, you'll only have a few minutes to answer questions or add specifics. Select from your portfolio items that match the desired competencies for the particular interview. Two approaches can be used in an interview to discuss your portfolio. One approach is to tell the interviewer up front that you have a portfolio and ask if you can show it. Or, you can wait

Catherine Bolivia's cover letter. FIGURE 8.6

120 Stapley Street
San Francisco, CA 94105
May 15, 2003

Ms. Diana Thomson
Director of Marketing
Optico Corporation
4333 West 56th Avenue
San Francisco, CA 94000

Dear Ms. Thomson:

The introduction of the FXY-203 at Optico must be creating exciting opportunities within the Marketing Department. After exploring the Optico website, it is apparent that Optico is marketing specifically to consumers for the first time. I would like to be part of this effort. You will require someone to develop marketing strategies that increase profits, as well as ensure that your marketing events are organized and within budget.

Recently, I completed a bachelor's degree in business administration with an emphasis in marketing. As my resume indicates, my degree, along with my work experience in sales and accounting, prepared me well for the specific tasks outlined in your job description. During my internship at the American Heart Association, I worked with a team to create the advertising materials for a direct marketing campaign. I researched the marketing data and recommended the targets of the campaign. I would like to use my skills to help you organize events that result in on-time, within-budget marketing solutions. If you are looking for a marketing assistant who is willing to work hard, is a team player, and will flourish in a creative environment, please consider me for the position.

I look forward to speaking with you further about my background and qualifications. I will call you during the week of May 19 to set up a convenient time to meet. Thank you for your consideration.

Sincerely,

Catherine Bolivia
cbolivia@hotmail.com

FIGURE 8.7 *Jennifer DiCarlo's cover letter.*

JENNIFER DICARLO

August 31, 2003

Ms. Jessica Owens
Director of Engineering
Bradford and Associates
4557 West London Road
Boston, MA 98700

Dear Ms. Owens,

Brad Peterman suggested that I contact you regarding an entry-level engineering position. I worked with Brad on my Senior Design Project. He was the primary engineer for the City of Tempe assigned to this traffic improvement issue. He felt there could be a good match between my skills and your firm. I am very interested in working for a firm with such a strong history of supporting women civil engineers.

I recently graduated from Arizona State University with a BS degree in Civil & Environmental Engineering. I have experience working on projects involving steel structures, surveying, highway design, and geotechnical foundations. My computer skills are excellent. I am familiar with most engineering software. People tell me I have a real aptitude to pick up technical computer programs quickly.

I grew up on the East Coast and would be very interested in relocating to the Boston area. I will call you next week to set up an appointment to discuss my qualifications in further detail. I am planning on being in the Boston area the second week of September. Thanks for your time and consideration.

Sincerely,

Jennifer DiCarlo
Attachment

12345 MAIN STREET • TEMPE, ARIZONA 12345-6789 • PHONE (123) 456-7890
FAX (123) 098-7654 • E-MAIL JENN@MYCOMPANY.ORG

Kesha Moore's cover letter. FIGURE 8.8

430 North Monroe
Southridge, SC 45701

Home 415 893-7800
Cell 415 667-9870
kesha.moore@scnet.org

Kesha Moore

September 22, 2003

Ms. Janet Iwaoka
Director of Information Technology
Southland Express
PO Box 43000
Southland, SC 67800

Dear Ms. Iwaoka,

As I was researching Southland Express, I was very impressed by the online services offered to your software users. However, customers who aren't technically inclined may prefer to call a live person who can walk them step by step through solutions. I can provide not only fast and accurate help desk services, but I also can make customers smile. I feel that I can become an outstanding help desk technician for these reasons:

- Through my online research, I identified your most common problems and already know how to solve many of them. As part of my AS Degree from Alpha Technical Institute, I became skilled at quickly identifying and solving software and hardware conflicts.
- I can help you develop repeat customers. I found that by learning my regular customers' names at Taco Bell and by providing genuinely friendly service, my customers consistently came back. I know how to smile across the phone.
- Count on me to always go the extra mile. Earning a 4.0 GPA while working full-time demonstrates my commitment and work ethic.
- Save money on training costs with a technician who is up-to-date on the most current technologies.

I recently graduated from Alpha Technical Institute with an Associate degree in Computer and Electronics Technology and am anxious to begin using my skills to help your customers. My attached resume details my abilities. Next week I will call you to discuss how I can help Southland Express provide outstanding customer service. Thanks for your time and consideration.

Regards,

Kesha Moore

until the skill demonstrated by an item in the portfolio emerges in the interview. Then, show the portfolio item and describe how the project reflects your ability in this area. If there isn't time to show your portfolio in the interview, ask the interviewer if you could leave it or send copies of items that are particularly relevant.

"Perhaps the biggest advantage of a portfolio is that it is tangible evidence of skill and achievements and provides an infrastructure to record your progress as a student. It reminds you to gather information and experience now about your course work, and experiences that will help your job search when you graduate."

CHRIS HELMS, Assistant Director of Career Services at Arizona State University

Obtaining References

References are a very misunderstood and misused tool in the job search process. Employers usually ignore written letters of reference. They're too easy to fabricate with desktop publishing. Employers want to call and speak to your references directly.

Always be on the lookout for good references. Most employers will request professional references. These are people who can attest to your professional skills—employers, coworkers, professors, and colleagues. Some employers ask for references other than former employers, so be prepared to include teachers and coworkers. Some employers request personal references. These refer to people who know you personally, preferably five years or more, who can vouch for your character. It's best to select professionally employed people to use as personal references. Never use your relatives; everyone expects your mother to give you a glowing report.

"I had a second interview scheduled for a position I really wanted. When I called one of my references to see if the employer had contacted her, she offered to call the employer directly. Imagine my surprise when I arrived to interview, to be greeted with "Your former boss says you walk on water." With that intro, I relaxed and sailed through the interview and into a new job. My former boss had called five minutes before my interview."

Lukewarm references can be as damaging as negative references. Ensure that yours are excellent by asking people if they feel comfortable allowing you to use them as a reference. Make sure to give them an opportunity to opt out. If they say yes, then help them help you. Provide your references with copies of your resume. Even if your reference knows you well, he or she should see the same piece of paper as your potential employer. Employers often ask references to verify dates or accomplishments. Your reference has to confidently answer these questions. Describe to your reference, preferably in writing, the types of positions that you are applying for. Check in with them frequently about your job search process. They may have other ideas or suggestions for you to follow up on.

Because it's not necessary to include reference information as part of the resume body, where does it belong? Create a separate piece of paper (same color and type as your resume) for your references. It's a good idea to list at least three personal and three professional references. After reading the example references worksheet in Activity 8.3, complete your own references worksheet.

References Worksheet — Activity 8.3

Ruby Slippers' Example:

Personal	*Professional*
Betsy Blake 348 E. Lake Road Manhattan, KS 68500 316-746-5678	Margaret Hamilton Vice President, First Bank of Kansas 1051 East Wilshire Drive Manhattan, KS 60428 mhamilton@first.com 913-555-5432
Rev. Lloyd Wizwerd 5690 N. 51st Avenue Wichita, KS 67432 lloyd345@aol.com 316-456-0987	William Burke Professor, Kansas State University 1683 West Main Street Manhattan, KS 66403 burke@ksu.edu 913-545-6516
Marvin K. Munichen 45 West Ridge Road Wilson, KS 67590 316-789-0001	J. Garland Owner, Specialty Graphics 44 Yellow Brick Road Wichita, KS 63090 judy@specialty.com 319-333-3345

Your Turn:

Personal References (People who can vouch for your character and have preferably known you at least five years.)

1. Name ______________________

Mailing address

____

____

____

E-mail ______________________

Work phone ______________________

Home phone ______________________

Number of years they have known you ______

2. Name ______________________

Mailing address

____

____

____

E-mail ______________________

Work phone ______________________

Home phone ______________________

Number of years they have known you ______

3. Name ______________________

Mailing address

____

____

____

E-mail ______________________

Work phone ______________________

Home phone ______________________

Number of years they have known you ________

4. Name ______________________

Mailing address

____

____

____

E-mail ______________________

Work phone ______________________

Home phone ______________________

Number of years they have known you ________

Professional References (People who can vouch for your professional knowledge.)

1. Name ______________________

Mailing address

____

____

____

E-mail ______________________

Work phone ______________________

Home phone ______________________

Relationship ______________________

2. Name ______________________

Mailing address

____

____

____

E-mail ______________________

Work phone ______________________

Home phone ______________________

Relationship ______________________

3. Name ______________________

Mailing address

____

____

____

E-mail ______________________

Work phone ______________________

Home phone ______________________

Relationship ______________________

4. Name ______________________

Mailing address

____

____

____

E-mail ______________________

Work phone ______________________

Home phone ______________________

Relationship ______________________

Application Tips

- Complete the application in ink. (Fill out a practice application in pencil. You can erase any errors and make sure the information is correct. Use this as a guide for completing an application you will turn in to an employer.)
- Pay attention to correct spelling and grammar. Some employers use applications as a type of literacy test to evaluate whether you can follow directions.
- Complete all questions and give appropriate information. Do not leave any spaces blank. If the information does not apply to you, write N/A, meaning *not applicable.*
- Always include correct names, addresses, dates of employment, salary information, and reasons for leaving previous jobs. Be positive about your reasons for leaving. Instead of saying "I didn't get along with my supervisor," say "I'm looking for a better career opportunity."
- List people who have given you permission to use them as your references. Employers will call your references and verify information about you. Include in your references professional people you know who will attest to your character.
- Neatness counts. Putting job information in writing should always reflect your best effort and work.
- Use any sections marked additional skills and knowledge or other qualifications to market your transferable skills as well as your personal qualities and characteristics that illustrate your qualifications for the specific position.

USING YOUR REFERENCES

Always bring extra copies of your resume, along with your references, to the interview, and be ready to provide your reference information when requested. Employers will want to check your information, and your references may make the difference between starting the job on Monday or not.

When you accept a position, be sure to inform all of your references. A handwritten note of thanks is appropriate.

Summary Points

- Writing an effective resume, prepared with careful thought and attention, is your opportunity to create a strong, lasting impression.
- The Information Age now requires preparing your resume for electronic as well as human eyes.
- Your resume should focus on ways your skills, accomplishments, and knowledge meet the needs of the employer.
- The cover letter is an opportunity to tell the employer *what you have to offer* in a conversational manner.

CHAPTER NINE

9 Developing Relationships

CREATING A PROFESSIONAL NETWORK

How can relationships help you achieve your goals?

How do you create a network of people to help you in your work search?

Do you need a mentor?

Now that you've established your career dreams, it's time to turn them into reality. Few people achieve their dreams alone. In today's interconnected world, it takes support and assistance from others to succeed. This chapter discusses ways you can develop relationships to achieve your goals. Connecting with professionals in your field can help you find opportunities when you're searching for work. Your network can give you important advice about how to meet with the people who make hiring decisions. By continuing these vital relationships, you'll be able to anticipate changes in your field and prepare for them.

Cooperation, Not Competition, Underlies Success

One of the most popular cultural myths in the United States glorifies the lone cowboy—the rugged individualist who raised himself up by his bootstraps, tracked down the bad guys, brought them to justice, and rode off into the sunset tipping his white hat. Very few others populate Louis L'Amour stories or western movies to help the hero. Part of the mystique of the cowboy is his ability to seize the bad guys single-handedly. The rugged individuals who settled the West or traveled north to work in new industries helped shape our country. Men and women competed against the elements and each other to settle the frontier. Our culture still worships the lone hero—the successful careers of Arnold Schwarzenegger, Tommy Lee Jones, and Bruce Willis attest to America's continued love affair with modern-day cowboys. They take you back to a simpler time when a cowboy could solve the town's problems single-handedly.

"Networking is very important when it's up to you to track down the companies you're interested in working for, and you have to find a way to get yourself invited for an interview. Using any connection you have is the best way to get your foot in the door at a company and get an interview. If you know someone who can make an introduction for you at a company, at least you can be sure that someone there will read your resume. Sending an unsolicited resume to a company's human resources department is the least effective way of getting yourself an interview."

RUSSELL A. BOSS, President and CEO, A.T. Cross Company

The American myth of the rugged individualist, however, no longer applies in the Information Age. Great new products are created by *teams* of people. Although the media has made popular icons of Bill

REAL-LIFE PERSPECTIVE

OLIVIA LARSON

Elementary Art Teacher

"One of the best pieces of advice I ever received occurred during orientation for my first professional job as an elementary teacher in a large urban school district. The chairman of our department gave us this advice. She said, 'This school district may employ thousands of teachers and tens of thousands of teachers work in our state, but don't let that fool you—it's a small world. Never say anything to anyone in the profession that you don't want to come back to haunt you. When you're frustrated or working with an inept colleague, don't ever talk about them at work. Share your frustrations at home. You never know who your next boss will be. If you stay in this profession long enough, it will become a small world. You will be surprised to find out you're reporting to the person sitting next to you now or next year's new teacher.' I've found that advice to be very true. You never want to burn bridges: Instead, concentrate on constructing new ones."

How Relationships Saved California Defense Workers

Here's a real-life example of why networking is so crucial in today's world of work. From the 1950s until the early 1990s, southern California's economy was based primarily on the defense industry. The area boasted several military bases, as well as manufacturing facilities for large defense contractors such as Boeing and General Dynamics. No one predicted the end of the Cold War. When military bases closed, thousands of defense employees lost their jobs. Southern California's economic recovery in the 1990s lagged behind the rest of the United States because of its dependence on military spending. During the late 1990s, southern California recovered by diversifying its economy. A surprising area of rapid growth was in multimedia companies that provide high-tech services to the entertainment industry. As aerospace engineers became aware of the growth, they developed relationships with multimedia producers. Now, instead of designing warheads, they design special effects. Former aerospace technicians help directors plan camera shots, and assemblers build special computers that handle the speed and huge memory needs of digital imaging. Most multimedia companies are small and add more employees according to demand. Companies grow from 200 to 1,000 employees during peak periods; then, they resize back to 200 when demand falls off. Animators earn between $50,000 and $150,000 annually—even with these uneven periods of employment. They have learned to prosper in this volatile environment by networking and sharing information about new projects.

Gates and Steve Jobs, none of these men or their companies would be successful without the organized teams that created, produced, and marketed their products. Cooperation, not competition, drives business today. Former competitors cooperate to develop new markets. Joseph Weber and Amy Barrett report in "The New Era of Lifestyle Drugs" that two pharmaceutical companies, Searle and Warner-Lambert, are cooperating with Pfizer, another pharmaceutical company, to co-market new drugs. Pfizer has the largest pharmaceutical sales force in the United States. It makes business sense to take advantage of their existing sales force rather than compete.

In the new economy, businesses strive for win-win relationships—shifting from competition to cooperation. For every winner in the past, there was a loser. Sales forces tried to beat out the competition and often beat up the buyer trying to make short-term profits. Today, suppliers and customers form long-term relationships so both can win. Companies realize they can't survive without their customers.

Successful people mirror this shift toward cooperation in their day-today relationships in the workplace. Employees inside a company treat each other with the same respect and courtesy that used to be reserved only for customers. The real winners today share information and knowledge to create results that an individual could never accomplish alone. Successful companies view themselves as dynamic, open systems where there is room for everyone to prosper. Managers coach and mentor their subordinates to roll out products or achieve department goals—then take their loyal protégés with them when they move on to new assignments.

Developing relationships will be the most important ingredient in achieving your personal goals. Skillful relationship-builders refine these two skills:

- Connecting with key people to exchange useful information
- Maintaining relationships over time

Successfully learning both skills will help you connect with people "in the know" about your profession, company, and industry.

WAYS RELATIONSHIPS CAN HELP YOU STAY EMPLOYABLE

Stay current with new developments in your field

Learn about future trends that will impact your profession

Discover new work opportunities

"Let someone else boast for you. Build relationships so people will do that."

MARTIN SMITH,
Team Leader, Honeywell

To keep pace with the rapid changes in the workplace, you need information from people outside your daily work environment. A network of professional colleagues will challenge and support you to develop new skills. Your network can give you feedback on your projects, your communication style, and your professional development. Learn to schedule time every week to maintain your professional relationships. When you want to change jobs, you'll be glad you did.

James Taylor and Watts Wacker, in their book *The 500 Year Delta*, call this the Age of Connectivity. They believe the real outcome of the Information Age is not the ability of computers to compile data rapidly, but the ability of people to interconnect—to gather information from many sources. Taylor and Wacker say the emergence of networks and the Web fused computing and communication—and connectivity was born. The productivity gains attributed to computerization resulted directly from interconnectivity, allowing many people within an organization to access information simultaneously. Employees have been able to improve products and services by having instant access to information that wasn't available before computers were networked.

Developing Relationships in College

College is the perfect time to begin developing professional contacts and relationships. You'll develop the interpersonal communication skills critical in today's team-based workplace.

Your peers. Nearly everyone you meet in college will one day be working, and some of them will be working in companies of interest to you—as potential suppliers, customers, or employers. Particularly important will be students in your major. Sharing notes, studying for exams, and participating in joint class projects build the foundation for positive relationships. Use these experiences to learn how to work with others, assert your viewpoint, and collaborate to achieve results.

Some students become competitive when the rounds of campus interviews start. However, you can really help each other by comparing notes about interviews. Find out what questions interviewers are asking. Which answers seem to get the best responses? Even sharing job openings pays off. A company that is a poor match for you might perfectly suit a colleague's needs. Sharing information with your peers can pay big dividends in the job hunt.

Stay in touch with classmates after college—you have already built a network that can lead you to others in your field. Sharing first-year work experiences will help each of you achieve success early in your career.

"If I receive a resume cold, without a personal referral, it almost automatically gets forwarded to human resources without getting any personal attention from me. I simply don't have time to read unsolicited resumes and respond to them. If the resume comes with a personal referral from someone I know, however, then it has a much better chance of getting personal attention."

HOWARD LINCOLN, chairman, Nintendo of America, Inc.

Program advisors. Meet regularly with your program advisor to develop a relationship. The more your advisor knows about your work goals, the more he or she can help you select the courses most beneficial to you. Advisors communicate with employers in your field of study. They can explain trends in the workplace and recommend courses to increase your employability. Advisors may also be aware of internships, co-op experiences, and employers looking for job candidates in your field.

Career center counselors. Most colleges have career centers where you can access information about career fields, internships, job search techniques, and on-campus interviews. A career center counselor can help you find work related to your field while you're in school. Many career centers maintain a link to the campus home page on the Internet. Although career center Internet sites are useful, they cannot provide the personal relationship that a counselor can.

Professors. Many students only think to contact their instructors when they are having trouble with an assignment. Instructors, however, can also be invaluable in helping you prepare for your future career. If you share your dreams with them, they can help you identify resources that will help you achieve your goals. Many instructors serve on community boards, consult with businesses, and read numerous publications about workplace trends. See "Developing a Mentoring Relationship" at the end of this chapter for ideas on how you can develop a mentor relationship with a professor.

Clubs. Your campus has many clubs for students to learn more about careers related to their field of study. Clubs also provide a setting where you can develop relationships with people who will be working in your profession.

Alumni association. You may be surprised at how many new graduates are active in alumni clubs. Fellow alumni are usually willing resources for information about current trends and opportunities in your field.

Developing Relationships to Help You Find Work

When you think of networking, you may picture yourself at a party shaking hands with as many contacts as possible or calling people to ask if there are openings in their company. Networking involves more than this;

REAL-LIFE PERSPECTIVE

NIK HARRIS

When Nik Harris moved from Phoenix, Arizona, to Washington, D.C., to look for a job right out of college, she knew only a few people through interning for Senator John McCain. She turned to the National Capitol Chapter of the Arizona State University Alumni Association. "The chapter has many social events throughout the year, including watching our teams play football and basketball on big screen TVs. People in the alumni association gave me support during my job search, leads on people to network with, and the opportunity to talk about home. I might not have stayed in Washington long enough to find my first job if it hadn't been for them."

it involves developing professional relationships with people you may or may not know, and it's the best way to look for work. (See Activity 9.1.)

You may have heard that the *hidden job market* is the market you should tap into to find work. The hidden job market refers to all of the work that needs doing that hasn't been advertised. If you wonder whether this job market exists, or whether it's worth pursuing, consider the following scenario. For a moment, put yourself in the shoes of a manager who just received a resignation from a valued employee. What would you do if you were the manager faced with this dilemma? First, you might ask employees in your department if they know someone who could do the work. (Like other managers, you'd probably feel more comfortable hiring someone others recommend than an unknown person who looks good on a resume.) If this doesn't lead to a referral, you'd ask other managers, contacts, and professional colleagues. As a last resort, you'd call the human resources department and advertise the position. Why? You dread the typical hiring scenario: Sorting through the onslaught of resumes, conducting rounds of interviews, and checking references. By networking, you can become that candidate who is recommended before the job is advertised.

The first step in developing a network is to start with the people you already know. You may be thinking that you have been busy with school, work, and internships and haven't had time to develop a network, but everyone knows people who can help them in their search for work. Every day, you meet and exchange information with many people. You'd be surprised who may know someone in your field or someone who works at a company where you'd like to work—it might even be your pal at Radio Shack. You won't know unless you ask.

WAYS TO EXPAND YOUR NETWORK

- **Join a professional association.** Many associations have student memberships. All of them welcome new graduates or people aspiring to work in their profession. *The Encyclopedia of Associations,* available in most libraries, lists all major professional associations. Visit www.ipl.org/ref/AON for a searchable directory of business-related associations.

Creating Your Network

Activity 9.1

Instructions: Fill in as many names as you can in each of the circles—be creative. Don't worry about addresses and telephone numbers now; you can look those up later. Stretch your imagination to list as many people as possible, including teachers, advisors, friends of your parents, bank tellers, auto mechanics, ministers, and so on.

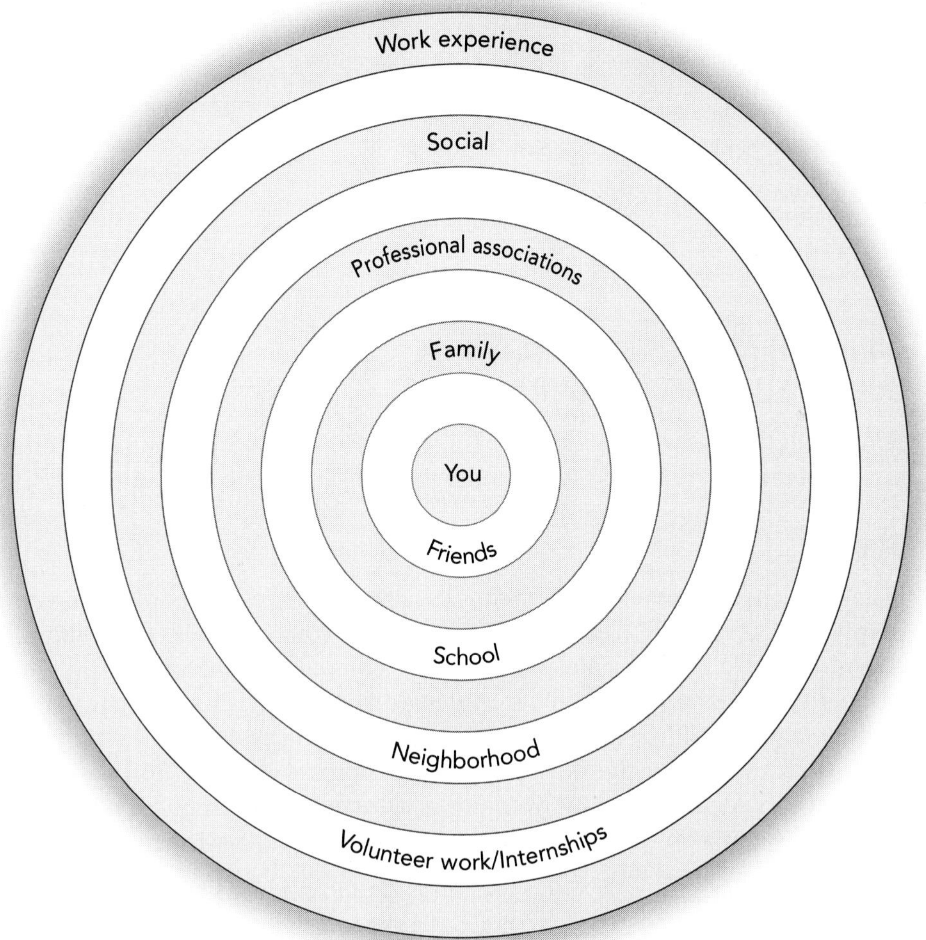

- **Talk to speakers at conferences or professional meetings.** Call ahead and ask if conference speakers have time to meet with you after their presentations.
- **E-mail or call authors of articles in trade journals or magazines.** Authors spend time writing articles to gain visibility and recognition. Sometimes, they appreciate hearing from people who have read what they wrote. They may have good ideas about who else you could talk to about your job search.
- **Join a discussion list geared to your profession or industry.** Go to www.listz.com for a listing of discussion groups on the Internet. After you join a group, spend a few weeks reading the postings. Send a private e-mail asking for career advice to individuals who post

interesting comments. Make sure to read the FAQs (frequently asked questions), and follow the etiquette guidelines for the group. Many groups welcome questions from students and recent graduates. Follow up responses to your questions individually. Acknowledge and thank everyone for their advice and assistance.

- *Join Company of Friends sponsored by* Fast Company *magazine.* Visit its website at www.fastcompany.com/cof/index.jsp and enter your name, location, contact information, and professional interests. They'll respond with information about Fast Friends in your area.

"Obviously, if you know someone at a company you're interested in working for, that helps. I think everyone knows people out there who can provide introductions for him or her into companies. If you network correctly, you should be able to at least get your foot in the door at a company and get yourself an interview."

SIDNEY SWARTZ, Chairman, CEO, and President, The Timberland Company, in *First Job, Great Job*

See Activity 9.2

CONNECTING WITH YOUR NETWORK DURING YOUR WORK SEARCH

Remember that networking is requesting and receiving information from others. People rarely turn down the simple request: "I'd like to ask your advice."

Step 1

Using the chart provided in Activity 9.3, list the names of people who can help your job search. Then, rank the names on your chart in the left-hand column. Give a 1 to people who work in companies where you want to work; give a 2 to people who can put you in touch with a company or a person in your field; give a 3 to everyone else. Call the 1's and 2's on your list first. They will be the most helpful. You probably have more 3's than 1's. That's okay; it points out your need to network. The people who you rated as 3's can also help you. Use a script like the following:

> "Hello, this is ________________. I'm calling to see if you know anyone who works at ___________ company. I'd like to ask them a few questions about the company."
>
> or
>
> "I'm calling to see if you know anyone who works in the ___________ field. I would like to ask them a few questions about their background."

Add any names you receive to your list; they will rate as a 1 or 2. Telephone the person and schedule an appointment to meet with them. You will find it much easier to connect with them if you use the name of the person who referred you. Use a script like the following:

> "Hello, my name is ___________. I spoke with ___________ about working in the field of ___________. S/he recommended I contact you because of your background in ___________. I am wondering if I could spend 15 minutes talking to you about your experience? I'd like your advice about what I should do to get started in this field. When would it be convenient to meet with you?"

Ways to Expand Your Network

Activity 9.2

Instructions: Check the ideas in the table that you could use now to expand your network. Add to the table other ideas to increase your network. Next, write down whom you will contact to begin expanding your network.

✓	WAYS TO EXPAND MY NETWORK	WHOM I CAN CONTACT
	Asking people I know to find contacts in my profession	
	Joining a professional association	
	Subscribing to a discussion group	
	Joining a student organization	

Activity 9.3 Keeping Track of Your Network

Rank	Name	Organization	Title	Date of Contact	Date Thank You Sent	Phone/E-mail

Networking is *not* asking for a job; it's asking for information. Your questions in the networking interview differ from research interviews because you have already decided on a profession or field of work. Now, you are using the law of averages to your advantage: The more people you talk to, the more likely you will be in the right place at the right time—when an opening exists. Ask for advice, not a job. If you ask for a job, particularly over the telephone, it's easy for the other person to say no. If you ask for advice, most people are flattered and will usually agree to meet with you. Ask whether they prefer to meet at a nearby coffee shop or in their office.

Step 2

Plan your interview—what do you want to achieve from this contact? Here are some possibilities:

- Find out (from their perspective) what it's really like to work in this field or organization.

- Learn what skills, training, and entry-level or part-time experience would help you enter the field.
- Find out how to acquire needed skills or experience.
- Learn *insider* information about an organization. Ask them to describe the company culture.
- Obtain feedback on your resume, your interviewing style, and other job-hunting advice for this field.

"There is so much connectivity in my career. Every new position I have found because of making connections. I'm always looking for people I can learn from. I have always made it a point to ask people how they got there. Let people know what you want. Life is about connectivity—there are no accidents."

SUSAN COURTNEY, V. P. Administrative Services, Central Arizona College

Step 3

Research the company and industry before you meet with the person. Become familiar with the company's products and services, organizational structure, and competitors. Candidates who don't bother to do their homework don't appear genuinely interested in the company. Your research will demonstrate your motivation as a professional job-seeker.

- Utilize research books, trade journals, and periodicals from the library. Also use *Dun & Bradstreet* or *Standard & Poor's* directories.
- Request literature (and an annual report if the company is publicly traded) from the company's public relations department.
- Use online resources like the company's home page, Hoover's Guide, or any of the large job-posting services.

Step 4

Prepare for each interview. Summarize your background by using the commercial you developed in Chapter 7. Write it down in case your nerves interfere with your thinking. Prepare written questions to take to the interview.

POSSIBLE QUESTIONS TO ASK

- How did you get started in this profession?
- What kinds of skills are most important in your work?
- What kinds of problems do you solve?
- What types of experience are needed for working in this field?
- What advice would you give people entering this field?
- Would you recommend other people I could talk to about work in this field? (Always, always ask this question!)

Build on the information you gather, and let your contacts know you are working hard on your job search. Check the validity of ideas you've heard about with others. For example: "Sally Brown at XYZ Company suggested I start by working through a temporary agency. Do you agree? What agency does your company use?"

- *Secret strategy.* Ask every person you talk to for the names of three other people you could call to continue your research. This exponentially increases the number of people in your network.
- *A word of caution.* If you told the person on the telephone that you were seeking information, don't play *bait and switch*; that is, don't walk into the information interview and ask for a job. The person will feel used.

Step 5

Write a personal thank-you note to every person you interview. Enclose a copy of your resume.

Step 6

Stay in touch with your network. Some networkers believe it takes four or five contacts with a person before they will recommend you for a position. Select the people whom you think can be the most helpful and keep them informed of your progress. People are impressed when you follow through on their suggestions. Call and briefly let them know you followed their advice, and tell them what happened. Ask for any other suggestions. Often, your conversation will trigger new ideas. Now, they may be willing to call a colleague to see if there is an opening.

WHAT PREPARATION IS NECESSARY FOR THE FUTURE?

"I believe that a person must continue to learn new skills, new or better ways to work. Keep your mind open to new ideas, and move around to new jobs every two or three years. Move out of your comfort zone, and learn many aspects of your organization. This will prepare you for better job opportunities when they present themselves. I believe in networking as the way to keep in touch with people that you have worked with in the past. Keeping a network or link going can be of help to you when promotions become available—and you need that information to keep you informed of job openings. I also believe in mentoring, which will also help in your career preparation."

GINGER MURDOUGH, Executive Partnering Administrator, Arizona Department of Transportation

HOW DISCUSSION GROUPS CAN HELP YOUR JOB SEARCH

Marcia J. Eagleson is Assistant Director of Career Services at Georgia Southern University. She contacted a discussion list on behalf of a blind student interested in a journalism career. She asked the list for names of organizations and other resources that might help the student in her job search. Here are the responses she received within days of posting her inquiry:

1. NFB-BPJ, the Blind Professional Journalists List—www.nfb.org/nfb-bpj.htm (any interested students can join through this website)
2. The American Foundation for the Blind, 15 W. 16th Street, New York, NY 10011 (212-620-2079)
3. Job Accommodations Network (1-800-526-7234)

REAL-LIFE PERSPECTIVE

HOW PERSISTENCE PAYS OFF

After relocating to Phoenix, Arizona, Kelly Duffy-Bassett applied for a position advertised in the newspaper as a trainer for a nonprofit agency. Being new in town, she hadn't yet developed a network, but she knew the power of networking. After mailing her resume, she called the agency and asked to speak to someone about the job opening. When the hiring manager was unavailable (which is often the case), she didn't give up. Instead, she asked to speak to one of the employees in the position. She asked several questions about the position, talked about her background, and shared how she could use her skills at the agency. The staff person, impressed with her knowledge and skills, immediately went to the manager and recommended that she interview Kelly. That call made a big difference. Kelly's resume was pulled out of the discard pile. Because she could talk about the organization and how she could help solve its problems, she interviewed well and was hired over candidates with more work experience and local references.

4. *Successful Job Search Strategies for the Disabled: Understanding the ADA* by Jeffrey G. Allen
5. *Job Strategies for People with Disabilities* by Melanie Astaire Witt
6. American Press Institute—www.newspaper.org

Mentors

A mentor serves as a trusted advisor who shows interest in your professional growth and development. Mentors not only supply valuable information; they also build an ongoing relationship with you. They share their experiences to help you solve problems or develop skills. A mentor can explain the organization's culture—"the way we do things around here."

Homer described the first recorded mentoring relationship in the *Odyssey*. Before leaving for the siege of Troy, Odysseus appointed a guardian to protect his family during his absence. For 10 years, the guardian acted as advisor, teacher, friend, and surrogate father to Odysseus's son, Telemachus. The guardian's name was Mentor. In ancient Greece, it was common to select an older male to mentor each boy so he would learn and emulate the knowledge and values of his mentor.

The craft guilds formed during the Middle Ages used masters to mentor their apprentices in their crafts or businesses. The apprentice advanced to journeyman and then became a master himself by taking an exam or producing a work of art. Through this structure, craft guilds con-

How to Keep a Relationship Going

- Send articles about developments in their industry or field. No one has the time to read everything that applies to them.
- Send discussion list or e-zine information that might interest them.
- Share openings that aren't right for you.
- Give occasional progress reports about your job search or new job.
- Attend professional association meetings, conferences, and company-sponsored community projects.

trolled the quality of work and passed on valuable connections and customers.

In modern times, unions and trades still use the roles of master, journeyman, and apprentice to pass on skills to new employees. Many industrial companies, however, abandoned this structure as the mentoring relationship evolved into the employer/employee relationship. For many years, organizations created training programs to pass on skills; unfortunately, these programs rarely provided individuals to help the trainees adapt skills learned in the classroom to the workplace. Some companies recognized this gap and developed formal mentoring programs for promising employees.

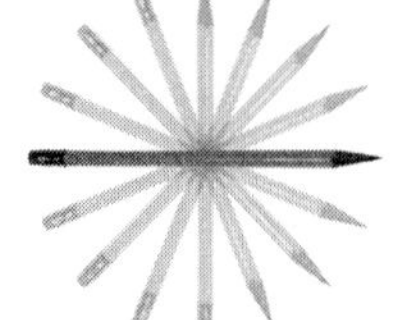

A recent study found that 80 percent of top executives received assistance from mentors early in their careers. Their mentors groomed them for advancement by giving them advice and providing opportunities to develop necessary skills. (See Activity 9.4.)

"It's who you know—most of the time, that's the truth. Because I know particular people I'm able to do things I never would have done—like write a book."

JUDITH BARRETTE, Director of Organizational Development and Training, Arizona Department of Transportation

BENEFITS OF MENTORING

Improved performance on the job. Mentors give feedback on how well you're meeting expectations. They can give you tips for improving your skills that otherwise might take years to figure out on your own.

Greater visibility. Mentors may suggest special projects or recommend you for teams to increase your visibility with senior management. Assignments like these are often difficult to obtain by yourself.

Increased work satisfaction. Mentors help their protégés see the big picture of how their work fits into the goals of the organization. When you know the value of your work, your satisfaction increases.

More rapid promotions. Because your mentor will help you acquire the right skills and increase your visibility, your chances for promotions increase.

Insider knowledge. In some companies, only insiders know who the essential players are and where the company is headed in the future. Your mentor can share this information with you.

The Information Age demands complex skills such as decision making, process improvement, continuous learning, and team participation. Sharpen these skills with suggestions from your mentor. Ask for feedback on what worked and what you should do differently next time.

GETTING STARTED WITH A MENTOR

Read "Ways to Find a Mentor" on page 234. Using the strategies described, select three or four people to contact as a potential mentor. Decide what you would like to learn from the person during your first conversation.

Don't say, "Will you be my mentor?" Ask for specific advice: "Sue, if you have some time to talk soon, would you explain to me why we don't

Are You Ready for a Mentor? Activity 9.4

Consider these questions before becoming a mentee. You may need more time to define your career focus before pursuing a mentoring relationship. Think about your answers and give thoughtful responses.

1. Am I focused on the kind of help I want from a mentor?

2. Am I willing to spend the time meeting with a mentor?

3. Will I take to heart and follow the advice a mentor gives me?

4. Do I welcome feedback from others on my strengths and areas that need to be developed?

5. Do I learn from others and appreciate their ideas?

6. Am I willing to set goals and measure my progress?

use Promo as a supplier?" "Dan, could we set up a meeting soon so I could ask your advice about the actual skills I need to become an account rep?" "Sally, I didn't understand some of the things that occurred at our last staff meeting. Could I have a few minutes of your time soon so you could explain to me what happened?"

Listen and assess the conversation. If you get a brief two-minute lecture, this person is not mentor material. He or she may be impressed with your initiative, and you may be able to periodically ask other questions to increase your knowledge; however, mentoring involves more than this. If, on the other hand, your first question leads the other person to ask questions about your goals and interests, you have identified a potential mentor!

Ways to Find a Mentor

- Meet with your favorite college professor. Discuss ways he or she could help you.
- Ask someone in your network for ideas on people you could contact to be your mentor.
- Ask the membership chairperson of a professional association to recommend a mentor.
- Discuss mentoring opportunities with someone you meet during an internship.
- Contact a discussion list on the Internet, and establish private e-mail connections.
- Contact your career center advisor for mentor ideas. Some campuses have formal mentoring programs with instructors, alumni, or community business leaders.
- Contact your program advisor and ask for mentoring ideas.
- Check out your part-time job; there may be a possibility for a mentoring relationship there.
- Ask your boss for advice and support. The best way to begin is to discuss goals for your current position. If the relationship doesn't develop into a mentoring one, ask him or her to suggest someone who might have the time and interest.

DEVELOPING A MENTORING RELATIONSHIP

Schedule several meetings with your potential mentor to become acquainted and to share interests, values, and goals. Remember, the person does not need to be your boss—he or she can be working anywhere in the company. Plan each meeting by developing specific questions or targeting the kind of advice you'd like. When you schedule the meeting, let it be known what you want to discuss, as in the examples shown above, for the first meeting. As the person gets to know you, ask for assignments or ideas that will add to your professional growth. You might never have to formally ask the person to be your mentor—just find ways to keep the relationship moving forward.

Your mentor has many professional responsibilities and time constraints. When you meet, always have a specific goal. Concisely explain what it is you want to know; it doesn't take a lot of time to get good advice. If possible, meeting often with your mentor with small requests, rather than overwhelming him or her with a long list in one meeting, is best. Parceling out your questions gives the relationship time to develop. You'll also have time to digest what you've heard and follow through on the suggestions you received. Be prepared to answer questions about your dreams and goals. The more your mentor knows about you, the more likely it is that he or she will think of you when an opportunity presents itself that would help you achieve your goals.

Tip: If a senior person asks you to perform a special assignment—seize the opportunity, even if it's not in your job description. The person may repay your efforts. Many informal mentoring relationships get started this way. After completing the project, schedule a meeting with the person who gave you the assignment. Discuss the project, and ask for feedback on how you could improve next time. Let the person know you welcome other assignments, and describe the kinds of skills you'd like to develop.

REAL-LIFE PERSPECTIVE

ISABELLA MORI

When Isabella Mori finished her B.A. in psychology, she immediately used the mentoring service at her college, Simon Fraser University in Vancouver, Canada. "Not only did my mentor encourage me to keep on trying to find a position that combines both my employment counseling experience and my experience working with people with disabilities, she also gave me some very useful contacts and suggestions, as well as a very good description of her own experience at her job." A great question Isabella asked her mentor was, "Can you tell me who has their ear to the ground in terms of what's happening in social service agencies in Vancouver?" She got the names of people at a legal aid agency and a research institute.

Isabella also listened to her mentor's needs. Her mentor mentioned that fund-raising wasn't her forte, although it's part of her job. Isabella reciprocated by sending her mentor some information as well as the name of another agency that was looking for some partners for a multi-agency fund-raising project. Good going, Isabella!

Summary Points

- Cooperation and interconnectivity have replaced competition in the Information Age.
- Relationships are the key to employability. Use your college years to learn how to develop long-term relationships. Class projects, school organizations, internships, and work provide opportunities to learn how to interact with people while accomplishing a task.
- Develop relationships with positive people for encouragement and support.
- Form relationships that help you stay employable by learning about new developments in your profession. Your network can keep you tuned into new work opportunities.
- Advisors and professors have a wealth of information about the world of work. Seek their advice about the best strategies to help you prepare for your profession.
- Use information interviews in your job search. Be proactive, take charge, and don't leave your job search in the hands of other people.
- Identify people to mentor you in your professional development.

CHAPTER TEN

10 Organizing Your Work Search

FINDING MEANINGFUL WORK

Which work options are right for you?

What are the best ways to look for work?

How do you negotiate and evaluate job offers?

How do you succeed at your new job?

How do you view your search for work? Are you eager to discuss your education, training, and experience with employers? Or, do you feel grateful someone, anyone, would hire you? Most people have felt both ways at some time during their work search. You can expect your work search to be a roller coaster of emotions. Sometimes, you will feel hopeful and confident, eager to tell people how you can contribute to their organization's goals. Other times, you'll dread getting up in the morning. Suddenly, despite work experience and an excellent education, you may feel apprehensive. Often, when your self-confidence takes a nosedive, you may begin to think you're lucky to receive an offer—any offer. You lose your focus and find yourself frantically scanning the want ads to apply for any position you can find. This frantic approach can lead to missed opportunities and a sense of urgency surrounding your work search.

The more precisely you define what you're looking for, the easier it is to find work. If you have a clear focus of what you want, you can do the research and preparation that will help you stand out from other applicants. Having a focus and sticking to it will actually shorten the length of your search.

Beginning your actual search for work is the culmination of all your hard work throughout this book. You've analyzed your skills, researched career fields, learned how to communicate your value, and developed a resume. This chapter is all about getting and staying focused on *your* goal. We've assembled the strategies that successful job hunters use—strategies that optimize your time and lead you to the kind of work you want. We'll show you how to get organized and how to re-energize your search if you get stuck. We know you'll be successful, so we've ended this chapter with tips for success. You'll learn how to survive and thrive during your first critical year.

Preparing for Your Work Search

Resist limiting yourself to searching for job titles and job descriptions. Think of what you have to offer an employer. This broader perspective will help you discover more ways to work and more opportunities. Think of yourself as *You, Inc.* Market the skills you can offer to an employer. You've identified your features (skills and knowledge) and benefits (value you can bring to a company). You developed this information into your marketing brochure—your resume. You know how to sell your services through your interviewing skills, and you have identified a network that can help you reach your potential customers. You are ready to act! The next step is to scan the world of work to find organizations that need what you have to offer. Who are your potential customers, and what are their needs? Who needs the skills, abilities, and knowledge you can provide?

"The days of the mammoth corporations are ending. People are going to have to create their own lives, their own careers, and their own success. Some people may go kicking and screaming into the new world, but the key is: you're now in business for yourself."

WILLIAM BRIDGES, *JobShift*

THE HIDDEN JOB MARKET

Make sure you're tapping into the *hidden job market,* not just accessing traditional work search methods. Whether you are looking for a job, contract employment, or free agent work, learning about opportunities through coworkers, faculty, friends, and relatives is the most successful way to seek employment.

Employers and job-hunters usually approach employment from opposite directions. Employers consider classified advertising as the strategy of last resort, while most job-hunters turn to the classified ads first. Advertised positions account for less than 15 percent of all job openings; yet, 90 percent of all job seekers apply for these advertised openings. Most employers prefer to hire someone they know or someone who has been recommended by someone they know. Most job hunters tend to focus their efforts on answering want ads offered through the Internet or the newspaper, or they rely on placement agencies, like their school's career center or headhunters. Solicit assistance from friends and colleagues before you seek work through strangers. Use your network to uncover the hidden job market and identify openings that will lead to interviews and

Strategies for a Successful Job Hunt

Know what you want. Successful job-hunters have a good idea of the work they're seeking. Employers are interested in applicants who can explain why they're seeking a particular position, what they find interesting about the work, and why they chose the company to work for. Conducting a random job search will waste your time, and potential employers are not interested in hearing, "I'll do anything!"

Be proactive—take initiative. Searching for a job is a full-time job. Devote the time and energy it will take to land the work you want. Instead of waiting to be discovered, create a job search plan with specific activities to do every day.

Focus on the needs of the employer. View the job from the employers' perspective. What can you do to help solve *their* problems?

Conduct information interviews. Use this strategy to talk to potential employers. Ask to talk to someone in your field, and ask job-specific questions like:

"What types of projects challenge you?"

"What advice do you have for someone entering the field?"

"Could you recommend someone else I could talk to?"

This approach will supply you with relevant information, and you may be invited to interview for an opening or referred to someone who may have openings.

Contact individuals who can hire you directly. Find out who has the authority to hire you. These are the people you should be talking to, even if it's just to say you're sending your resume.

Target your resume and cover letter. With each contact you make, ask if you can send a resume; include a cover letter that specifically addresses the particular needs of the position. Your resume and cover letter should emphasize skills and activities that relate to the job you want.

Be persistent and don't give up. Follow through on your job leads. You may not receive a response to your telephone calls immediately, but persistence pays off. You are communicating your interest in the position through continuous contact and follow-up.

Remain positive and confident. Looking for a job is hard work. Rejection is part of the process. Just when you feel like giving up, remember, there is a right job out there for you.

the work you want. A successful marketing strategy requires effort in all areas. On the one hand, 7 out of 10 good jobs come from personal contacts. At the same time, you can't ignore the fact that 30 percent of people do get their jobs through traditional methods.

Figure 10.1 illustrates how people actually find work. These recent figures are provided by the Department of Labor. Various researchers have been asking this question for over 30 years. In good economic times or bad, the results are always about the same.

How do these figures apply to you? Spend about 74 percent of your time networking and making direct contact with employers (we combined "other" and "informal"). Spend about 14 percent of your time responding to Internet and newspaper ads. Spend about 12 percent of your time at your college career center and employment agencies. So, if you're able to job hunt full-time and you spend 30 hours a week doing that, 22 hours should be spent networking and making direct contact with employers.

"You can create a great advantage for yourself in your job target fields if you identify prospective employers, not on the basis of employment ads, but by contacting enough of the right people in the right firms and uncovering opportunities that are not (and may never be) public knowledge."

TOM JACKSON, *Guerrilla Tactics in the New Job Market*

FIGURE 10.1 *How American workers find jobs.*

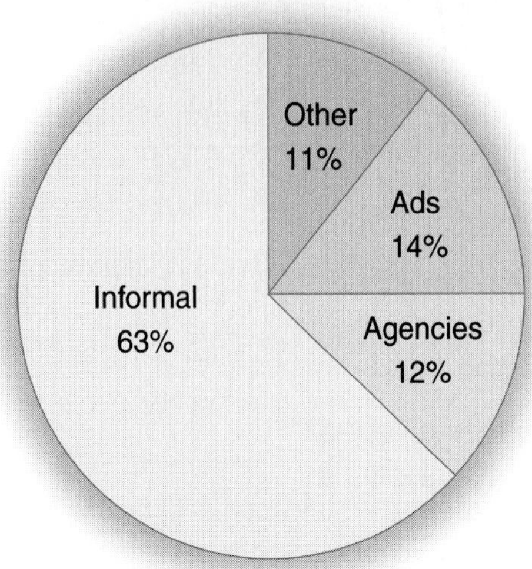

Source: U. S. Department of Labor.

The Work Search Process

THE WORK SEARCH PROCESS

1. State your goal
2. Identify target organizations
3. Research your targets
4. Make contact
5. Follow up

1. STATE YOUR GOAL

Begin planning your work search by clearly defining the patterns in your career kaleidoscope and deciding on your work goal. State your goal broadly enough so you can generate many possibilities for your work. Instead of declaring, "I want a job at XYZ Company in the marketing department," say, "I want to work in marketing." A broad view gives you the opportunity to examine many work possibilities, generating ideas you probably would never think of otherwise. Too often, we only think of obvious work choices, overlooking a wide range of likely prospects.

Your goal should be realistic—that is, achievable now. If you have a new degree (and little related experience), ask for advice about how to start your new career from instructors, career center advisors, and professionals. Submitting a few questions to relevant discussion lists on the Internet is a good way to query professionals for advice. If you're working as an intern or work-study student, ask your supervisor and coworkers for advice.

SAMPLE WORK SEARCH GOALS

Entrepreneur—Find a way to work from home using my computer skills.

Free agent—Find contract work using editing and writing skills.

Core employee—Find an entry-level position in marketing.

Record your goal in Activity 10.3 on page 249.

2. IDENTIFY TARGET ORGANIZATIONS

Compile a list of industries, companies, and opportunities for work. Don't worry about whether they're realistic options at this point; your goal is to generate as many ideas as possible. Don't do this alone; brainstorm with others. Ask your professors, colleagues, career center personnel, friends, and relatives

Are You Ready?

Activity 10.1

Use this checklist to help you assess your work search readiness. Your answers to the following questions will give you important clues about what to do next. Answer each question "Yes" or "No." Then, take the time to turn each "No" into "Yes."

I. WHAT DO YOU KNOW ABOUT YOURSELF AND YOUR PREFERENCES?

Ⓨ Ⓝ 1. Can you clearly state your career goal?

Ⓨ Ⓝ 2. Can you explain why this field interests you?

Ⓨ Ⓝ 3. Can you name five skills used by people working in this field?

4. For each of these skills, can you:

Ⓨ Ⓝ • Describe a time when you used it and explain the actions you took?

Ⓨ Ⓝ • Explain the benefits of your actions?

Ⓨ Ⓝ 5. Have you defined your geographical preferences?

Ⓨ Ⓝ 6. Have you decided on the types of companies where you'd like to work?

Ⓨ Ⓝ 7. Are you familiar with the professional associations and publications in your field?

II. WHAT DO YOU KNOW ABOUT EMPLOYERS?

Ⓨ Ⓝ 8. Can you name at least 10 types of employers that might offer the kind of work you're seeking?

Ⓨ Ⓝ 9. Do you know four or five resources to help you find the answer to Question 8?

Ⓨ Ⓝ 10. Can you list at least four resources that could help you discover potential employers in a particular geographical area?

Ⓨ Ⓝ 11. Have you talked to at least three people who are working in your field of interest with the purpose of learning what they do?

III. ARE YOU READY FOR CONTACT?

Ⓨ Ⓝ 12. Have you prepared your one-minute commercial?

Ⓨ Ⓝ 13. Have you identified a network of people who can help you reach employers in this field?

Ⓨ Ⓝ 14. Do you use more than just advertised listings as a source of job leads?

Ⓨ Ⓝ 15. Does your resume emphasize experiences related to skills used in this field?

Ⓨ Ⓝ 16. Have you asked for feedback on your resume from someone working in this field?

Ⓨ Ⓝ 17. When you apply to an employer, do you address your cover letter to a specific person?

Ⓨ Ⓝ 18. Have you researched the products, services, or programs of the employers to whom you are applying?

Ⓨ Ⓝ 19. Do you know the questions employers are likely to ask in an interview?

Ⓨ Ⓝ 20. Can you clearly state why you are interested in working for each employer to whom you apply?

21. Have you used any of the following methods to prepare for an interview:

Ⓨ Ⓝ • Role-playing with a friend or relative?

Ⓨ Ⓝ • Practicing in front of a mirror?

Ⓨ Ⓝ • Writing out answers to typical interview questions?

for ideas. For additional ideas, scan professional journals, discussion lists on the Internet, employer directories, and the telephone directory. Develop a list of at least 40 potential work opportunities, which you'll list in Activity 10.3.

For example, if you're interested in a marketing position, your list might include names of service businesses, including advertisers, publishers, health care organizations, and financial institutions. You might also choose to look at opportunities in marketing with transportation, communication, and manufacturing companies.

You may have discovered a single industry or type of business that really interests you. That's good because it gives you a clear focus. However, the opportunities in your geographical area may be limited. To expand your possibilities, complete the Mind Map Activity explained in Chapter 5. The mind map will broaden your view and help you identify other related work options. For example, you may want to work as an accountant for a pharmaceutical business and you know pharmaceuticals are scarce in your area. Map out the companies who are either *customers or suppliers* of pharmaceuticals, such as biomedical equipment manufacturers, laboratories, drug-testing companies, hospitals, and doctors' practices. You now have a much broader range of choices related to your original target that need accountants.

Another strategy to expand your list of options is to target small companies—an approach some job hunters overlook. As Figure 10.2 illustrates, more jobs are created by small companies than any other sector. We hear a lot about corporate mergers and acquisitions, as well as the fallout of dot-coms, but established small companies are thriving and growing in number. Some people may be reluctant to apply for positions in small businesses, fearing there is less job security; in fact, companies in the Fortune 500 employ fewer people now than 20 years ago. It can be exciting and rewarding to be involved in growing a small business. There is less bureaucracy and fewer organizational layers to figure out. You're likely to have direct access to the owner of the company. Also, jobs are less structured, so you may have more opportunity to work on a variety of assignments and projects that interest you.

Identify the Optimal Work Environment

If you're not sure about your career goal, go back to Chapter 4 to review your career kaleidoscope.

Imagine yourself at work. You are doing the kind of work you've always wanted to do; imagine your surroundings. What do you see? Are there lots of people representing many departments, doing many varied tasks? Does the company's e-mail system and intranet link you to other employees around the country and even around the world? Are you part of a large corporation with many divisions or part of a smaller business with 100 or less employees? Are you working in government—at the federal, state, county, or city level? Do you see yourself as part of a publicly or privately funded group? Providing a service or earning profits for stockholders? Or, is the business your own, with your unique workplace design? Narrowing down the type of organization you want to work for, the location where you want to work, how you prefer to approach the work (e.g., core employee, free agent, etc.), and the culture that suits you best will help select the best fit—for you.

You may want to declare yourself a free agent, avoiding altogether the traditional work environment. You're in charge of choosing which clients you want to work with and which projects you want to work on. As a free agent, you have ultimate control over your work life.

More and more companies are offering more flexible work options. Do you want to work part-time, perhaps 25 hours a week, instead of 40? Or, as a full-time core employee, would you prefer flextime hours instead of the traditional 9 A.M. to 5 P.M.?

"The free agent's work ethic: If we're going to spend half our lives working, we insist that the work be fun—serious fun."

DANIEL PINK, "Free Agent Nation," *Fast Company*

Corporate cultures can vary significantly between government, nonprofit organizations, and private industry. Every organization has its own customs and habits—collectively known as *corporate culture.* Some customs are linked to formal systems—pay for performance; monetary rewards and bonus options; rapid advancement and power; work environments emphasizing independence, freedom, and autonomy in making decisions and solving problems. Other customs are more informal; think of them as the typical do's and don'ts or the unwritten rules—risks are rewarded and mistakes are tolerated; breaks and lunch hours are flexible; everyone has access to information or only those with a need to know have access. These habits and quirks are important to learn. You'll discover some customs are easy to research and identify before you accept a work offer. Other corporate idiosyncrasies can only be discovered over time as you listen and observe the "way we do things around here." One way to observe corporate customs before you begin work in a particular environment is to pay attention in the job interview:

- Are you being interviewed by an individual or a team?
- Are there pictures on the walls, family photographs, and plants?
- Are corporate posters hanging on the walls? What messages do they convey?
- Is (are) the interviewer(s) relaxed?
- Is the dress code formal or corporate casual?
- Are you offered a tour of the area, opportunities to meet potential coworkers, and a glimpse of the physical location where you'd be working?

3. RESEARCH YOUR TARGETS

Now you're ready to find out which of these work ideas offer the most promise. Which employers offer the best work fit for you? Through research, you'll find these answers. Researching the best options is *not* searching the want ads or the mega-job sites on the Internet. It's finding out information that will help you decide on the companies you would prefer to work for. Stay focused on your work goal. Gather specific information about the companies on your list to determine if they're viable options; determine which would offer you the most satisfying work and which work environments you would prefer. Decide if a particular organization looks interesting enough to pursue further. At the same time, if an organization seems intriguing, look for information you can use to focus your cover letter, resume, and interview. Use the NAB process (refer to Chapter 7) to help you identify the employer's needs and strategies to successfully interview.

The skills you're developing as you conduct your work search—organizational skills, writing skills, research skills, communication skills—and, above all, gaining experience in your ability to look for the work you want will be assets throughout your career.

Researching employers has two main benefits:

1. To see if you're interested in working for a particular company or organization
2. To prepare for an interview—employers expect work candidates to know about their company

Check out: *Don't Send a Resume* by Jeffrey J. Fox (New York: Hyperion, 2001) for more info on targeting companies.

Activity 10.2 Choosing Work Options

Narrowing down the type of organization you want to work for, where the work is located, how you prefer to approach the work, and the environment that suits you best will help you select the best job fit. These are important considerations in making a job choice. Answer the following questions to help you focus your work search.

1. Circle the type(s) of organization you want to target for your search:
   a. Large corporation
   b. Small business
   c. Government
   d. Nonprofit organization
   e. High-tech start-up company
   f. My own company

2. I will research companies in:
   a. Urban areas
   b. Suburban areas
   c. Rural areas

3. I would rather work as a(n):
   a. Free agent
   b. Part-time employee
   c. Core (permanent) employee
   d. Entrepreneur

4. Circle the type(s) of companies you will target for your search:
   a. Global
   b. National
   c. Regional
   d. Local

5. What's important to me in choosing a *corporate culture* is a work environment that:
   a. Emphasizes monetary rewards
   b. Provides learning opportunities
   c. Gives opportunities for meaningful work and autonomy

Write your optimal work environment in Activity 10.3.

An anatomy of employment growth. FIGURE 10.2

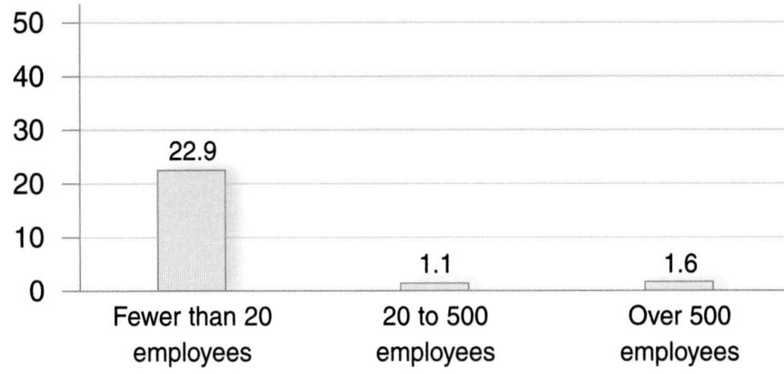

Source: Small Business Administration.

Taking time to research information about the company helps you write your cover letters and resumes and successfully interview. Recruiters are impressed with candidates who know something about the organization. To demonstrate to employers how your skills and abilities meet their needs, you must know specific information about their business.

Three important research tools can help you uncover information: the Internet, print resources in the library or career center, and members of your network. If you don't have direct access to the Internet, use the computer of a friend, in the library, or at a campus location. Some of the directories listed on the following page are also available in print.

Good organization can help you stay focused on your work goal. Develop a system to manage all of the information that you are collecting. For example, Anne developed a simple table like the one shown below to keep her job-hunting information easily accessible. She added information as she made each contact with a target company, dating each entry. This allowed her to easily track and follow up with all companies.

Of the 6.85 million private sector jobs, 76 percent occurred in companies with fewer than 500 employees.

Check out: "Using the Internet for Research to Support Your Job Search" at www.rileyguide.com

DATE	COMPANY	CONTACTS	ACTION
5/28	Arise, Inc 4542 E. Balloon Ave.	andrea@arise.com 750-890-7890 ext 6002 Andrea Owens, VP of Mfg.	5/20—called and requested info 5/29—sent e-mail 6/05—mailed letter
5/30	Program Administrator Ambulatory Surgery Centers (ad in paper)	AmSurg Corp 4920 S. Wendler Drive Suite 214 Tempe AZ 85282 Contact Bonnie Wentz 602-600-0100	5/31—set up interview for 6/8 @ 11am with Kari Lindsay (1 1/2 hrs) 6/9—sent thank-you letter 6/14—offered position (not enough money) 7/1—sent e-mail

Internet Resources to Research Employers

Use any search engine to determine the URL for these Internet sites.

- *The employer's website.* The place to start.
- *American Stock Exchange.* Search its list of companies by stock symbol or alphabetically by company name.
- *America's Job Bank.* Find contact information for companies directly by using this site's search engine, which will allow you to search by industry and/or geographic location.
- *Big Book.* Quickly find information about more than 16 million U. S. businesses. Search by company name, category, city, and/or state.
- *BizWeb.* More than 23,000 companies are categorized and listed by the goods or services they provide in more than 180 categories.
- *Companies OnLine Search.* Search for information on more than 100,000 public and private companies. Search by company name, city, state, industry, ticker symbol, and/or URL. It is sponsored by Dun & Bradstreet.
- *Company Profiles.* Sponsored by Jobtrak Corporation, this meta-list of companies is organized alphabetically and contains links to hundreds of online company home pages.
- *Employer Directory.* Browse profiles alphabetically and/or by category or region. This site is sponsored by JobWeb.com.
- *EDGAR Database of Corporate Information.* It performs automated collection, validation, indexing, acceptance, and forwarding of submissions by companies and others who are required by law to file forms with the U. S. Securities and Exchange Commission.
- *Fortune 500. Fortune* magazine lets you view its database of information using a variety of categories. You can also search by company to obtain Fortune 500 rankings, sales/revenue, profits, assets, etc.
- *Getting a Job.* This database, sponsored by StudentCenter.com, contains more than 35,000 companies that you can sort by name, location, and industry.
- *Hoover's Online.* A great source for job seekers needing company information, this site provides free access to a Corporate Directory, which lists information on thousands of companies.
- *Social-service.com.* A great resource for the non-profit sector.
- *Thomas Register of American Manufacturers.* Access this website's search engine to search the 155,000 companies in their database classified under more than 57,000 product and service headings.
- *Wall Street Research Net.* Search for U. S. or Canadian companies (from the NYSE, NASDAQ, AMEX, and OTC exchanges) alphabetically or by entering either the company name or stock symbol.
- *Yahoo!'s Corporate Directories.* Enter the name of the company you want to find and let its database of listings do the rest.

Anne also created a file for each company (you can use file folders or a notebook). She filed copies of the letters she sent and relevant research data. Then, if a company called, she could quickly go to that file and talk confidently about how she could contribute. Develop the kind of system that works best for you. You'll want a system that's flexible enough so that you can add the names of new target companies when your networking contacts provide you with leads.

One challenge during this process is finding a balance so you can optimize your efforts. Pursuing one or two companies at a time doesn't give you much choice. On the other hand, it's difficult to really stay connected with more than 10 or 15 companies at a time. Another challenge is monitoring how you're spending your time. Try to resist "busywork" that won't yield good results. Some job searchers spend hours searching job boards and classified ads and never find time to contact their network for promising leads and introductions to people who can hire them. Don't let that happen to you! Prioritize your activities to maximize your time.

Resources Available in Print

Business librarians can help you find information on almost any company. Many libraries have special sections to assist job-hunters. Libraries also offer online access, including databases of articles from local newspapers. This can be a great source for information about a local company branch or small private companies in a specific geographic area. Your career center may also have a library of resources, including annual reports of the companies that are recruiting on campus.

- *The Almanac of American Employers.* This resource lists 500 companies. The information you will find includes the company's recent financial performance, salaries and benefits, company divisions, academic backgrounds the company wants in its applicants, and future growth projections (Publisher: Corporate Jobs Outlook).
- *Dun & Bradstreet Employment Opportunities Directory—The Career Guide.* This is a one-volume directory that lists employment information about more than 5,000 companies (Publisher: Dun & Bradstreet, 3 Sylvan Way, Parsipany, NJ 07054).
- *Standard & Poor's Register of Corporations, Directors and Executives.* This directory covers approximately 55,000 public and private companies. The directory is published annually in three volumes. Volume 3 provides the reader with brief data on key executives (Publisher: Standard & Poor's Corporation, 25 Broadway, New York, NY 10004).

Many other directories are available for you to browse. Visit your library and decide which ones will benefit you the most.

As you research and gather information, consider the pros and cons of each choice, and how the facts you uncovered fit with your career kaleidoscope—what's important to you. For example, after completing his research, Grant decided to focus his work search in marketing to education—targeting community colleges and associations that advocate for education and lobbying firms whose clients are schools, colleges, and textbook publishers. He narrowed his options and submitted his resume to 20 specific organizations he felt would be a good work fit. Grant contacted his network and began asking people if they knew anyone who works for the organizations on his list. He has narrowed the target of his work search and is preparing to talk to potential employers.

Connect with Your Network

This is your ultimate goal—talk to people who have the authority to hire you. Use your network to help you identify decision makers in the organizations you have targeted. Don't worry about whether there's an opening

For tips on contacting your network, review Chapter 9.

at the time. If you can get your foot in the door to talk to the right person (a decision maker), he or she might even create a position for you. At a minimum, you can learn about potential opportunities, strategies for becoming better qualified, and names of other individuals you can talk to.

"Of the people who found jobs through personal contacts, 43.8 percent of them had new positions created for them."

MARK GRANOVETTER, ***Getting a Job: A Study of Contacts and Careers***

Identify who the decision maker is for your work in each organization on your list. Call the organization, and find out who is responsible for the work you want to do. Don't ask, "Who hires potential candidates?" They may refer you to the personnel department. If you go through personnel, you'll be in competition with all the other job applicants. Remember, the personnel department only prescreens applicants. The decision maker is the manager responsible for the work.

When Sean began looking for work as a physical therapy aide, he identified five area hospitals where he was particularly interested in working. Sean called each hospital and identified the director of physical therapy. After sending his resume directly to each of the directors, Sean called all of them to discuss why he wanted to go to work in their hospital. Bypassing the personnel system, Sean obtained several job offers to consider.

After completing your research, enter the most promising options in Activity 10.3.

JOB SEARCH TIP

While you're job hunting, make sure your answering machine always has a professional response.

4. MAKE CONTACT

Now that you have researched potential employers, it's time to make contact and get busy landing the job you want. Successful candidates—people who are hired to do the work they want at a company they've targeted—use a variety of techniques to contact employers. You should use a combination of strategies to help you learn what employers are looking for and ways to contact them. Now that you have more information about your work goal and the companies you want to work for, reexamine your resume and make any changes based on your research. Practice the one-minute commercial you created in Chapter 7 and you're ready to make contact!

REAL-LIFE PERSPECTIVE

CHARLES CORNELL

When Charles Cornell graduated from the University of Michigan with a degree in finance, he decided he wanted to relocate to the Southwest. Though he had interned in college and developed a number of professional contacts, they were all in the Chicago area. They couldn't offer Charles any help in approaching decision makers in Phoenix, Arizona. So, Charles called his alumni association in Michigan and asked for information about the University of Michigan alumni association in Phoenix. When Charles found out that one did not exist in Phoenix, he offered to start one for the School of Business graduates. The placement office gave him a list of graduates living in Phoenix, and Charles began making contacts—not to look for work, but to develop an alumni association. Through his efforts, Charles soon knew people who could introduce him to decision makers working in more than half of the companies on his list.

Work Search Targets

Activity 10.3

My goal

My optimal work environment

Potential employers

My best targets—narrow your list to the 20 most promising options

Favorite Job Boards

- www.monster.com: The largest job board on the Web.
- www.flipdog.com: Pulls in jobs posted on company websites.
- www.rileyguide.com: Margaret Dikel, a librarian, evaluates and links to job boards sorted by industry and specialty. A good place to find specialty and niche job boards.
- www.careerbuilder.com: Sign up for e-mails to notify you of openings that match your skill sets.
- www.collegejournal.com: *The Wall Street Journal* hosts this excellent resource for students on all aspects of looking for work—from cover letters to interviewing. This links to *The Wall Street Journal's* career site: www.careerjournal.com.
- www.americasjobbank.com: National site compiling all state unemployment office listings. Because employers can post here for free, it is a good source for jobs when the economy is tight.
- www.collegegrad.com: Excellent entry-level job bank combines with outstanding job hunting resources geared toward college students.
- www.aftercollege.com/: Job board for recent grads.
- www.black-collegian.com/: The online site of the magazine dedicated to college students and professionals of color.

Contact Methods to Reach Employers

- **Contact small and medium size companies.** You can begin your campaign by sending a cover letter and resume, then following up with a phone call.
- **Visit your targeted employers.** If you don't know anyone in the company, you might make a stronger impression by dropping in than by putting your resume in the mail. If you can't talk to a manager when you visit, leave your resume, ask for his or her name, and follow up with a phone call.
- **Contact your network.** Ask members of your network for (and keep them posted in your progress):

  Names of people who work in the field you've chosen or companies you've targeted

  Job leads and possible work opportunities

  Advice about your job search
- **Contact hiring managers directly.** Bypass the personnel department and contact the manager of the department where you'd like to work. Ask if you can meet to discuss how you can add value to their department.
- **Broadcast the news.** Don't hesitate to tell everyone you meet that you're looking for work. Relate your one-minute commercial. Tell them about the kind of work you want and the types of companies you've targeted. You can do this during social gatherings, standing in line at the video rental store, or other places you visit.

REAL-LIFE PERSPECTIVE

LISA MARTIN

After graduating from college with a degree in biochemistry, Lisa Martin started working for a pharmaceutical firm in her college town. After five years, she still found the work challenging and exciting, but she wanted to move to Albuquerque, New Mexico. Lisa made the move and started her job search. One day she took some clothes to the dry cleaner. While talking to the counter person, Lisa mentioned she was looking for work. The person asked Lisa a few questions, and then said, "My sister-in-law works at the university here, and she's been looking for someone with your background for over a year. Here's her name and phone number." Lisa made the phone call and was hired. Lisa says, "You never know who can give you a promising lead. Be willing to tell everyone you can what you're looking for—it will pay off!"

Contact Methods to Learn the Qualifications Employers Seek and the Language They Use

- **Classified advertisements.** Reading want ads can be discouraging because they are written to attract only the most qualified candidates. With that in mind, apply for positions for which you are reasonably qualified, even if you don't quite measure up to everything listed in the ad.
- **College Placement and Alumnae Offices.** Check the jobs listed at your college career center in person or online. Visit campus job fairs to meet employers.
- **Campus Recruiters.** Find out from your college career center when recruiters will be on campus. Bring copies of your resume and be prepared for a brief interview.
- **Job Hot Lines.** In most cities, large employers, government agencies, and nonprofit organizations have job hotlines. Ask a research librarian for a list of them. Call the hot line for job vacancy information.
- **Internet Job Boards.** Most people have the best luck using job boards that specialize in their career field. Professional associations sponsor some of the best.

5. FOLLOW UP

Follow up on your interviews—without follow up, you may miss work opportunities that may be waiting for you. Follow up consists of two strategies:

- *Staying in touch* with hiring managers after your initial contact. You can call on the phone, e-mail, and send letters. Follow up helps managers remember you and the solutions that you can offer. It also helps you know how the hiring process is proceeding.

Sample thank-you letter after an interview.

Mr. Mark Campbell
California Research Labs
1234 Calle Brisa
San Jose California 95125

April 5, 2004

Dear Mr. Campbell,

Thank you for taking the time to discuss the computer analyst position at California Research Labs with me. I appreciate the opportunity to learn more about the company and am convinced that my background and skills coincide with your needs.

I am so pleased you agree that my internship with Lucent Technologies helped prepare me with the computer skills and language applications necessary for the job. Taking a tour of the facility was extremely valuable. I know I would enjoy working in this high-tech environment. The digital equipment you've installed keeps your employees up-to-date with the latest advances in technologies. With the high demands of continuous technological change, being a quick learner, like me, is a plus in your work environment.

In addition to my skills and experience, I will bring exceptional work habits to the position. My ability to take initiative and work as a team member will fit in well with the position.

I look forward to learning of your decision soon. Thank you again for the wonderful opportunity to become part of the California Research Labs team.

Sincerely,

John Jenkins

- *Sending thank-you letters.* No matter what work search strategies you use, send thank-you letters to everyone you meet. After an interview, try to mail your thank-you letter the same day. A unique approach is a handwritten note on nice stationery. Restate your interest in the job and mention any other ideas you have about solving their problems. Your letter is another chance to present your strengths and their relevance to the employer.

By following the work search process we've described in this chapter, you'll develop the skills you need for an effective work search and gather

Ten Ways to Get Started — Activity 10.4

Instructions: In the space below, write down the first 10 things you will do to start your job search. For example, you might write down: research my top 10 targets; visit the career center to get a schedule of on-campus interviews; call Joe Brown to ask questions about Big Star Technology; look for advertised positions in marketing; talk to Dr. Nakar and ask for contacts.

ACTION I'LL TAKE	TARGET DATE
1. ____________	____________
2. ____________	____________
3. ____________	____________
4. ____________	____________
5. ____________	____________
6. ____________	____________
7. ____________	____________
8. ____________	____________
9. ____________	____________
10. ____________	____________

enough information to shine in job interviews. Mastering the work search process will not only result in an offer—it will also result in the right work for you! To start your search, complete Activity 10.4, Ten Ways to Get Started.

What About Salary?

You should think about salary before going to your first hiring interview. The first thing to recognize is that starting salaries are a function of the economy. We heard many stories of fantastic salary offers and signing bonuses during the late '90s. As the economy slowed, those fantastic offers disappeared. Rather than guessing your worth or the current state of the job market, do some research. Salaries vary widely in different parts of the country, so seek information about salaries in your location. Salary surveys are available online and through professional associations. The best source, of course, is someone already working in the company.

How much do you need to earn? Activity 10.5 will help you determine your monthly budget. Write down realistic amounts of your actual spending. If you don't usually track your expenses carefully, keep a small notebook handy for the next two weeks and jot down every penny you spend. Then, double those amounts to estimate your monthly budget. Once you've entered the figures in the table, you can mark the areas where you could pare down expenses.

E-MAIL ADVICE

As a job-seeker, it's best to choose an e-mail address name that is professional and business-like. For example, Robin Michaels could select Rmichaels@aol.com. if America Online was her service provider.

Activity 10.5 Your Monthly Budget

Instructions: List the dollar amounts you think you will need in each expense category.

MY MONTHLY BUDGET	
Expense	*Amount*
Housing (rent or mortgage + utilities)	$
Food (groceries + eating out)	$
Clothing (purchases + cleaning)	$
Automobile/transportation (payments + gas)	$
Insurance	$
Childcare or child support	$
Education loans or expenses	$
Bills and debts (credit cards, stores, loans, etc.)	$
Savings	$
Amusement/discretionary spending (movies + reading + other entertainment, gifts + vacation	$
Total amount you need each month	$

Negotiating Offers

You will ultimately be faced with the dreaded questions about salary. "How much should I ask for?" "What am I worth?" One thing is for sure—*never* discuss salary until the position has been offered. This is not always an easy rule to follow. In your first interview, the personnel analyst may ask you what salary you want. Be aware of two things:

1. Every position has a salary range. Research it before the interview by calling the personnel office and asking about the range.
2. The interviewer may try to get you to state a figure early in the interview process and expect you to stick to it. Remember, you usually can't negotiate up from the lowest figure you name.

Here's how to answer salary questions in the first interview: "I'd like to know more about the responsibilities before I discuss salary." Sometimes, the interviewer will not be satisfied with this answer and will ask the question again. If that happens, there are two possible responses:

- Respond with a question if you don't know the salary range: "What is the salary range for this position?"
- If you know the range, state that you are comfortable with it and will be prepared to discuss the exact salary when you know more about the position.

There seem to be two different strategies companies use when it comes to offering salary. Some companies spend time and effort researching salaries offered by their competitors. Their first offer is their best offer—that is, there isn't room to negotiate pay. Most companies offer a salary range and are willing to negotiate. Always assume that you can negotiate. Research indicates that 80 percent of the time job applicants can negotiate a higher salary or better benefits.

In order to negotiate, you must have done your homework. Know what the typical salary range is for the type of position and that area of the country. Salary surveys are available online and through professional associations. The best source, of course, is someone already working in the company. Start in the mid-range, leaving yourself room to compromise if it's necessary.

For example, if you were relocating, you might explain that because the cost of living is higher in the new city, you believe you need a higher salary to stay even with your financial needs. Ask if there is any room to adjust the salary to account for this cost-of-living difference. If this company has given its best offer, the person will say so. If there is room for negotiation, you will probably be asked what salary you have in mind.

Follow our strategy—it will pay off! If you can't negotiate the stated salary range, think about things besides salary that would make the job worth accepting. Additional benefits you can negotiate include:

- Signing bonus
- Telecommuting
- Flextime
- Time off to attend professional association meetings and seminars
- Training or education
- Moving allowance (if you will relocate to another city)
- Performance-based bonus
- Stock options
- Relocation costs
- Vacation

EVALUATING BENEFITS

Employee benefits vary from company to company. Many companies offer a cafeteria of benefits, allowing employees to choose what they like best from a variety of plans. If you have health insurance through your spouse's employer, you may prefer to select other benefits, such as child care assistance. Benefits are constantly changing as companies scramble to remain competitive. Here are some of the most common benefits, demystified.

- **Stock options.** The company offers the employee stock options. This allows the employee the opportunity to buy a certain amount of company stock at a certain price for a specified time period, such as five years. Employees may buy at any time, pocketing the difference between the option price and the stock.

REAL-LIFE PERSPECTIVE

BONNIE BURKE

Bonnie accepted a position as an advisor at a university because she knew she'd enjoy the work. Her salary was less than she was offered for a position in the private sector, but one benefit from her new employer made all the difference. College tuition is free. Bonnie is working on her master's degree at no cost to her. When she added that benefit to her salary, she realized the compensation was about equal. She believes she made the right choice—she has a job she loves, and she's continuously learning.

- **Health insurance.** Most companies pay for medical insurance for full-time employees. Coverage can vary dramatically. Some companies pay 100 percent of health insurance costs for the employees and their families. Other companies may pay only 50 percent (or some other portion) of the cost of health insurance coverage for the employees and contribute nothing toward the coverage of dependents.

  Health insurance options also vary extensively from company to company. Options include medical savings accounts, HMOs, PPOs, dental and orthodontic coverage, eyeglass coverage, and so forth.

- **Life insurance.** Some companies offer term or whole life insurance to employees. Usually, the policy terminates when employment ends.

- **Vacation, sick leave, and time off.** Many companies now lump together vacation, sick leave, and time off, calling it *paid time off,* and you can use it as you wish. You may be able to negotiate another week of vacation or *mental health days* in lieu of higher salary.

- **Signing bonuses.** Signing bonuses may be offered to high-demand employees. This negotiated amount varies but is often 20 to 25 percent of the annual salary. Typically, it's paid to the employee upon successful completion of the probationary period or after one year.

- **Child care assistance.** Some large companies offer on-site day care to dependents of the employee. Other companies offer pretax savings accounts to meet child care expenses; the company may or may not contribute money to the account.

- **Tuition reimbursement.** Many companies offer tuition reimbursement for additional education. Check to see if the courses have to be related to your current job or can help prepare you for a lateral move or promotion. Rules for reimbursement vary, so find out the individual company's policy.

- **Relocation benefits.** These are often reserved for experienced applicants. The company may pay the cost of your move, provide temporary housing, help you with a down payment on a house, and even buy your current house if it isn't sold in a reasonable amount of time.

EVALUATING JOB OFFERS

Some job seekers believe that once they've negotiated salary and benefits, they're obligated to accept the position. When they receive their first solid job offer, they *immediately* say yes. This isn't necessary—remember, you're going to be spending the next few years of your life working for this company; you'll want to carefully consider the offer. In addition, the company will be investing time and training to bring you onboard. It would prefer you say no, rather than invest in you if you're going to be dissatisfied. When a job is offered to you, always ask for a day or two to think about it. Both you and the employer will be glad you did.

There is more to evaluating a position than just looking at salary and benefits. Remember to consider your kaleidoscope elements (see Chapter 4 and Activity 10.6) and the goal statement you wrote at the beginning of this chapter. Think about the values and preferences that are most important to you when analyzing the position, and determine if it's right for you.

WAYS TO READ A COMPANY

When it comes to judging out-of-this-world job offers, Professor Maura Belliveau, who teaches at Duke University's Fuqua School of Business, gives this down-to-earth advice: Don't believe everything you read or much of what you hear. She has assembled a guide to help her students *interview* companies and learn what makes them tick. In "Four Ways to Read a Company," she shared some of her tips with *Fast Company* (1998).

1. Know some answers before you ask questions. "The best information about a company comes from the people who know the intimate details—current employees, former employees, customers—but these people may not know *you*. How do you persuade them to be frank? By becoming as informed as possible *before* you talk with them. The more you know, the more likely it is that people will consider you someone worth spending time with."

"One of my students evaluated a consulting firm. She wanted to talk about office politics, a sensitive topic. Before she visited, she found a 50-

What Makes a Job Great?

1. Does the job mirror what you love to do? What are your passions? Will you be spending most of your day engaged in the activities you enjoy doing the most? Would you continue to do the work even after you inherited a large sum of money?
2. Will you work with people who will help you soar? Who will be your leader, the person you count on for direction, guidance, and support? Good jobs are ones with supervisors who encourage you to grow and develop. Find jobs with good mentors to help you succeed.
3. Will you have the opportunity for continuous learning? Will you have the opportunity to learn and develop new skills and competencies? Select the job that gives you opportunities to work on many projects, challenges you, and helps you stay on top of new developments.
4. Does the job invite rapid change? Choose a job in an environment that is growing and changing. It will force you to keep up with the rate of change.
5. Does the company have a good reputation? Look for a job in a company that displays world-class business practices. Is the company respected as a leader in the field? Exposure to an industry leader will prove invaluable when you're ready to search for your next job.

Activity 10.6 Checklist for Evaluating Offers

Instructions: Use this checklist to help you decide on a position. Space is provided in each category for you to add factors that are important to you.

THE EMPLOYER

- ◯ Fits with my work goal
- ◯ The right size, growth rate, market potential for me
- ◯ Good facilities and working conditions
- ◯ Work activities appeal to me
- ◯ Desire to work there for a period of time
- ◯ Demands of job compatible with my lifestyle
- ◯ ______________________
- ◯ ______________________
- ◯ ______________________

MANAGEMENT AND COWORKERS

- ◯ Stable management
- ◯ Professional workforce
- ◯ Compatible with the management style I prefer
- ◯ I think I can work well with my immediate supervisor
- ◯ Job expectations and responsibilities are realistic
- ◯ Largely promote from within
- ◯ ______________________
- ◯ ______________________
- ◯ ______________________

POTENTIAL FOR CONTINUOUS LEARNING

- ◯ Provides opportunities for training, tuition reimbursement
- ◯ Opportunity to attend conferences, seminars for professional development
- ◯ Opportunity to learn new skills
- ◯ Opportunity to work on new projects
- ◯ ______________________
- ◯ ______________________
- ◯ ______________________

COMPENSATION

- ◯ Starting salary, long-term outlook satisfactory
- ◯ Satisfactory benefits (e.g., insurance, profit sharing, tuition, retirement)
- ◯ ______________________
- ◯ ______________________
- ◯ ______________________

LOCATION

- ◯ Cost of living
- ◯ Distance to work
- ◯ Geographic area, environment
- ◯ ______________________
- ◯ ______________________
- ◯ ______________________

page history of the firm on its website. She absorbed that material. She had a better understanding of the firm's evolution than some of the people she talked to, which meant that they were more likely to answer her questions honestly."

2. You're often just two degrees of separation away from the best sources of information. "It's easy to say, 'I want to talk to people with inside knowledge, but I don't know anyone on the inside.' Work your networks and you'll be amazed at who you know. If you've gone to business school, you have fellow alumni who work for that company or in that industry—or know people who do. Get their telephone number through the alumni directory. Chances are they'll be candid with you."

REAL-LIFE PERSPECTIVE

RUDY TAN

Rudy has followed the advice in this chapter, using many resources for his job search. His hard work has paid off—he received two job offers! Now, he has to decide which one to accept. One offer is with a large telecommunications firm, working in a department that is developing Internet services. The second offer is with a small start-up company, which is also developing Internet technology. When Rudy compared the pros and cons of each position, he still couldn't decide which offer to take. The salary and benefits were comparable. The main differences were company size and the opportunities for learning. Rudy believed he would have more autonomy and responsibility at the smaller company and would receive more opportunities for learning. As Rudy evaluated the offer from the large telecommunications firm, he knew from past experience he would fit into the corporate culture. However, this position would probably only offer training directly related to the work he performed. After careful consideration, he decided to take the position with the smaller company. He knows his decision to go with the smaller company is riskier—it's just getting off the ground—but he believes it's a better fit for him.

3. Appearance matters. "Don't just look at where people work. Watch *how* they work—simple things like how a receptionist greets strangers can be illuminating. Organizations convey something about themselves in their selection of front-line staff. Companies with strong cultures stand out from the moment you walk onto the premises."

4. Look for heroes, listen for stories. "Every company has *heroes*, people who embody the core values. And, every company has *stories*—anecdotes that employees share with outsiders. What are the stories about? Big wins? Great service? Political battles? The stories that people inside a company share tell you a lot about the company itself."

Succeeding at Work

You've made it! Now what? Once the excitement wears off, you'll realize your first year on the job is a time of transition. It takes some time to adjust to your new professional status. And it will take some time for you to earn the rights and responsibilities of a full-fledged professional. During this period, you will be scrutinized as people around you determine your potential. If you start out demonstrating that you're an outstanding performer, more doors and opportunities will open.

Your first task is to understand your immediate supervisor's expectations. Let's face it—some managers know better than others how to explain the "big picture"—the goals of the department and how you and your responsibilities contribute to them. If your manager doesn't provide that information right away, then take the initiative and ask. Your work performance will be evaluated, and it certainly helps to know the standards by which you'll be judged.

Remember to display the right attitude and show enthusiasm in everything you do, whether it's your first professional job or an opportu-

Job Do's and Don'ts

Do's

- Show up ready to work on your first day with enthusiasm.
- Build positive relationships, especially with customers, coworkers, and your boss.
- Develop work savvy—learn the unspoken rules.
- Master the competencies of your job.
- Become a team player.
- Make a good impression by keeping your commitments.
- Continuously learn. Ask for new assignments once you've mastered your responsibilities.
- Find a mentor.

Don'ts

- Agree to do the impossible. If you're not sure you can deliver, don't promise.
- Cross the ethical line.
- Tell dirty, racist, or sexist jokes.
- Fall behind the technology curve—become proficient in the use of technology in your work.
- Take sole credit for a team effort.
- Go it alone. Ask for help when you need it.
- Try to work without a calendar or pocket planner.
- Burn bridges—you never know who your next boss will be or when you'll need that person's help.

nity for career advancement. In this textbook, we have stated that career planning is a creative, flexible process evolving over time. You'll likely experience many work opportunities as you build your career and look for ways to contribute to the workplace. Continue to use the career management strategies you've learned in this text to help you anytime during your career journey. Good luck!

Summary Points

- The job search process involves thinking of yourself as a unique product—*You, Inc.*
- Accessing the *hidden job market* is more effective than traditional job search methods.
- Focusing your search begins with knowing what you want and what work environment best suits you.
- Researching employers will help you learn whether this company suits you and how to market your skills toward their needs.
- When you evaluate a job offer, consider more than salary and benefits. What is the environment like and how well does the work fit your goal?
- The first year of your new work is an exciting transition. Learn your supervisor's expectations right away and then perform at the highest level you can.
- You've learned valuable lifetime skills; use them whenever it's time for a career change.

References

CHAPTER 1

Boyett, Joseph and Conn, Henry. 1991. *Workplace 2000.* New York: The Penguin Group.

Boyett, Joseph and Snyder, David Pearce. 1998. "Twenty-First Century Workplace Trends." *On the Horizon.* Published online at www.horizon.unc.edu.

Bridges, William. 1994. *JobShift.* Reading, MA: Addison-Wesley.

Conza, Anthony P., as quoted by Jason Rich. 1996. *First Job, Great Job. America's Hottest Business Leaders Share Their Secrets.* New York: Macmillan Spectrum.

Coplan, Jill Hamburg. 2001. "Making the Case for Telecommuting." *BusinessWeek Online,* April 11.

Foner, Philip S. 1980. *Women and the American Labor Movement—From World War I to the Present.* New York: The Free Press, a division of Macmillan Publishing Inc.

Hammonds, Keith, et al. 1997. "Non-Standard Jobs: A New Look." *Business Week,* September 15, p. 96.

Kelly, Kevin. 1997. "New Rules for the New Economy." *Wired,* September, p. 142.

Land, George and Jarman, Beth. 1992. *Breakpoint and Beyond, Mastering the Future Today.* New York: Harper Business.

McKenna, Regis. 1997. *Real Time: Preparing for the Age of the Never Satisfied Customer.* Boston: Harvard Business School Press.

Mendels, Pamela. 2000. "Allowing Temps to Organize." *BusinessWeek Online,* September 14.

"The Promise of Productivity," 1998. *Business Week,* March 9, pp. 28–30.

Rifkin, Jeremy. 1995. *The End of Work.* New York: G. P. Putnam.

Smith, Robert H. 1969. *This Fabulous Century 1900–1910, the Golden Interlude.* New York: Time-Life Books.

Smith, Robert H. 1969. *This Fabulous Century 1910–1920, the Golden Interlude.* New York: Time-Life Books.

Taylor, James and Wacker, Watts. 1997. *The 500 Year Delta.* New York: HarperCollins.

CHAPTER 2

Bateson, Mary Catherine. 1989. *Composing a Life.* New York: Atlantic Monthly Press.

Bolles, Richard. 1978. *The Three Boxes of Life and How to Get Out of Them: An Introduction to Life–Work Planning.* Berkeley, CA: Ten Speed Press.

Bridges, William. 1994. *JobShift.* Reading, MA: Addison-Wesley.

Land, George and Jarman, Beth. 1992. *Breakpoint and Beyond, Mastering the Future Today.* New York: Harper Business.

Michalko, Michael. 1991. *Thinkertoys: A Handbook of Business Creativity for the 90's.* Berkeley, CA: Ten Speed Press.

Reich, Robert, as quoted by Richard Koonce. 1996. "The Changing Landscape of the American Workplace: An Interview with Labor Secretary Robert Reich." *Training and Development*, December, pp. 25–28.

Seligman, Martin. 1991. *Learned Optimism.* New York: Knopf.

Senge, Peter. 1995. *The Fifth Discipline: The Art and Practice of the Learning Organization.* New York: Doubleday.

Taylor, James and Wacker, Watts. 1997. *The 500 Year Delta.* New York: HarperCollins.

CHAPTER 3

Crispell, Diane. 1998. "The Lure of the Entrepreneur." *American Demographics*, February. Available online at www.demographics.com.

Fields, Debbi, as quoted by Jason Rich. 1996. *First Job, Great Job. America's Hottest Business Leaders Share Their Secrets.* New York: Macmillan Spectrum.

Higgins, James. 1994. *101 Creative Problem-Solving Techniques.* New Management Publishing Co.

Lieber, Ron. 2000. "Start-Ups: The Inside Stories." *Fast Company*, March, p. 284.

Michalko, Michael. 1991. *Thinkertoys: A Handbook of Business Creativity for the 90's.* Berkeley, CA: Ten Speed Press.

Yang, Jerry, as quoted by Jason Rich. 1996. *First Job, Great Job. America's Hottest Business Leaders Share Their Secrets.* New York: Macmillan Spectrum.

CHAPTER 4

Gottfredson, Gary and Holland, John. 1996. *Dictionary of Holland Occupational Codes* (3rd ed). Lutz, FL: Psychological Assessment Resources.

Holland, John. 1985. *Making Vocational Choices: A Theory of Vocational Personalities and Work Environments* (2nd ed). Englewood Cliffs, NJ: Prentice Hall.

Land, George and Jarman, Beth. 1992. *Breakpoint and Beyond, Mastering the Future Today.* New York: Harper Business.

Waldroop, James, as quoted by Alan Webber. 1998. "Is Your Job Your Calling?" *Fast Company*, February/March, p. 110.

CHAPTER 5

Belasco, James. 1993. *Flight of the Buffalo.* New York: Warner Books.

Bishop, Peter. 1998. "Thinking Like a Futurist." *The Futurist,* June/July, pp. 39–42.

Carey, John; Freundich, Naomi; and Gross, Neil. 1997. "The Biotech Century." *Business Week,* March 10, p. 74.

Cornish, Edward (Editor). 1996. *Outlook '97—Recent Forecasts for the Futurist Magazine for 1997 and Beyond.* Bethesda, MD: World Future Society.

Drucker, Peter. 1993. *The Effective Executive.* New York: Harper Business.

Fulton, Katherine. 1996. "A Tour of Our Uncertain Future." *Columbia Journalism Review,* March/April, pp. 19–26.

Halal, William, et al. 1997. "Emerging Technologies: What's Ahead for 2001–2030." *The Futurist,* November/December, pp. 20–28.

Haldane, Bernard. 1996. Quoted in "Ten Rules for Living in the Age of Joblessness." *William Bridges & Associates Newsletter,* Vol. 6, No. 1.

Hines, Andy. 1996. "Scenarios for Infotech Workers." In *Exploring Your Future—Living, Learning, and Working in the Information Age.* Bethesda, MD: World Future Society.

Kaye, Beverly and Farren, Caela. 1996. "New Skills for New Leadership Roles." *The Leader of the Future.* The Peter F. Drucker Foundation. San Francisco: Jossey-Bass.

Mans, Charles and Sims, Henry. 1995. *Business Without Bosses.* New York: John Wiley and Sons.

Melcher, Richard A., et al. 1998. "Grains that Taste Like Meat?" *Business Week,* May 25, p. 44.

Naisbett, John. 1998. "Report from the Futurist." *Fast Company,* December/January, p. 44.

Olesen, Douglas E. 1996. "The Top Technologies for the Next 10 Years." *Exploring Your Future,* World Future Society, pp. 67–71.

Salter, Chuck. 1998. "This Is Brain Surgery." *Fast Company,* February/March, p. 149.

Schwartz, Peter. 1991. *The Art of the Long View.* New York: Doubleday.

U. S. Department of Labor. 2000–2001 *Occupational Outlook Handbook.* Washington, D. C.: U. S. Government Printing Office.

Wacker, Watts. 1997. "How to Be Your Own Futurist." *Fast Company,* December/January, p. 34.

World Future Society. 1996. "The art of forecasting—A brief introduction to thinking about the future." *Why Study the Future?* Bethesda, MD: Author.

CHAPTER 6

Andriola, Tom. 1998. "Career Survival 101: Work in the Future." Published online at www.getajob.com.

Basta, Nicholas. 1991. *Major Options: The Student's Guide Linking College Majors and Career Opportunities During and After College.* New York: HarperCollins.

Belasco, James. 1993. *Flight of the Buffalo.* New York: Warner Books.

Bronner, Ethan. 1998. *The New York Times,* July 5.

Bronner, Ethan. 1998. "Voracious Computers Are Siphoning Talent from Academia." *The New York Times,* June 25.

Brown, Arnold. 1997. "The Next Economy and What It Means for Education." 76245.2554@compuserve.com, Weiner, Edrich, Brown, Inc. Published online at horizon.unc.edu.

Challenger, John, as quoted by William O'Hare and Joseph Schwartz. 1997. "One Step Forward, Two Steps Back." *American Demographics,* September, p. 53.

Covey, Steven. 1989. *The Seven Habits of Highly Effective People.* New York: Simon & Schuster.

Johnson, Kirk. 1998. "In the Changed Landscape of Recruiting, Academic and Corporate World Merge." *The New York Times,* December 4.

Mulpuru, Sucharita. 2002. "Learning in the Real World Classroom," *BusinessWeek Online,* October.

National Association of Colleges & Employers. *Salary Survey Fall 2002 and Job Outlook 2002.* Bethlehem, PA: Author.

Resler, David H., as quoted by Gene Koretz. 1998. "U. S. Workers Get Smarter—Experience and Schooling Pay Off." *Business Week,* March 9, p. 7.

Taylor, James and Wacker, Watts. 1997. *The 500 Year Delta.* New York: HarperCollins.

U. S. Department of Labor. 2000. "Scans Report." Washington, D.C.: U. S. Government Printing Office.

VanDerWerf, Martin. 1998. "Enrollment growing in online courses." *Arizona Republic,* November 16, p. E1.

www.studentcenter.com. "Career Options for English Majors." Available online.

CHAPTER 7

Allen, Claudia (Editor). November 1997. *Job Outlook '98.* National Association of Colleges and Employers. Bethlehem, PA: Author.

Mieszkowski, Katharine. 1998. "Eunice Azzani, Head Farmer." *Fast Company,* December, p. 129.

Rich, Jason. 1996. *First Job, Great Job. America's Hottest Business Leaders Share Their Secrets.* New York: Macmillan Spectrum.

Sullivan, John. 1998. "How to Look Experienced Right Out of School!" Available online at JohnS@sfsu.edu.

CHAPTER 8

Fisher, Ann. 1997. "Stupid Resume Tricks." *Fortune,* July 21, p. 119.

CHAPTER 9

Boss, Russell, as quoted by Jason Rich. 1996. *First Job, Great Job. America's Hottest Business Leaders Share Their Secrets.* New York: Macmillan Spectrum.

Lincoln, Howard, as quoted by Jason Rich. 1996. *First Job, Great Job. America's Hottest Business Leaders Share Their Secrets.* New York: Macmillan Spectrum.

Swartz, Sidney, as quoted by Jason Rich. 1996. *First Job, Great Job. America's Hottest Business Leaders Share Their Secrets.* New York: Macmillan Spectrum.

Taylor, James and Wacker, Watts. 1997. *The 500 Year Delta.* New York: HarperCollins.

Weber, Joseph and Barrett, Amy. 1998. "The New Era of Lifestyle Drugs." *Business Week,* May 11, p. 318.

CHAPTER 10

Belliveau, Maura. 1998. "Four Ways to Read a Company." *Fast Company,* October, p. 158.

Bridges, William. 1994. *JobShift.* Reading, MA: Addison-Wesley.

Conley, Lucas. 2003. "Where Are the Jobs?" *Fast Company,* March, p. 34.

Crispin, G. and Mehler, M. 2000. *CareerXRoads 2000.* MMC Group.

Fields, Julie. 2000. "Still Seeking Job Seekers." *BusinessWeek Online,* Feb. 12.

Fox, Jeffrey J. 2001. *Don't Send a Resume.* New York: Hyperion.

Granovetter, Mark. 1995. *Getting a Job: A Study of Contacts and Careers.* Cambridge, MA: Harvard University Press.

Imperato, Gina. 2000. "Get Your Career in Site," *Fast Company,* March, p. 322.

Jackson, Tom. 1993. *Guerrilla Tactics in the New Job Market.* New York: Doubleday Dell.

LaBarre, P. 1999. "The New Face of Office Politics," *Fast Company,* October, p. 80.

Pink, Daniel H. 1998. "Free Agent Nation." *Fast Company,* December/January, pp. 131–151.

Index

My Kaleidoscope Elements

As you complete the assessment activities in Chapters 3 and 4, write your preferences in the shapes below.

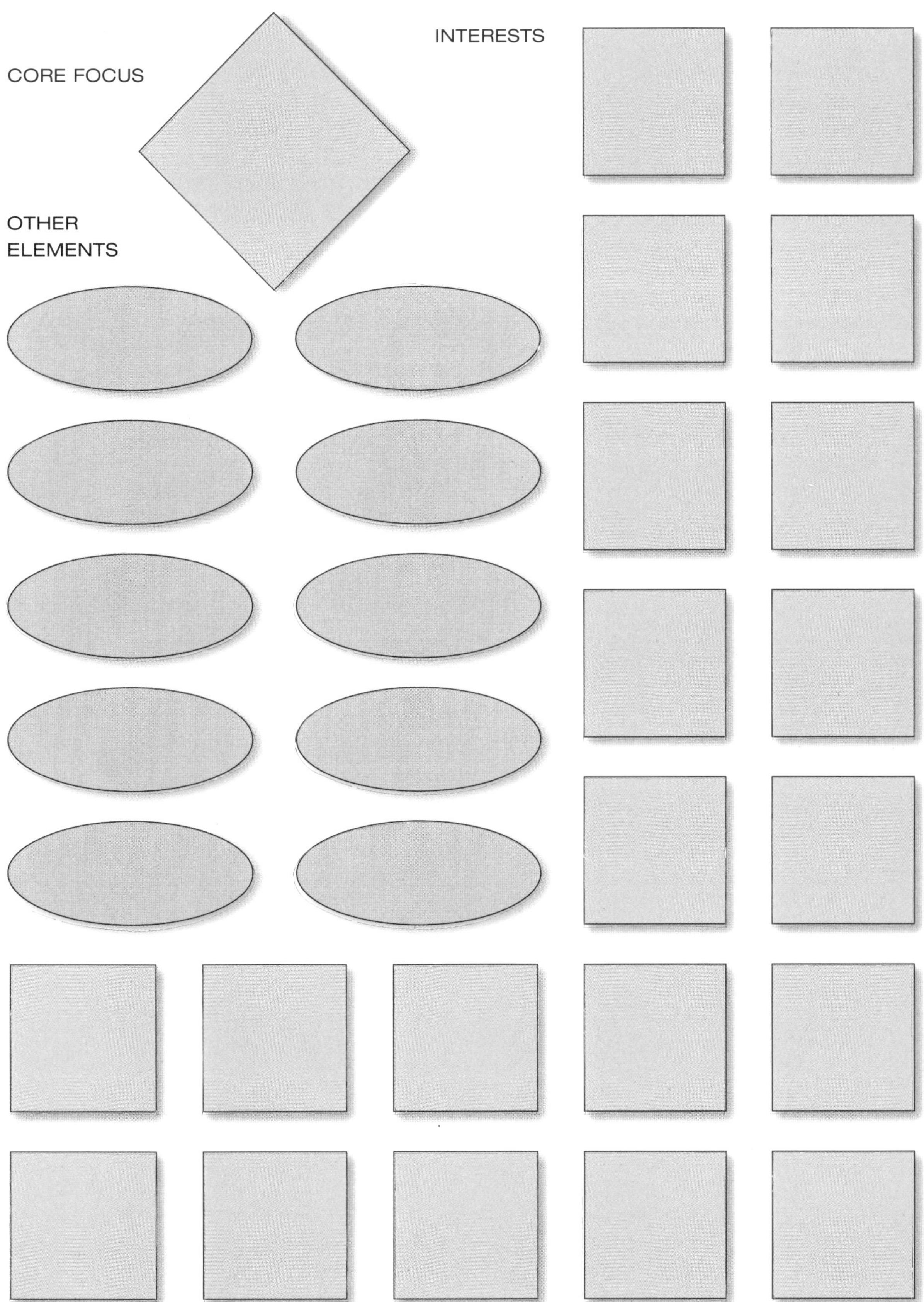

My Kaleidoscope Elements

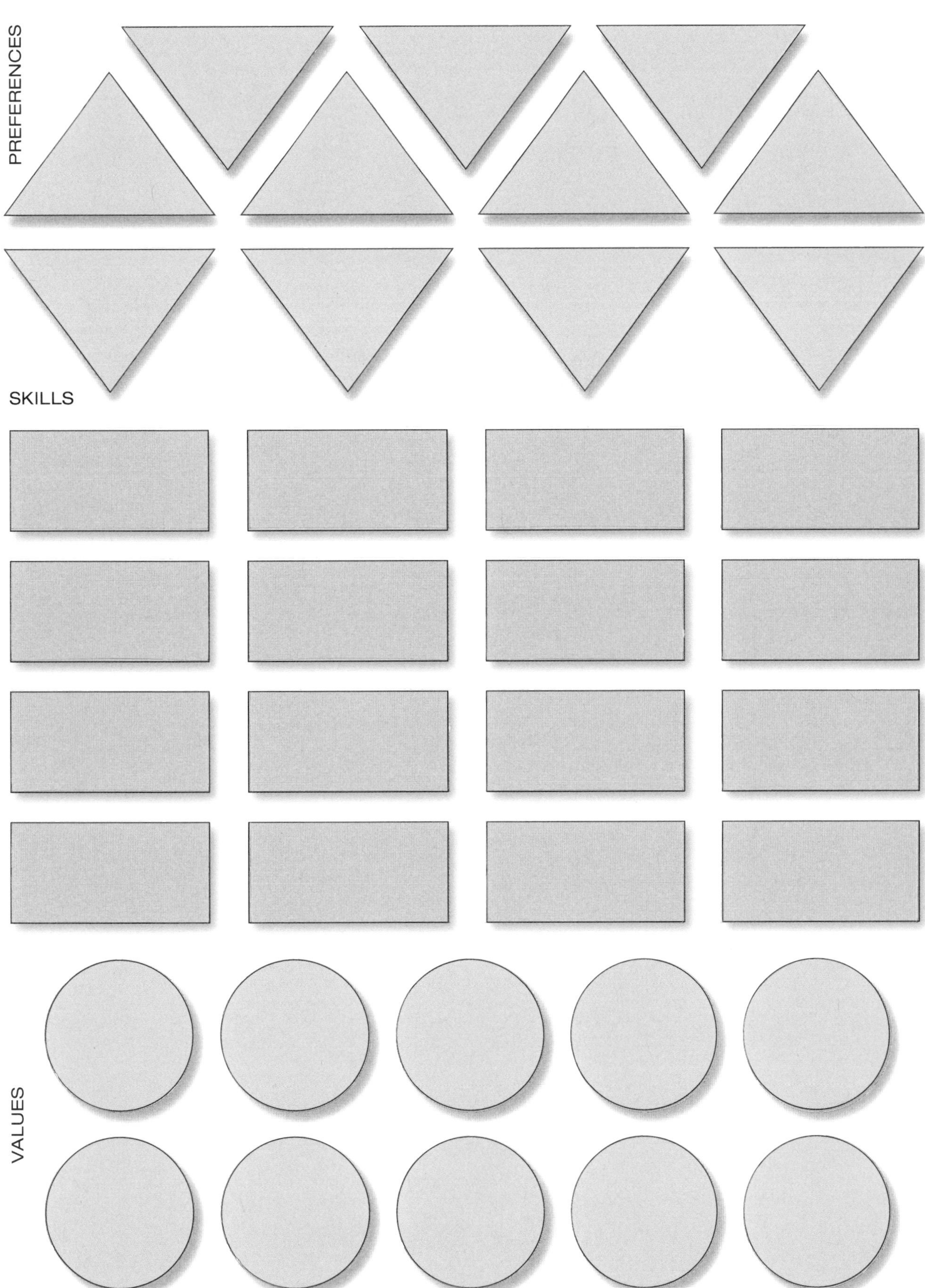